Treating
Addiction

Treating Addiction

Beyond the Pain

Collected Works, 2000–2016

EDWARD J. KHANTZIAN

FOREWORD BY MARTIN WEEGMANN

ROWMAN & LITTLEFIELD
Lanham • Boulder • New York • London

Published by Rowman & Littlefield
A wholly owned subsidiary of The Rowman & Littlefield Publishing Group, Inc.
4501 Forbes Boulevard, Suite 200, Lanham, Maryland 20706
www.rowman.com

Unit A, Whitacre Mews, 26-34 Stannary Street, London SE11 4AB

British Library Cataloguing in Publication Information Available

Library of Congress Cataloging-in-Publication Data

Names: Khantzian, Edward J., author.
Title: Treating addiction : beyond the pain / Edward J. Khantzian ; foreword by Martin Weegmann.
Description: Lanham : Rowman & Littlefield, [2018] | Includes bibliographical references and index.
Identifiers: LCCN 2017053100 (print) | LCCN 2017053495 (ebook) | ISBN 9781538108598 (electronic) | ISBN 9781538108574 (cloth : alk. paper) | ISBN 9781538108581 (paper : alk. paper)
Subjects: LCSH: Substance abuse—Treatment.
Classification: LCC RC564 (ebook) | LCC RC564 .K5354 2018 (print) | DDC 362.29—dc23
LC record available at https://lccn.loc.gov/2017053100

∞™ The paper used in this publication meets the minimum requirements of American National Standard for Information Sciences—Permanence of Paper for Printed Library Materials, ANSI/NISO Z39.48-1992.

Printed in the United States of America

Contents

Foreword

Martin Weegmann

As it strips a course through bodies, minds, and relationships, addiction remains a baffling disorder, and there is much that we do not know, and may never know, about it. No area of the human drama is left untouched by its effects, and at its worst, addiction resembles a locked vault with no obvious way out. To convey such challenging realities, I often open workshops on addiction with words from Edward Khantzian and Mark Albanese (2008, xv), who write, "Addiction is consuming in the depth to which it affects individuals, and extensive in the breadth to which it affects persons from all walks of society." Enough said.

When Edward asked me to write this foreword to his new book, I not only was delighted but also felt the rush of closeness, personal and professional, that has kept us connected since the early 1990s, on different sides of the big pond. When I set out as a clinical psychologist navigating the field of substance misuse, I chanced upon his name and took the step of writing to him—yes, letter writing was not that unusual once upon a time! I realize in retrospect that I was reaching out for a framework of understanding to match the realities with which I was faced and one congruent with a humanist perspective that tried to see the person, and their core suffering, behind the disorder. Stigma, of any kind, in mental health upsets me. Edward's appreciative and considered response provided the encouragement I needed and so began a long-term association and friendship, including conferences (in London) and joint publications. That is something of our history, but what of his?

On the personal side, his Armenian heritage has played its part. Asked about this in a journal interview (2006; reproduced here as chapter 12 of this volume), he observes, "I believe my mother's appreciation of human suffering which she endured and witnessed during the Turkish genocide, and my father's convictions about a more just social order, combined to stir in me an early sensitivity about what is disordered in human nature and society." So, too, in a more proximal way, was his involvement in reforming the Cambridge Hospital to respond to another scene of societal devastation—the heroin epidemic of the late 1960s and early 1970s. Edward demonstrates a lifelong sensitivity to the experience of those who live on the margins, and of what he is fond of describing—and by way of inspiration from sociology—as a "plea for marginality." In this he has faced a considerable career task, challenging stigma from society about substance misuse, but also, equally, from within the psychiatric and psychoanalytic communities. Thus, it has been common to regard people suffering from substance misuse as no more than "addicts" full stop, as fatally flawed individuals, containers of psychopathology and little more, and as menacing and inherently "difficult cases." By contrast, instead of seeing them as "difficult people," even hopeless, Edward prefers to see those with substance misuse as especially troubled, caught up in cycles that entail self-loss and, along with it, despair and desperation. But these are also cycles that can be interrupted by periods of abstinence and/or longer term, if not permanent, recovery. Chemical careers can be superseded by change for the better. There can indeed be life after addiction.

In a revealing joke at a conference I used to organize—Psychotherapy of Addiction (London)—Edward referred to the popular stereotype of the Armenian as trader and rug merchant, moving with wares from town to town. He suggested that the "self-medication hypothesis" was his one and only ware. In response, I added that it was a warmly received and influential ware in many quarters, academic and clinical, and, moreover, that he was a model salesperson, in this case, of an idea. In my view, the self-medication hypothesis offers us a guiding sensitivity and constitutes a rich paradigm of research.

This book is testimony to that illuminating idea and the many ways in which Edward has sought to define, defend, and refine the hypothesis over the years. His writing is a model of clarity, and his claims are refreshingly free from the dogma of one position or another within a field often divided by them. In many ways, the self-medication hypothesis is a traveling theory that has all the advantages of pragmatism and offers a wide scope of application.

In addition, I would praise Edward's much needed modernization of the psychodynamic perspective in addiction, how such a perspective assists us in understanding and helping those whose lives are characterized by extremes and distortions—lives bent to the purpose of chemicals, emotions warped by shortcut solutions, and relationships compromised by reliance upon inanimate objects. As I am interested in literary history, I was delighted to come across some passages from the first and most famous of the genre of "drug confession," by Thomas de Quincey (1821), an opium eater. Of his drug of choice, once discovered, he declares, "Happiness might now be bought for a penny, and carried in a waistcoat pocket" (21). Yet, in a section that expresses a version of the self-medication view, de Quincey observes of his dependence, "It was not for the purposes of creating pleasure, but of mitigating pain in the severest degree, that I first began to use opium as an article of daily diet" (6).

Much of Edward's book is a fleshing-out of how it is that people respond to pain within their lives and seek refuge in substances, even, and invariably, at the price of producing new sorts of pain that they had not bargained upon. With his formulations, we are, I believe, helped to know that significant bit more about the nature of addiction and to adopt a clinical stance that seeks to meet our clients with the least prejudice and optimal responsiveness.

Thank you, Edward, for your dedication to the field and to all the clients whom you have served (and still do), and this over such a long period of time.

Martin Weegmann
Clinical Psychologist, Group Analyst, Author
London, August 2017

References

De Quincey, T. (1821/2013). *Confessions of an English Opium-Eater and Other Writings.* Oxford: Oxford University Press.

Khantzian, E., and Albanese, M. (2008). *Understanding Addiction as Self Medication: Finding Hope behind the Pain.* Lanham, MD: Rowman & Littlefield.

Acknowledgments

As I indicated in my 1997 collected works, *Treating Addiction as a Human Process*, acknowledgments are about the people and institutions that have made it possible for a person to do his/her work. My experience over the past 20 years since then allows me to again affirm that conviction, and in this respect, I have continued to be enormously blessed. Starting with mentors and colleagues at Massachusetts Mental Health Center and, subsequently, at the Cambridge Hospital, Tewksbury Hospital, and Harvard Medical School, I have had sustained encouragement and support to pursue my commitment to pursue a humanistic understanding and treatment of individuals who have succumbed to addictive disorder. In 2008, we (with Mark Albanese) were fortunate to meet and have the guidance of our editor, Sarah Stanton at Rowman & Littlefield, in publishing our book, *Understanding Addiction as Self-Medication*; she later supported my wish to publish this volume and passed me on to my subsequent editors, Molly White and Megan Manzano at Rowman & Littlefield. Most recently, the contributions of Katie O'Brien to these efforts were crucial. I am grateful for and deeply appreciate their diligence and careful attention to all aspects of production in bringing the book to press. As the pages in this book reveal, I have been most fortunate to have my comrade in arms, Martin Weegmann, to continue to embrace ideas that go beyond simplistic explanations that fail to get at the roots of addictive suffering. Jesse Suh, in a previous book and in this one, provided invaluable empirical data to support the self-medication hypothesis of addictive disorders. Over the greater part of the past 50 years, I can single out Mark Albanese and Jan Kaufmann as singularly special colleagues and friends along the way. Their continuous efforts and support have been invaluable sources of encouragement and validation, and for that I am deeply grateful. And finally, there are few (if any) pages in this book that have escaped the devotion and watchful eye of my life companion, CarolAnn Khantzian.

Introduction

A HUMANISTIC UNDERSTANDING
OF ADDICTION

In the first edition of my book *Treating Addiction as a Human Process*, published in 1999, the central theme was that addiction is rooted in human psychological suffering and is not about seeking pleasure or self-destruction, an unfortunate and not infrequent characterization of and misunderstanding about addiction. My studies and treatment of addictive disorders and behavior over these past 15 years have not convinced me otherwise.

Almost without exception, life histories of human discomfort, disconnection, and unhappiness leave those so burdened vulnerable to the appeal of addictive drugs, including alcohol. In this volume composed of previously published papers, with added commentary and reflections, I will present evidence (practice based) from five decades of study and treatment with substance-dependent individuals that effective treatment is based on an appreciation of these core issues.

Early psychoanalytic and psychodynamic formulations of addictions were heavily influenced by instinct theory, thus emphasizing pleasure and self-destructive drives to explain the motivation for overuse and misuse of addictive substances. Much of this is outdated, and modern theories (structural, object-relations, self-psychology, and attachment theory) significantly depart from such formulations. Unfortunately, and more than we would like to consider, these early characterizations linger and influence how we think of and react to addictive behavior. And they play a significant role in the stigma associated with these conditions. Karl Menninger, in his 1938 book *Man against Himself*, referred to addictive behavior as a form of "chronic suicide"; others have cynically referred to addiction as "suicide on the installment plan"; countless accounts in lay and scientific articles and reports refer to the "euphoria" or "high" obtained from addictive substances; and much of the neuroscientific literature continues to study and focus on how addictive drugs are reinforcing on the "pleasure and

1

reward centers" in the brain. Although there is merit and validity in such views and approaches, they fail to consider the human psychological vulnerabilities and suffering that is so central a part of addictive disorders. As I have repeatedly stressed throughout my career, no explanation of addictive disorders is complete without such consideration. In this overview, and subsequently, I stress that what is needed to better understand and treat addictive disorders is an empathic understanding of what addictively prone individuals endure that makes addiction so powerfully compelling. Such a perspective provides a compassionate and humanistic appreciation of addictive conditions for those who experience it and for those who witness it.

Part I

THE INTERNAL TERRAIN OF ADDICTION: PSYCHODYNAMICS

In my experience, addiction represents an attempt by individuals to cope with confusing and/or unbearable feelings, or to deal with external realities that are threatening or overwhelming. Albeit long-term addiction solutions cause harm and physical deterioration, in the short run they produce relief of painful feelings; thus, the effect of the drugs becomes welcome, and for the susceptible, they ultimately become addictively compelling. In this section, I spell out and expand on how the internal workings of individuals prone to addiction operate in such a way that they are likely to be captured by this effect of addictive drugs.

Chapter 1 was written by invitation for the journal *Neuropsychoanalysis*. This journal is committed to integrating findings from neuroscience and psychoanalysis to explain human troubles and behavior. It is based on an assumption (to which I emphatically subscribe)—namely, that the domains of neuroscience and psychoanalytic theory and practice complement each other, and that they need not and do not compete. Such a focus is especially refreshing because it stands in stark contrast to the countless polarized formulations that are prevalent on the nature of addictive disorders. Furthermore, integration of the domains enriches our understanding of problems such as addictive disorders and has important implications for adopting effective treatment. For example, medication-assisted treatments (MATs) such as methadone maintenance and buprenorphine, which derive from neurobiological studies, can be crucial in stabilizing addiction to opiates, thus allowing and making more effective psychosocial interventions that predispose to and perpetuate addictive adaptions.

The chapter was a target or lead article with commentaries by two distinguished neuroscientists, Dr. Yak Panksepp and Dr. George Koob, the latter currently being the director of the National Institute of Alcohol Abuse and Alcoholism (NIAAA), as well as three prominent psychoanalysts. In my lead article, I described how over four decades of studies and treatment of addictions I had adopted an evolving perspective that initially emphasized addiction as a *special adaptation* that provided susceptible individuals a means to cope with internal emotional distress originating from traumatizing, neglectful environments. Subsequently, this perspective evolved for me to articulate the *self-medication hypothesis* (SMH) of addiction wherein I spelled out and emphasized how addictive drugs become appealing and compelling because, first and foremost, they relieve a range of painful and unmanageable feelings, and second, that there is considerable degree of specificity or preference for an individual's drug of choice. I then spelled out how the self-medication perspective stimulated me to adopt a more overarching perspective of *addiction as a self-regulation disorder*—namely, that addictively prone people have major problems in knowing and managing their emotions, their sense of self and self-esteem, difficulties in interpersonal relations, and difficulties in regulating their behaviors, and in particular, their self-care. And finally, I considered what it is in the *person(ality)* that causes individuals prone to addiction to experience their feelings and to behave in such ways that makes addiction more likely.

The subsequent chapters in this section of the book explore in more detail the psychodynamics of addictive vulnerability. In chapter 2, the collaboration with my esteemed colleague, Martin Weegmann in the United Kingdom, allowed us to reflect with one another on how modern psychodynamic theory more readily allows an appreciation of underlying difficulties with the self-regulation problems of addicted individuals avoiding early psychoanalytic explanations that were more speculative, sweeping, and theory based. Martin Weegmann and I agree that there is a need for a different language than that provided by early theory such as "primitive fixations . . . oral dependency . . . pre-oedipal problems, etc.," a language unlikely to gain the needed alliance with our patients in helping to engage with them to understand their addictions. We both agreed that the contemporary language of "developmental deficits, sectors of vulnerability/distortion, retreats, psychosocial adversity/opportunity, affect dysregulation, etc." is more appropriate, empathic, and effective for treatment to identify the vulnerabilities in addicted individuals that rendered them susceptible.

Chapters 3 and 4 focus on specific populations and areas of dysfunction operative in addictive disorder. For example, in chapter 3, we consider how and why there is such a high co-occurrence of disorders such as posttraumatic stress disorder (PTSD), schizophrenia, attention-deficit/hyperactivity disorder (ADHD), and depressive disorders with substance use disorders. This chapter explores in more detail the importance of the comorbid conditions associated with addiction, and how the SMH model for understanding addiction underscores an appreciation that the comorbid conditions are invariably and significantly intertwined. In chapter 4, we elaborate in more detail on an area of behavioral problems that is insufficiently appreciated—namely, deficits in "self-care"—wherein addictively prone individuals fail to experience fear and worry, and fail to appreciate the cause-consequence relationship in the face of potential or real danger. The chapter explores how such thinking and feeling deficits add flesh and substance to the observations about "impulsivity" in addicted persons. In the final chapter of this section, chapter 5, I explore how attachment deficits and self-medication issues interact with and complement each other to more effectively explain how and why addiction is more likely, and how the integration of these two paradigms can lend to more effective treatment.[1]

1. This grew out of an invitation by Sir Richard Bowlby, the son of John Bowlby, to give the 20th John Bowlby Memorial lecture in 2013 because of his conviction that my body of study and work complemented the work and findings of his father, John Bowlby, an honor that I enthusiastically accepted.

CHAPTER 1

Understanding Addictive Vulnerability

AN EVOLVING PSYCHODYNAMIC PERSPECTIVE

Substance use disorders (SUDs) are among the most pervasive and devastating psychiatric disorders and public health problems of our times. Until recently they have also been considered refractory to treatment. Three developments in this past half century, however, have given rise to the prospect that addictive problems are better managed and treated. Although lacking much significant data to substantiate its efficacy, the enormous growth and acceptance of Alcoholics Anonymous (AA) over the last half of the 20th century suggests it has made a major impact on helping alcohol dependent individuals. Second, the "heroin epidemic" starting in the 1960s forced clinicians and investigators to see, evaluate, and treat many opiate-dependent individuals. Finally, the widespread influx of cocaine into our society over the past two decades and the concurrent abuse and dependence on other addictive substances over this corresponding period have forced us as a society, scientists, investigators, and practitioners to address these problems. Many of the treatments that have emerged have proven to be effective.

Even though SUDs are considered "chronic and relapsing" disorders, there is evidence to suggest that these disorders are at least as manageable and/or treatable as other chronic and relapsing diseases such as diabetes and hypertension (McLellan et al. 2000). Biological and psychosocial treatments have been developed that have proven to be effective if employed with the right timing and matching to patients needs and conditions (Khantzian 1988). More often than not the biological and psychosocial treatments have been most effective when they have been combined. In some instances, effective treatments (e.g., methadone maintenance) have led to a better understanding of SUDs and, in other instances, a better understanding (e.g., contemporary psychodynamic and cognitive behavioral psychology), and more effective treatments (e.g., individual and group psychotherapy and relapse prevention approaches) (Flores 1998; Khantzian et al. 1990; Marlatt and Gordon 1980). This review will emphasize an evolving psychodynamic perspective of addictive vulnerability which the author believes has had important implications for a better understanding and more effective treatments.

In the traditions and practice of psychodynamic psychiatry, resistance to treatment and relapse are constants, and if appropriately appreciated and managed, become opportunities for deepening an understanding of what governs patients' dilemmas, and in the instance of this paper, what governs patients with addictive behaviors. Hansel (1997) in a recent report highlights works, starting with Freud, how psychoanalytic theorists have repeatedly considered a fundamental paradox in clinical practice and the nature of psychopathology. Namely, as much as patients present with inner conflicts and struggle to grow and change, inner forces resist them. Hansel uses the contemporary interactive paradigm as an example of how new models for understanding and treatment are necessitated when clinicians' existing methods fail to ameliorate conflict (pain) and to produce psychological maturation. Not surprisingly, this shift is not dissimilar to the case with individuals suffering with addictive disorders who often seem to desperately need and want help, yet repeatedly continue to defeat their best intentions, and that of others, to change and get better. It is also significant and consistent with Hansel's interactive paradigm that addictive disorders seem to have become more manageable and understandable (probably in that order) over the last 50–60 years. This has mainly occurred as large (12-step programs) and small groups (psychotherapy) have developed as mainstays of treatment of these disorders (Khantzian 1985a, 1990, 1995, 2001a). Such approaches rest on core corrective elements which contain and transform addictive behavior and depend on interactive elements which are central to the dynamics of large and small therapeutic group experiences and have also been incorporated in individual psychotherapy (Khantzian 1985a, 1988, 1999; Krystal 1988; Woody et al. 1983, 1995).

Contemporary psychodynamic approaches for SUDs have improved therapeutic outcomes because clinicians have better incorporated interactive and supportive elements into therapy. The classical traditions of uncovering techniques, passivity, the blank screen, and strictly interpretive modes are not appropriate or beneficial in meeting the needs of addicted individuals. The developmental vulnerabilities, discussed in this review, suggest the need for greater support, empathy, structure, and active dialogue with the treating clinician in addressing the nature of their vulnerability to addiction (Khantzian 1995).

The evolving psychodynamic perspective in this report spans more than four decades. It draws on findings from the psychiatric literature and longitudinal and epidemiological studies, where appropriate, which complement the psychodynamic perspective. This perspective incorporates elements of contemporary psychoanalytic models deriving from structural, self, and object relations theory. It primarily draws on a perspective that focuses on developmental deficits effecting ego structures, sense of self, and the quality of relations with others. In the author's experience, this perspective has evolved through four stages—namely, viewing addiction as (1) a special adaptation, (2) an attempt to self-medicate and/or change unbearable or confusing affect states, (3) evolving into an understanding of addictions as a self-regulation disorder, and finally, (4) an exploration of the nature of the "disordered person(ality)," which predisposes individuals to become, remain and relapse to addictive behaviors.

A Case Vignette

The following case illustrates many of the themes that this report will highlight. It is apparent that the patient, who is presented, suffered with intense and extreme emotions. He also suffered with self-esteem problems and difficult interpersonal relations. His impulsive and risky behaviors also revealed poor self-care in that he invariably failed to anticipate the consequences of the dangers of his actions and activities. The case also reveals the short-term adaptive effects of addictive drugs and how they can relieve emotional suffering as well as counter certain restricting personality characteristics.

> **Arnold:**[1] When Arnold first came to see me he was 29 years old, and he had just started treatment in a methadone maintenance program. I followed him in psychotherapy over the subsequent 10 years, during which time he ultimately achieved abstinence from his dependency on all narcotics. Following him over this period of time provided the opportunity to appreciate the nature of his suffering and his personality organization. The long-term therapy also allowed time to observe him both during times when he was actively using, as well as an extended time when he abstained from all drugs, thus making it possible to compare how the drugs affected him, as well as how he behaved and reacted when he was free of drugs. The opiates had become his drug of choice over the past five years before he came to see me, but starting in early adolescence he heavily used and abused sedatives and stimulants (amphetamines). His long-standing shaky self-esteem and tenuous capacity to relate to others lent a self-effacing and reticent quality to his interpersonal dealings, including the way he related to me in his psychotherapy. These qualities lent to an appealing and likeable aspect of his personality that combined elements of charm and vulnerability. Nevertheless, by history, and

---

1. The case of Arnold is a composite one to preserve the patient's anonymity. It is based in part on a case reported in recent a publication (Khantzian 1999) but further modified for the purposes of this publication.

based on his day-to-day encounters and activities reported in therapy, it was clear he had another side. Arnold could be ruthless, sadistic, and disavow any need for help and care from others. In contrast to his generally gentle and solicitous veneer, he revealed a penchant to be aggressive if not violent, as he disclosed his keen interest in active and risky involvements in athletics, martial arts, and speedy high performance motorcycles and automobiles. As a result of his violent and risky behaviors he frequently suffered injuries of various sorts, many of which I witnessed when he came for his psychotherapy. He was often quick to play down or dismiss with bravado the nature or seriousness of his injuries.

In his adolescence, he used both depressants and amphetamines to overcome his shyness and restricted emotional life. The depressants would disinhibit him and he could more easily relate to his peers. He said that the amphetamines made him feel powerful and helped him to overcome feelings of vulnerability and weakness in social situations and contact sports. As he continued to use amphetamines he realized it helped as well to counter his low self-esteem and inertia, aspects of which indicated a longstanding depression. The progressive reliance on the stimulants empowered him and frequently resulted in brutal, punishing fights. As time went on, however, he realized that amphetamines caused him enormous dysphoria and fear, especially how much it heightened his sadism, whether it involved beating up a person or an emerging cruelty to his pet cats. As he approached his mid-20s and the uncontrollable violence and rage was interfering with his friendships, work, and life in general, he discovered and subsequently became dependent on heroin. In contrast to the amphetamines and sedatives, he was immediately impressed with the containing and calming effect of narcotics; he was aware of a marked diminution in his rage and aggressivity, and he felt more organized, in control, and able to work.

In the course of his therapy, he and I better appreciated how much the extremes and flip-flopping of his emotions derived from his growing-up years. During those years he was both shamed and devalued, and subjected to verbal and physical abuse by his mother, a person who apparently had her own problems with aggressivity and impulse control.

The Literature

An extensive review of the psychoanalytic literature would go beyond the scope of this chapter. There is an extensive review of the works of early psychoanalytic investigators who mainly emphasized the pleasurable aspects of drug use and their symbolic meaning (Brehm and Khantzian 1997; Khantzian 1974; Khantzian and Treece 1977' Rosenfeld 1965; Yorke 1970). The growing "heroin epidemic" beginning in the 1960s stimulated a resurgence among a handful of psychoanalysts to pursue, from a contemporary psychoanalytic perspective, an understanding of substance use disorders (SUDs) and what some treatment implications might be of such an understanding (Blatt et al. 1984; Khantzian 1972, 1978, 1985b; Krystal and Raskin 1970; Krystal 1988; Milkman and Frosch 1973; Wieder and Kaplan 1969; Wurmser 1974). These works, consistent with developments in more contemporary psychoanalytic theory, focused on structural (ego) factors, developmental difficulties, and disturbances in self and object relations. With some notable exceptions, it is surprising and unfortunate that since the 1970s there has been so few contributions from psychoanalysts addressing the dynamics of SUDs. This paucity of psychoanalytic reports on addictions is especially discouraging, given that addictive disorders have become one of the most overriding psychosocial problems of our time.

One might argue that this void exists because the psychoanalytic paradigm does not make as good a fit or does not have as much to offer as, for example, a neurobiologic one to explain the nature of addictive disorders. Proponents of this latter perspective, as a case in point, argue that addiction is a "brain disease" and that addictive drugs "hijack the reward centers of the brain" (Leshner 1997). Notwithstanding this paradigm shift and the great utility of a neurobiologic perspective, it can just as well be argued that drugs of abuse "hijack the emotional brain" (Khantzian 2001b). Any theory or explanation of addiction that does not address what it is in the workings of the mind (i.e., the inner psychological terrain) and a person to predispose and cause them to repeatedly relapse to addictive drugs is incomplete.

Although too few in number, recent psychoanalytic reports offer new and fresh perspectives validating the relevancy and utility of a psychodynamic perspective. Khantzian and Wilson (1993) and Schiffer (1988) have more clearly elaborated on the nature of the repetition compulsion in the addictions (i.e., why individuals repeat addictive behavior despite the pain), and Dodes has elaborated on narcissistic rage and helplessness in additive disorders, and a view of addictions as a subset of compulsions (Dodes 1990, 1996). Clinical and empirical studies have also provided evidence that substance dependency is basically a self-regulation disorder (Khantzian 1990, 1995, 1999; Wilson et al. 1989). From an object relations perspective, original contributions by Johnson (1993, 1999), Kaufman (1994), and Walant (1995) have explored the early childhood origins of an addicted individual's difficulty in establishing and maintaining adequate connections to and dependency on others and, as a consequence, turning to a dependency on drugs as a substitute for his/her troubled relationships in adult life.

Substance Abuse as an Attempt to Cope

PSYCHOPATHOLOGY AS AN ADAPTATION[2]

In the author's experience, substances of abuse are and become compelling because in susceptible individuals they help to cope with unbearable painful feelings and/or to adapt to external realities that are otherwise unmanageable. That is, albeit in the long run drug dependency becomes a problem in itself, in the short run, addictive drugs work and become a special adaptation in response to a range of human problems. In an early publication, Khantzian and his associates (1974) suggested that opiate-dependent individuals used their drug to deal with human problems involving emotional pain, stress, interpersonal problems, and dysphoria. Gold (2000) succinctly captured this emphasis in the author's work by stating, "Every human problem has a reason and represents an attempt to solve a problem" (2000, 1892). This view of psychopathology is entirely consistent with a recent publication by Nesse (2000) who similarly suggested that depression might serve an adaptive purpose. This adaptive perspective of psychopathology has been a mainstay in psychoanalytic thinking dating back to Freud, and in a sense consistently challenges alike the theoretician and clinician to ponder what purpose or role symptoms and psychopathology play in our patients' adjustments to their inner psychological and external realities.

Dating back to the 1950s, Gerard and Kornetskey (1954), and Chein et al. (1964) in their pioneering book *The Road to H*, emphasized that adolescents employ drugs to adaptively cope with overwhelming anxiety as they approached adulthood in the absence of adequate preparation, models, and prospects. Chein and his associates concisely summarized, that addiction was "adaptive and functional." Wieder and Kaplan (1969) extended this perspective by underscoring the role drugs play for adolescents in reducing distress and maintaining psychological homeostasis. They anticipated the self-medication hypothesis by proposing that individuals take drugs not to seek "kicks" but more to exploit the physical effect of the drug to deal "with the particular conflicts and defects in a person's psychic structure throughout his development—[and act as]—a structural prosthesis" (Wieder and Kaplan 1969, 428). Extending the work of Wieder and Kaplan, Milkman and Frosch (1973) empirically tested and demonstrated that addicts "preferentially" used different drugs to compensate for shaky ego defenses and to augment preferred styles of adaptation—that is, the calming and dampening effects for opiate dependent individuals, and the expansive and

---

2. Although the term "adaptation" in the strict psychoanalytic sense refers to adjusting to inner psychological life, it is used interchangeably here with the term "cope" to refer the problems addicted individuals have in adjusting to a range of internal and external life challenges.

activating effects for stimulant users. Wurmser (1974) stressed "defects in affect defense" and how narcotic dependent individuals used opiates to cope with overwhelming feelings of rage, shame, and loneliness. Along somewhat different lines, but seminal in conception, Krystal (1988) and Krystal and Raskin (1970) described how addicted individuals used addictive substances to cope with affects (or feelings) that are undifferentiated (e.g., feelings of anxiety cannot be distinguished from depression), somatized, and not verbalized.

As the foregoing analysis suggests, addictive drugs are employed, at least initially, to cope or deal with a range of painful emotions and developmental deficits. Many of these formulations were developed independently and began to converge and coalesce with each other during the 1970s. Some of this convergence of ideas that there was an adaptive purpose being served by addictive drugs was facilitated during that period by a series of technical review conferences sponsored by the National Institute on Drug Abuse (Blaine and Julius 1977).

DEVELOPMENTAL DEFICITS:
SUD AS A SPECIAL ADAPTATION

The psychoanalytic evidence that substances of abuse serve an adaptive purpose and are linked to developmental deficits is supported by longitudinal studies which provide empirical evidence and implicate emotional dysregulation and behavioral disturbances dating back to childhood (Brook et al. 1992; Kellam et al. 1991; Moss et al. 1995; Shedler and Block 1990). These studies are important in that they track over time patterns of family interaction, tolerance and expression of emotions, and behavioral adjustments. They shared in common findings that linked substance use and abuse, including "gateway drugs," to documented co-occurring disturbed emotional and behavioral patterns.

From a psychodynamic perspective, resorting to addictive drugs, more than anything, represent attempts at self-correction that ultimately fall short. As will be elaborated upon subsequently, drug-dependent individuals, in their drug use, are continuously trying to regulate their emotions, sense of self, relationship with others, and their behaviors. In the absence of substances as a means to cope, such individuals are repeatedly troubled and/or overwhelmed by their emotions, self-image, relationships and behaviors. The more they rely on drugs to solve their problems, another problem develops, which has been referred to as "disuse atrophy" (Khantzian 2001b), a term familiar to neurologists and orthopedic surgeons, referring to how a muscle or limb shrinks because of casting and/or disuse. The mind and its development, much like a limb, depends upon unencumbered use and, in this respect, is much like our physical anatomy. The more an individual uses drugs to cope with his/her emotions and self-other relations, the less likely they are to grow and develop in their psychological capacities and ability to meet life challenges. It is for this reason, as well as biological ones involving addictive process, that dependency on drugs progresses. As a result, one's drug of choice becomes more and more necessary, or other drugs are adopted to get by. Aside from the consuming and harmful physical consequences of SUDs, this "disuse atrophy," and related diminishing capacities to cope, plays a crucial role in attempts at self-correction with drugs that so cruelly fail.

THE ADAPTIVE PERSPECTIVE
AND THE TREATMENT ALLIANCE

All too often friends, family, and even clinicians try to warn patients with SUDs about the harm they are doing to themselves with their continuous use of sub-stances. Unwittingly, such warnings foster more defensiveness and play into patients' sense of shame. The clinician begins to be viewed more as interrogator or adversary rather than someone to be helpful and on the patient's side. As previ-ously indicated, the patient has had a short-term realization that their substance helps them to cope. The inroad to helping a person appreciate the negative and harmful results of drug use is not best achieved by pointing out, initially, what the drug(s) does *to* them. It is more alliance producing (i.e., getting the patient to feel you are on their side and with them) to at least initially explore what the drug does *for* them. Repeatedly, the author has had the discovery in taking this tack that not only does it help the patient and clinician to understand the suffer-ing that compels their drug use, but it also leaves the patient, often for the first time, feeling more understood. This twofold understanding becomes the foun-dation for a more mutually trusting relationship that makes a basis for further exploration of the patient's SUD and the acceptance of treatment options that the exploration and understanding suggests is indicated.

Over the past couple of decades, the "stages of change" model, introduced by Prochaska and DiClemente (1985), has been helpful to many clinicians in enhancing motivation for treatment of SUD. Taking an initial approach that explores patients' perceived "benefits" of substances becomes an important as-pect of engaging them in the treatment process. It fosters self-reflection in which the patient over time better considers in the treatment relationship the benefits of their drug use weighed against its cost. The patient shifts from a posture of denial or apparent oblivion that s/he has a problem ("pre-contemplation"), to one where s/he more realistically assess the self-harm and interference with life goals ("contemplation"). The patient is then more ready to take active measures to pursue a treatment plan. The simple but often important query, "What does the drug do for you?" more often becomes crucial in initiating this process.

DRUG EFFECTS: GENERAL AND SPECIFIC

Based on developments spanning four decades, the author believes there is a parallel in developments in psychopharmacology in clinical practice and the use of psychoactive substances in "street" psychopharmacology. When I began my training in psychiatry in 1964, we referred to two classes of psychopharmacologic drugs—namely, "major" (for major mental illness) and "minor" (for minor mental illness) tranquilizer. The operative term was "tranquilizer," connoting the general calming actions of the main agents being used, namely phenothiazines and benzodiazepines. However, during that same period antidepressants (tricyclic antidepressants) were also just coming into use. As a consequence of this latter development, clinicians were less inclined to consider these drugs as psychoactive agents which had the general effect of reducing or ameliorating distress associated with psychiatric conditions. Instead, they had more specific effects on the symptomatology of psychiatric conditions. As a result, a new nomenclature was adopted which designated the specific actions of the drugs, thus the modern terminology—anti-psychotic, anti-anxiety, and anti-depressant drugs. This shift in terms and the way of thinking about how these drugs worked (we were at the same time identifying the neuro-transmitter/receptor systems that corresponded to each class of drugs—i.e., dopamine, GABA, nor-epinephrine, serotonin, etc.) placed growing emphasis on the psychopharmacologic specificity of the drugs we were adopting in clinical practice.

When the author first began evaluating and treating opiate dependent individuals coming to a methadone program in 1970, at first I speculated from a psychiatric (and psychodynamic) perspective that beyond the so-called high or kicks derived from these drugs, there was a more general muting and pain (psychological) relieving action of these drugs that might be important. Patients as well referred to a general "mellowing-calming" effect that the drugs produced. However, as increasing numbers of patients were evaluated, and partly based on the aforementioned evolving changes in our terminology for psychopharmacologic agents which influenced my thinking, I began to consider that the opiate dependent patients were drawn to opiates for more specific reasons than ameliorating general states of distress and psychological suffering. It was this latter shift in my thinking and perceptions about the motives for drug use that lead me to increasingly consider the importance of psychopharmacologic specificity in an individual's "self-selection" (Khantzian 1975) of their preferred drug(s), a key factor in my considering that patients evolve into choosing a drug to self-medicate particular states of distress.

Substances as Self-Medication

One of the most defining aspects of addictive disorders is that substance abusers, with an unrelenting and tragic persistence, use, become dependent upon, and relapse to their drug of choice despite the consuming and devastating consequences on their lives. At some point, such a process cannot leave anyone who witnesses it without asking the fundamental question, "Why is this so?" For clinicians and scientists, it gets to basic issues of causation or etiology. Since first beginning to work with patients suffering with SUDs, I have wrestled with explanations on behalf of my patients and my own need to understand the determinants of this most vexing clinical and social problem. In pursuing this need to explain and understand, I have been guided by the paradigm and perspective in which I have been trained and am most comfortable—a psychodynamic one. Obviously, there are other paradigms or models that pertain and have powerful explanatory value, not the least of which is a biological one. This is especially so given the enormous advances that have been made in the neurosciences which have allowed investigators to fathom the structures and functions of the brain with an unimaginably sophisticated technology. This latter approach yields a special kind of data in unraveling the addictive equation. As already indicated, the clinical/psychodynamic approach harvests equally valid data but, it is of a different kind. Ultimately, the challenge is to integrate the data that the different approaches yield. Subsequently I will comment on the nature of this challenge but, in this section will elaborate on the self-medication hypothesis which has evolved out of a psychodynamic viewpoint and has produced an important explanation for a major determinant of SUDs.

THE SELF-MEDICATION HYPOTHESIS (SMH)
OF SUBSTANCE USE DISORDERS

There are two basic and important aspects of the SMH—namely, (a) addictive substances relieve human psychological suffering, and (b) there is a significant degree of psychopharmacologic specificity in the appeal of addictive drugs. Although this claim seems intuitively correct and is supported by clinical experience and empirical data (Glass 1990), it is a claim that is also controversial and disputed (Frances 1997; Gold and Miller 1994; Miller 1994). Because ones' drug of choice is not always available, individuals substitute other drugs or manipulate their dose to approximate a desired effect. For example, a person might use obliterating doses of alcohol to dampen rageful feelings when opiates are not available. In another instance a moderate dose of alcohol might help to activate a person if cocaine is not affordable.

PSYCHOPATHOLOGY: THE CART-HORSE DEBATE

Although the SMH is principally based on clinical work with substance-dependent individuals, there is now extensive psychiatric and epidemiologic literature that examines the relationship between psychopathology and SUDs. An extensive review of the studies would go beyond the scope of this report. However, this paper will highlight some considerations, based on this recent literature, which are relevant to the validity of the SMH. Khantzian (1997) and others (Nunes and Quitkin 1997) have reviewed the literature on the relationship between psychopathology and SUDs. Presumably, such studies might shed light on whether there is a causal relationship between psychiatric disorders and SUDs. The distinction between what condition is primary or secondary (i.e., what came first) is repeatedly raised in these studies and for the most part is inconclusive and leaves the "cart-horse" debate unsettled.

The works of Vaillant and Schuckit and their respective associates have further complicated the debate (Schuckit 1985, 1986, Schuckit et al. 1990, 1994; Vaillant 1983; Vaillant and Milofsky 1982). Longitudinal studies by Vaillant and follow-up studies by Schuckit and associates both indicate that genetic factors more than psychopathology play a greater role in the development of alcoholism, and that albeit states of distress are apparent with alcoholism, they are not enduring traits. Their work suggests that psychopathology is more likely a consequence of SUDs than its cause, and psychiatric distress associated with alcoholism clears once abstinence is established. Their findings would of course tend to invalidate the role of psychopathology in the evolution of addictive disorders. Khantzian (1997, 1999) and others (Donovan 1986; Zucker and Gomberg 1986) have critiqued the works of Vaillant and Schuckit. Schuckit's work on the role of anxiety and depression in alcoholic patients, like Vaillant's work, variously overlook, do not measure, or dismiss the importance of depressive and anxiety symptoms that predate or co-occur with alcohol dependence. Furthermore, Schuckit's sample was a preselected one in which patients with comorbid psychopathology were excluded, thus biasing the findings. Both Donovan and Zucker and Gomberg make the point that large-scale studies do not code for or identify environmental and personality factors, and along similar lines, the author has contended that subtle factors relating to self-comfort, interpersonal relations, and self-esteem are not considered or measured (Khantzian 1997). The recent longitudinal studies previously cited (see Brook et al. 1992; Kellam et al. 1991; Moss et al. 1995; Shedler and Block 1990) also indicate that emotional distress and behavioral dysregulation predate the development of SUDs, extend back to childhood, and are at distinct variance with the findings of Schuckit and Vaillant.

More recent evidence suggests that there is a significant relationship between psychiatric disorders, especially mood disorders, and SUDs, and when treated with antidepressants, there is an appreciable improvement in mood and a diminished tendency to use substances (Cornelius et al. 1997; Greenfield et al. 1998; Mason et al. 1996; McGrath et al. 1996; Nunes et al. 1996, 1997; Petrakis et al. 1998; Roy 1998; Roy-Byrne et al. 2000; Willens et al. 1999). The epidemiologic catchment area study (ECA) (Regier et al. 1990) and the national comorbidity survey (NCS) (Kessler et al. 1997) provide evidence that the association between psychopathology and SUDs is greater than would be expected by chance. From this author's vantage point, the convergence of findings from the longitudinal studies previously cited, the diagnostic/treatment studies, and the ECA/NCS epidemiologic data provide further bases to support the SMH.

UNDERSTANDING THE APPEAL OF ADDICTIVE DRUGS: THE CLINICAL CONTEXT

In the author's experience, individuals do not simply self-medicate comorbid psychiatric conditions. More precisely, they self-medicate states of subjective distress and suffering that may or may not be associated with conditions meeting DSM-IV criteria for a psychiatric diagnosis. More than any other source, the SMH derives from clinical work with hundreds, if not thousands, of patients evaluated by myself and other clinicians of a similar orientation.

I have elaborated elsewhere (Khantzian 1985a, 1988, 1999, 2001; Khantzian et al. 1990) on the modes and techniques employed in psychodynamic approaches to SUDs. A detailed review here goes beyond the scope of this chapter. "The clinical context" is described here briefly to demonstrate how the treatment approach can yield valuable data about addictive vulnerability by attuning to the patients' inner psychological life and observing and experiencing how they interact with others.

The author's findings about the suffering and characterological problems that cause individuals to self-medicate are based on a modified psychodynamic psychotherapeutic approach. Employing supportive techniques, and a semi-structured treatment relationship, provides access to the patient's inner life and permits a natural unfolding of the patient's particular ways of experiencing and expressing emotions. (Similar techniques employed in group therapy are equally revealing.) Such an approach allows patients to also display characteristic patterns of defense and avoidance that both reveal and disguise the intensity of their suffering, their confusion about their feelings, or the ways in which they are cut off from their feelings. Empathically engaging patients in this way builds an alliance that allows them to develop an understanding of how their suffering, defenses, avoidances, and separation from their feelings interact with the specific action of the drugs that they use or prefer. From the author's perspective a modified psychodynamic approach yields rich and ample clinical data that can explain why substances of abuse in general or a particular drug can become so compelling in a person's life (Khantzian 1997, 1999).

THE SMH: ITS EVOLUTION AND LIMITATIONS

It is not likely that an individual sets out to become addicted to a particular drug. Rather, in the course of experimenting with various substances of abuse an individual "discovers" the special augmenting, activating, or pain ameliorating properties of a specific drug and increasingly comes to rely on that action of the drug which appeals to them. Substances of abuse are not universally appealing. As much as a drug can have very compelling and appealing effects, it is also true that individuals are just as likely to experience a drug as aversive, especially if it heightens or makes worse a feeling state they might otherwise self-medicate with a preferred drug.

Contemporary psychodynamic theory in application to SUDs paralleled developments in modern psychoanalytic thinking by laying less emphasis on drives and unconscious conflicts, but placing greater emphasis on appreciating the importance of affects, the development of ego and self structures, and the quality of and capacity for relationships and connections to others. Such a focus was sparked by Gerard and Kornetsky (1954) and Chein et al. (1964) in the 1950s. But it was not until the 1970s, with the advent of the heroin epidemic that more definitive psychodynamic studies began to appear, which explored how and why addictive drugs had such appeal for certain individuals.

The contemporary psychodynamic focus on affects and their vicissitudes in patients with SUDs was a fundamentally important development in appreciating self-medication as a primary motive in drug seeking dependence and relapse. Although addicted individuals often experience affect life as being cut off, absent, and nameless (discussed subsequently), they are more likely to experience feelings as overwhelming and unbearable (Khantzian 1985). Wurmser (1974) referred to "defects in affect defense," and on a similar basis Wieder and Kaplan (1969) referred to drugs as a "prostheses—[or]—corrective" to deal with painful emotions. In an early publication Khantzian (1974) described how opiate addicts relied on the anti-aggression action of opiates to mute the disorganizing and threatening states associated with violent and rageful feelings. These formulations shared in common an appreciation of the use of addictive drugs as a means to cope with painful and threatening emotions. Wieder and Kaplan (1969) were the first to appreciate and articulate that there was a degree of pharmacologic specificity in the drug an individual preferred, introducing the term, "drug of choice." As previously indicated, along similar lines, Milkman and Frosch (1973) referred to the "preferential use of drugs," and more recently Spotts and Shontz (1987), intensively studying a sample of cocaine addicts, provided further empirical support for patients' specific drug preference, coining the term "drug of commitment." Khantzian (1975) originally referred to this preferential pattern of drug use and dependence as a "self-selection" process. Based on the evolution of these concepts, and subsequent developments supporting factor(s) of psychopharmacologic specificity, the author reported a basis for the SMH of addictive disorders (Khantzian 1985). More currently, Khantzian (1997) further clarified the SMH hypothesis and explored its relevance to nicotine dependence, schizophrenia, and posttraumatic stress disorders (PTSD). The more recent update of the SMH elaborated on the themes of deficits in ego capacities, troubled self-other relations, and self-care, which caused individuals psychological suffering, and as a consequence of such distress, individuals discovered how the action of each class of drugs differentially ameliorated or relived a range of painful feeling states.

It would seem intuitively and phenomenologically apparent that cocaine is distinctly different in its effects compared to opiates, which in turn are distinctly different than the effects of alcohol. Kosten (1998) argues against these apparent differences and psychopharmacologic specificity because of the frequency with which dopamine connections involving the ventral tegmental region and the nucleus acumbens have been identified repeatedly as the "final common pathway" with many abused substances. In the author's opinion, what is not sufficiently considered in the contention, beyond the apparent clinical observations, is how and what other intermediary neurochemical pathways (such as GABA, dopaminergic and endogenous opiate systems) might be involved to explain preferential patterns of use for addictive drugs. In the author's experience, the three main classes of abused substances—opiates, depressants, and stimulants—have powerful and distinct psychopharmacologic actions which can relieve or change different states of psychological suffering. The original motives for appeal of these drugs change when used chronically and heavily (i.e., addictive and neuroadaptive mechanisms increasingly dictate drug seeking behavior). However, the initial drug effects, and to some extent during heavy use, and then again with relapse, continue to be powerful determinants of substance dependence (Khantzian 1995, 1997, 1999). *Opiates* are very effective in countering and muting intense anger and rage and appeal to individuals who endure such feelings, and/or suffer with psychiatric conditions in which such affects dominate. (High or "obliterating" doses of alcohol can have similar effects, but obviously on a different basis—namely, a hypnotic action.) *Stimulants* appeal to high-energy and low-energy individuals; in the former case stimulants serve as augmenting agents, in the latter as activating or energizing drugs. Not surprisingly, such drugs appeal to patients with both bipolar and unipolar mood disorders (Khantzian 1995, 1997).

Predictably, they also appeal to individuals with attention-deficit hyperactivity disorder (ADHD) (Khantzian 1983, 1985). *Depressants* in low to moderate doses have appeal for individuals who are tense and anxious and, as Fenichel (1945) has suggested, might act as "super-ego solvents." However, it has been the author's experience (Khantzian 1995, 1997) and that of Krystal (1988) that depressants have even more appeal as an ego solvent. That is to say, individuals who are defensive and become very constricted in relation to dependency and nurturance needs experience the dissolving effects on their restrictive ego defenses as a magical and warm elixir.

This chapter has elaborated on how and why individuals self-select different drugs and manipulate drug dose when their drug of choice is not affordable or available, and why they switch from one drug to another (Khantzian 1997). These departures from one's preferred drug are used as arguments against the SMH. These are not the main or most compelling arguments against the SMH and its limitation. The two main arguments raised with the SMH are: (a) not all who suffer with pain and distress become drug dependent, and (b) there is as much, if not more, suffering as a consequence of drug use. These arguments raise interesting issues about protective factors against succumbing to SUDs, and what some of the psychological factors might be, beyond addictive mechanisms, as to what it is in our human nature that causes us to perpetuate suffering and self-harm an indisputable and not uncommon phenomenon (Farber 2000).[3] Struggling with these questions and issues raised by the SMH, I have found it necessary to adopt a superordinate or more overarching paradigm of the addictions as a self-regulation disorder.

Substance Abuse as a Self-Regulation Disorder

My early work emphasized pervasive and severe psychopathology as major determinants for individuals succumbing to and remaining dependent upon addictive drugs (Khantzian 1972, 1974). In part, this was a function of originally

---

3. Given the likelihood that biological and psychological factors are constantly interacting in addictive and compulsive processes, neuroscientists and clinicians might be challenged to further explore what the developmental neurobiological substrate might be for perpetuating self-harm.

working mainly with opiate-dependent individuals in a methadone treatment program, an admittedly more disturbed population, most usually suffering with both DSM-IV Axis 1 and 2 diagnoses (Khantzian and Treece 1985). As this work has evolved, I have been more impressed with sectors of vulnerability in the personality organization of drug-dependent individuals and related states of psychological distress that govern their addictive behavior. This perspective has evolved into a view that examines what it is that is disordered or dysregulated in a person, and differentiates what are the contributing factors and what are the essential ones. They are as follows:

• Disordered self-esteem—Contributory
• Disordered relationships—Contributory
• Disordered emotions—Essential
• Disordered self-care—Essential

DISORDERED SELF AND DISORDERED RELATIONSHIPS

Core issues of sense of self and troubled interpersonal relationships contribute in important ways to the predisposition for SUDs. These two contributory factors are discussed together because they are so interwoven with each other in explaining how states of discomfort and dis-ease about sense of self and others play into a tendency to resort to the effects of drugs. Substances, short term, can correct or substitute for a disordered sense of self and/or relationships. The self-psychologists and object relation theorists have made important direct and indirect contributions in appreciating the importance of disturbed self-other relations that are so often intertwined in the fabric of addictive disorders.

Kohut and his followers (Baker and Baker 1987; Goldberg 1978; Kohut 1971, 1977; Kohut and Wolf 1978; Ornstein 1978) made important contributions in understanding how the sense of self and narcissism have a normal developmental line and, when disturbed, the special ways in which they become manifest. Some of these manifestations are particularly evident in addictive processes, such as problems with over- or underevaluation of self, self-absorption, and, in the extreme, psychological disorganization and fragmentation. It should not be surprising that the differential action of each class of drugs could serve as antidotes or correctives to the dysphoric states engendered by such disturbances. Drugs also interact with many of the rigid characterologic defenses that are associated with such dysphoria (to be discussed later). Kohut appreciated well how drugs help to cope with inner dysphoria when he provocatively wrote, *the drug serves not as a substitute for loved or loving objects, or for a relationship with them, but as a replacement for a defect in the psychological structure* (1971, 46). For the purposes here, some of the most profound structural deficits affect ego-ideal formations, most notably involving the capacity for regulating self-love, self-esteem, and self-respect. Notwithstanding Kohut's disclaimer, it is little wonder that clinicians and substance abusers alike refer to the attachment to drugs as a romance or love affair.

Perspectives derived from object relations theory have shed additional light on how a troubled sense of self makes it less likely that one can attach to or depend on others. As a consequence, such individuals are more apt to resort to substances or other addictive behaviors for comfort and a sense of well-being (Flores 2001; Johnson 1993, 1999; Kaufman 1994; Walant 1995). Most contemporary psychodynamic investigators appreciate the preverbal developmental origins of why drug-dependent individuals experience so much discomfort about themselves and in their relationships with others. The problem is that the early-life derivatives of substance abusers' discomforts are not "encoded in words" (Gedo 1986, 206) but are expressed without conscious memories in perceptual-action-affect responses (Gedo 1986, Lichtenberg 1983). Along similar lines Fairbain (1944), the pioneering British psychoanalyst, proposed that libido was object seeking, not pleasure seeking, and that the child strives not for pleasure but for contact. Greenberg and Mitchell (1983), expanding on Fairbain's work, suggest that when early child-mother relationships are unsatisfactory and ungratifying, later in life they play out in painful, self-defeating relationships and attachments. These formulations provide theoretical underpinnings for the often observed difficulties that drug-dependent individuals display in establishing satisfactory relationships with and connection to others. Instead, more often they are self-sufficient, counterdependent, and isolative (Khantzian 1993).

Although this review has suggested that disordered self-esteem and disordered relationships are mainly "contributory," they are, nevertheless, important aspects of addictive vulnerability. But matters of how we feel about ourselves and relationships with others are more or less intact or disrupted for most of us; and for some, as disordered as they are in those prone to become addicted, but do not become addicted. For this reason, these vulnerabilities are not sufficient or essential to develop SUDS.

DISORDERED AFFECTS AND DISORDERED SELF-CARE

Difficulties in regulating emotions and self-care are two of the most basic and essential factors that coalesce and make more likely that an individual will experiment with and become dependent on addictive substances. As has been indicated, a disordered sense of self and disordered relationships contributes in important ways to the addictive process, but it is disordered emotional life and self-care that malignantly combine and become principal determinants of SUDs.

Individuals with SUDs suffer in the extreme with their emotions. They are either flooded with unbearable painful affects (emotions), or they are devoid of or cut off from their feelings. Both extremes are a source of distress and/or consternation to self and others. It is in this context that individuals have the experience that addictive drugs can either ameliorate their distress or change states of being devoid of feelings. For an individual flooded with violent or rageful feelings, opiates or obliterating doses of alcohol might be adopted. For others who suffer with states of anergia, anhedonia, or not feeling, the activating properties of a stimulant are often experienced as a welcome antidote. And for those who are cut off from or too tightly wrapped with their feelings, repeated low to moderate doses of alcohol or other depressants can often seem like a miraculous anodyne to experience and express feelings they otherwise cannot allow or articulate.

When an individual finds their feelings intolerable they self-medicate their pain and suffering. When they are confused by, cut-off from, or devoid of feelings, patients resort to drugs to change their feelings, even if using drugs causes more suffering or pain. In the former instance the operative motive is to *relieve* painful feelings; in the latter instance the operative motive is to *control* feelings. I have reviewed in more detail elsewhere (Khantzian 1995, 1997, 1999; Khantzian and Wilson 1993) how this latter instance of controlling and/or perpetuating pain is closely tied to affects that are inaccessible, cut off, and without words. Drawing on the observations of Sifneos (1967) and Nemiah (1970), Krystal (1988) has underscored the centrality of "alexithymia" in the lives of addicted individuals. Krystal's seminal works on tracing normal developmental lines for affects has provided a basis to understand that individuals with SUDs endure affects that are undifferentiated (i.e., they cannot differentiate anxiety from depression), and are somatized, and not verbalized. Along similar lines McDougall (1984) has observed how our "disaffected" patients are cut off from their feelings and instead substitute a range of impulsive and compulsive behaviors that are addictive in nature. Wurmser referred to the problem of "hypo-symbolization" to characterize addicted individuals' impoverished emotions and their incapacity for symbolization. Along these lines, Sashin (unpublished manuscript) catalogued "non-feeling responses" related to the inability to fantasize or tolerate distress.

I have elaborated on the elusive nature of feeling life and the lexicon of terms that capture this. The terms provide a basis for a partial explanation to the seeming contradiction that individuals self-medicate their pain with drugs at the same time they continue the pain and make it worse. Beyond the biological factors involved in the addictive process, clinical observations (Khantzian 1989, Khantzian and Wilson 1993, Schiffer 1988) suggest that there are important psychodynamic reasons why individuals with SUDs knowingly and unknowingly perpetuate their pain. Although early and more recent formulations have invoked masochistic motives (Menninger 1938; Schiffer 1988), the author has concluded that there are other more subtle but important positive motives. Addictions in part become a form of substituted suffering in that "patients exchange their preexistent world of feelings, which are out of control, vague, and confusing, and thus overwhelming, for a life revolving around drugs, in which they repetitiously produce relief and suffering, which enables them to feel more in control and less confused and overwhelmed" (Khantzian and Wilson 1993, 280).

Substance abusers not only suffer because they cannot contain or control their feeling life. They also suffer because they cannot contain or control their behaviors. This is notably evident in regard to their self-care. We have elaborated extensively elsewhere on this aspect of structural deficits in substance abusers that repeatedly threaten their well-being and survivability (Khantzian 1978, 1990, 1995, 1999; Khantzian and Mack 1983). Self-care deficits result in an individuals' inability to ensure their self-preservation. In addicted individuals, these deficits are evident in their incapacity to anticipate or avoid harmful and dangerousness situations, especially those associated with hazards involved in the experimentation with and use of addictive drugs. A distinctive aspect of this vulnerability is the inability to use appropriate judgment and feeling as guides in the face of danger. Substance abusers think and feel differently around danger and this is especially apparent around situations involving drug use. It is also evident in failures to avoid harm involving preventable medical, dental, financial, interpersonal and other preventable life problems. Numerous clinical cases have been reported (Khantzian 1978, 1990, 1995; Khantzian and Mack 1983, 1994) in which individuals failed to appropriately experience fear, worry, apprehension, or appreciate the consequences of the dangerous behaviors and practices leading up to and using addictive substances.

As the author's thinking evolved about what were the most significant and essential elements of addictive vulnerability, it became increasingly apparent that the need to self-medicate psychological pain and suffering combined malignantly with self-care deficits to make individuals susceptible to suffer SUDs. This evolving perspective also has helped to more clearly respond to a legitimate criticism of the SMH, namely that suffering alone (i.e., painful or confusing affects, troubled sense of self, and interpersonal grief) is not sufficient to explain the development of drug dependency. However, when accompanied by the dangerous, if not life-threatening consequences of co-occurring self-care deficits, individuals are more likely than not to succumb to addictive disorders.

Substance Abuse and the Disordered Person

Beyond understanding the nature of the suffering and the behavioral dysregulation involved in SUDs, explorations into the psychodynamics of addictive vulnerability has lead me to consider what the nature might be of the relationship between the personality organization of a substance-dependent individual and the predisposition to become and remain dependent on substances of abuse. The formulations presented in this section are more recent and should be considered preliminary in nature and in need of further clinical inquiry and empirical study.

There is a recurrent empirical association found between personality disorders and SUDs. However, in the author's opinion, there is more obscurity than illumination in clarifying this relationship, when and if it is considered it at all. Although the contemporary psychoanalytic literature makes frequent references to character traits and defenses, there have not been any systematic explorations of the part personality disorders play in the psychodynamics of addictive disorders. Clinical and epidemiologic studies document a high incidence of anti-social personality disorders (APD) associated with SUDs (Helzer et al. 1988; Kessler et al. 1997; Grande et al. 1984; Khantzian and Treece 1985; Koenigsberg et al. 1985; Regier et al. 1990; Rounsaville et al. 1982; Weiss et al. 1984, 1988). In a number of studies, however, the findings were not limited to APD alone, and there were high, if not higher, proportions of substance abusing patient diagnosed with borderline (BPD) and narcissistic personality disorders (Grande et al. 1984; Khantzian and Treece 1985; Koenigsberg et al. 1985; Nace et al. 1983, 1991; Weiss et al. 1984, 1988). To complicate matters further, Schuckit (1985) reported findings indicating that the diagnosis of APD decreased significantly when patients became abstinent from alcohol.

In work with patients the author has found it useful and heuristic to distinguish between personality disorder and the disordered person; the former is more descriptive and empirical, the latter is more dynamic and explanatory. In this section the focus will be on two areas of disordered personality, namely characteristic traits and defenses related to deficits in affect life and deficits in self-care.

SUBSTANCE ABUSE, SUFFERING/SELF-CARE, AND THE DISORDERED PERSON

Individuals with the diagnosis of APD, in the author's experience, are not happy people. This assertion runs counter to the stereotype of patients with APD as pleasure seeking, guiltless, destructive characters. Furthermore, in practice, I have not seen a pure type among substance abusers. In my opinion, the explanation of their unhappiness resides in their *disordered personality*, which may or may not be antisocial on closer examination. The disordered person is unhappy because they cannot regulate themselves without substances; but the more they use substances the more unregulated they become and the more they suffer.

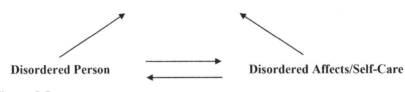

Figure 1.1.

The way a person is disordered in their personality interacts in important ways with resorting to substances and the ways in which such individuals suffer. As already indicated, there is considerable psychological pain as a consequence of an individual's disordered sense of self and their disordered relationship with others, which contributes to the development of SUDs. But it is the combination of disordered affects and self-care that malignantly combine to make substances repeatedly compelling and persistent. I have schematized this relationship in figure 1.1.

Experiences drawn from everyday life (often captured in drama or literature) and clinical practice suggest that the way a person is characteristically (i.e., the disordered person) causes them to suffer in, for them, typical ways. As an example, closed-off, restricted personalities more often suffer from anxiety (often of a tense nature) and depression. The more their anxiety or depression increases, the more they become disordered in their personality organization, heightening characteristic maladaptive traits and defenses. In the case of the self-care deficits, individuals vaguely sense their vulnerability to danger but instead posture with defenses of bravado and counterphobia. Such a heightening in defenses, in turn, only makes their suffering and self-care worse. On either side of the equation, the increasing maladaptive defenses or distress leaves the individual more susceptible to resort to substances of abuse.

SUBSTANCE ABUSE, DISTRESS AND CHARACTER TRAITS

As previously elaborated, individuals self-medicate their pain by using addictive drugs. But their pain is not the only reason for turning to drugs. We often refer to "denial" and related reactions of justifications and rationalizations as major component of resorting to addictive drugs. My clinical experience suggests more complex characterologic defensive patterns are involved. They arise and are in response to the particular ways the substance abusing patient suffers. Singling out the two most essential areas of vulnerabilities, disordered affects and self-care (listed in figure 1.2) are the elements involved in problems with affects and

(1)   ***Disordered Emotions (Affects)***

     a.   *Too much or too little feeling*
     b.   *Too much feeling* ⟶ *self- medication through substances*
     c.   *Too little* ⟶ *Perpetuation / control of suffering through substances*

Character Traits

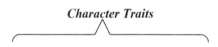

Action
Activity (including hyperactivity)
Circumstantiality
"Stimulus Seeking"
"Risk Taking"

(2)   ***Disordered Self-Care***

     a.   *Inability to insure self-preservation*
     b.   *Deficits in signal affects/cognition to guide behavior or action. Diminished or absent:*
         • *fear*
         • *apprehension*
         • *worry*
         • *judgement*
         • *appreciation of cause—consequences*
     c.   *Pervasive / global <u>vs</u>. susceptibility / vulnerability*

Character Traits

Counterphobic
Bravado
Aggressive posturing
Defensive self-reliance
Passive resignation

Figure 1.2.

self-care and the characteristic defenses which appear. It should be noted under self-care deficits that for some the deficits are global and pervasive. For others self-care functions are better developed, but subject to lapses and erosion under conditions of stress and distress.

Whether it is the case of physical disease or psychological disorder, our human/ biological nature causes us to respond with physiological reactions and/or psychological responses to defend against disease or disorder. The aggregation of granular leukocytes in an area of infection is a case in point of protective reactions to physical insult. Similarly, when we are vulnerable psychologically, we respond with characteristic personality traits and defenses. As with self-medication, such responses, short term, are consciously and subconsciously experienced as protective, but long term become maladaptive and self-defeating. It is for this reason that our treatments, to be effective, have to target both the suffering and the disorder in personality (i.e., the disordered person).

Substance abuse and personality disorders (or the disordered person) are co-occurring companions when individuals' sense of self, self-worth, and self-other relationships are faulty or inadequate, when they are unable to tolerate, know or express their feelings, and when they cannot use fear, anxiety, or judgment in guiding their behaviors or self-care. Treatments that work do so because they access and modify these vulnerabilities. The challenge is to understand what it is in the person (or personality) that is disordered and makes the occurrence of substance abuse more likely. Treating the substance-abusing patients requires us to deal with a person who suffers and to target their suffering and the person, and not the brain, synapses, or symptoms alone. Such an approach has implications for all our interventions, whether they be psychological, social, or biological.

Summary and Conclusion

This report has reviewed an evolving perspective of SUDs that is grounded in psychodynamic psychiatry. It has emphasized that addiction is a special adaptation and means to cope with a range of human psychological problems. This perspective has led the author to consider more specific reasons for why individuals repeatedly resort to drugs to alleviate their problems. Individuals have a discovery that short term they can reduce or control their suffering by self-medicating a range of distressful states, and that there is a considerable degree of psychopharmacologic specificity in a person's preferred drug. In response to questions raised by the SMH, an overarching perspective has been adopted of addictions as a self-regulation disorder. Finally, and more recently, the author has tried to examine how an individual's distress and drug effects interact with aspects of a person's characterological makeup to render drug use and dependence more likely and compelling.

Drugs of abuse are potent because they possess properties that can profoundly alter the brain and the mind. The way they do so have important implications for theory building and explaining how and why substances of abuse become so compelling. In my opinion, such explanations are too often presented as competing or in isolation with alternative theories. This is unfortunate in that it is likely there is more complementarity than competition in the predominant controversies in the study of the addictions. This is especially so with regard to the now prevailing ascendance of neuroscience and the study of the brain, and the lingering tendency to de-emphasize or ignore the findings from a psycho-social perspective and the workings of the mind and personality in health and disease.

As I have tried to argue elsewhere (Khantzian, 1999), we all need to strive for (and I "plead for") a "measure of marginality" as we adopt and advance our perspectives on understanding addictive vulnerability. That is to say, we all need to try and dwell in the "margins" (see Stonequist 1937) between the different paradigmatic domains in which we operate, and seek more ways to integrate those domains even as we focus upon and emphasize our preferred ones. Ultimately, I have suggested that probably the best we can do is to "[milk our perspectives for all they are worth] . . . [and then to] reside [at least for a while] in the margins of our different ways of thinking. The 'marginal person' in each of us can consider the potentials and limitations in one another's perspectives and then we must wait on the rare 'Renaissance person' who can ultimately bridge the different domains and explain how they all come together. This is how we advance our sciences and our civilization, and it is how we address what ails us as individuals and as a society" (Khantzian 1999, 666–67).

References

Baker, H. S., and Baker, M. N. (1987). Heinz Kohut's self-psychology: An overview. *American Journal of Psychiatry* 144:1–9.

Blaine, J. D., Julius, D. A., eds. (1977). *Psychodynamics of Drug Dependence*. Rockville, MD, National Institute on Drug Abuse.

Blatt, S. J., Berman, W., Bloom-Feshback, S., Sugarman, A., Wilber, C., and Kleber, H. (1984). Psychological assessment of psychopathology in opiate addiction. *Journal of Nervous and Mental Disease* 172:156–65.

Brehm, N., Khantzian, E. J. (1997). Determinants and perpetuators of substance abuse: Psychodynamics. In *Substance Abuse: A Comprehensive Textbook*, 3rd ed., edited by J. H. Lowinson, P. Ruiz, R. B. Millman, and J. G. Langrod, 90–100. Baltimore: Williams and Wilkins.

Brook, J. S., Whiteman, M., Cohen, P., and Tanaka, J. S. (1992). Childhood precursors of adolescent drug use: A longitudinal analysis. *Genetics, Society and General Psychology Monograph* 118:195–213.

Chein, I., Gerard, D. L., Lee R. S., et al. (1964). *The Road to H: Narcotics, Delinquency, and Social Policy.* New York: Basic Books.

Cornelius, J. R., Salloum, I. M., Eliler, J. G., et al. (1997). Fluoxetine in depressed alcoholics: A double blind, placebo controlled trial. *Archives of General Psychiatry* 54:700–705.

Dodes, L. M. (1990). Addiction, helplessness, and narcissistic rage. *Psychoanalytic Quarterly* 59:398–419.

———. (1996). Compulsion and addiction. *Psychoanalytic Association* 44: 815–36.

Donovan, J. M. (1986). An etiologic model of alcoholism. *American Journal of Psychiatry* 143: 1–11.

Fairbairn, W. R. (1944). Endopsychic structures considered in terms of object relations. In *Psychoanalytic Studies of the Personality.* London: Tavistock, 1952.

Farber, S. K. (2000). *When the Body Is the Target: Self-Harm, Pain and Traumatic Attachments.* Northvale, NJ: Jason Aronson.

Flores, P. J. (1998). *Group Psychotherapy with Addicted Populations.* New York: Haworth.

———. (2001). Addiction as an attachment disorder: Implications for group therapy. *International Journal of Group Therapy* 51:63–81.

Frances, R. J. (1997). The wrath of grapes versus the self-medication hypothesis. *Harvard Review of Psychiatry* 4:287–89.

Gedo, J. (1986). *Conceptual Issues in Psychoanalysis: Essays in History and Method.* Hillsdale, NJ: Analytic Press.

Gerard, D. L., and Kornetsky, C. (1954). Adolescent opiate addiction: A case study. *Psychiatric Quarterly* 28:367–80.

Glass, R. (1990). Blue mood, blackened lungs: Depression and smoking. *Journal of the American Medical Association* 264:1583–84.

Gold, M. S. (2000). Review of *Treating Addiction as a Human Process* by Edward J. Khantzian, M.D., Jason Aronson, 1999. *American Journal of Psychiatry* 157:1892–94.

Gold, M. S., and Miller, N. S. (1994). The biology of addictive and psychiatric disorders. In *Treating Co-existing Psychiatric and Addictive Disorders: A Practical Guide*, edited by N. S. Miller, 35–49. Center City, MN: Hazelden.

Goldberg, A., ed. (1978). *The Psychology of the Self.* New York: International Universities Press.

Grande, T. P., Wolfe, A. W., Schubert, D. S. P., Patterson, M. B., and Brocco, K. (1984). Associations among alcoholics, drug abuse, and anti-social personality: A review of the literature. *Psychological Reports* 55:455–74.

Greenberg, J. R., and Mitchell, S. A. (1983). *Object Relations in Psychoanalytic Theory.* Cambridge, MA: Harvard University Press.

Greenfield, S. J., Weiss, R. D., Muenz, L. R., Vagger, L. M., Kelly, J. F., Bello, L. R., and Michael, J. (1998). The effect of depression on return to drinking: A prospective study. *Archives of General Psychiatry* 55:259–65.

Hansel, J. H. (1997). The interactive paradigm and a psychoanalytic paradox. *Psychoanalytic Quarterly* 66:470–88.

Helzer, J. E., and Pryzbeck, T. R. (1988). The co-occurrence of alcoholism with other psychiatric disorders in the general population and its impact on treatment. *Journal of Studies on Alcohol* 49:219–24.

Johnson, B. (1993). A developmental model of addictions and its relationship to the twelve-step program of Alcoholics Anonymous. *Journal of Substance Abuse Treatment* 10:23–34.

————. (1999). Three perspectives on addiction. *Journal of the American Psychoanalytic Association.* 47:791–815.

Kaufman, E. (1994). *Psychotherapy of Addicted Persons*. New York: Guilford Press.

Kellam, S. G., Werthamer-Larsson, L., Dolan, L. J., Brown, C. H., Mayer, L. S., Rebok, G. W., et al. (1991). Developmental epidemiologically based preventive trials: Baseline modeling of early target behaviors and depressive symptoms. *American Journal of Community Psychology* 19:563–84.

Kessler, R. C., Crum, R. M., Warner, L. A., Nelson, C. B., et al. (1997). Lifetime co-occurrence of DSM-III-R alcohol abuse and dependence with other psychiatric disorders in the nation comorbidity survey. *Archives of General Psychiatry* 54:313–21.

Khantzian, E. J. (1972). A preliminary dynamic formulation of the psychopharmacologic action of methadone. In *Proceedings of the Fourth National Methadone Conference*. San Francisco: National Association for the Prevention of Addiction to Narcotics.

————. (1974). Opiate addiction: A critique of theory and some implications for treatment. *American Journal of Psychotherapy* 28:59–70.

————. (1975). Self selection and progression in drug dependence. *Psychiatry Digest* 10: 19–22.

————. (1978). The ego, the self and opiate addiction: Theoretical and treatment considerations. *International Review of Psychoanalysis* 5:189–98.

————. (1983). An extreme case of cocaine dependence and marked improvement with methylphenidate treatment. *American Journal of Psychiatry* 140:784–85.

————. (1985a). Therapeutic interventions with substance abusers: The clinical context. *Journal of Substance Abuse Treatment* 2:83–88.

————. (1985b). The self-medication hypothesis of addictive disorders. *American Journal of Psychiatry* 142:1259–64.

————. (1988). The primary care therapist and patient needs in substance abuse treatment. *American Journal of Drug and Alcohol Abuse* 14:159–67.

————. (1989). Addiction: Self-destruction or self-repair? *Journal of Substance Treatment* 6:75.

————. (1990). Self-regulation and self-medication factors in alcoholism and the addictions: Similarities and differences. In *Recent Developments in Alcoholism*, edited by M. Galanter, 8:255–71. New York: Plenum.

————. (1993). Affects and addictive suffering: A clinical perspective. In *Human Feelings*, edited by S. L. Ablon, B. Brown, E. J. Khantzian, and J. E. Mack. Hillsdale, NJ: Analytic Press.

————. (1995). Self-regulation vulnerabilities in substance abusers: Treatment implications. In *The Psychology and Treatment of Addictive Behavior*, edited by S. Dowling, 17–41. Madison, CT: International Universities Press.

————. (1997). The self-medication hypothesis of substance use disorders: A reconsideration and recent applications. *Harvard Review of Psychiatry* 4:231–44.

————. (1999). *Treating Addictions as a Human Process*. Northvale, NJ: Jason Aronson.

————. (2001a). Reflections on group treatment as corrective experiences for addictive vulnerability. *International Journal of Group Psychotherapy* 51:11–20.

————. (2001b). Addiction: Disease, symptom or choice. *Counselor* 2:46–50.

Khantzian, E. J., Halliday, K. S., and McAuliffe, W. E. (1990). *Addiction and the Vulnerable Self: Modified Dynamic Group Psychotherapy for Substance Abusers*. New York: Guilford Press.

Khantzian, E. J., and Mack, J. E. (1989). Alcoholics Anonymous and contemporary psychodynamic theory. In *Recent Developments in Alcoholism*, edited by M. Galanter, 7:67–89. New York: Plenum.

————. (1994). How AA works and why it is important for clinicians to understand. *Journal of Substance Abuse Treatment* 11:77–92.

Khantzian, E. J., Mack, J. E., and Schatzberg, A. F. (1974). Heroin use as an attempt to cope: Clinical observations. *American Journal of Psychiatry* 131:160–64.

Khantzian, E. J., and Treece, C. (1977). Psychodynamics of drug dependence: An overview. In *Psychodynamics of Drug Dependence*, edited by J. D. Blaine and D. A. Julius, 11–25. NIDA Research Monograph 12. Rockville, MD: National Institute on Drug Abuse.

————. (1985). DSM-III psychiatric diagnosis of narcotic addicts: Recent findings. *Archives of General Psychiatry* 42:1067–71.

Khantzian, E. J., and Wilson, A. (1993). Substance dependence, repetition and the nature of addictive suffering. In *Hierarchical Concepts in Psychoanalysis: Theory, Research, and Clinical Practice*, edited by A. Wilson and J. E. Gedo, 263–83. New York: Guilford.

Koenigsberg, H. D., Kaplan, R. D., Gilmore, M. M., and Cooper, A. M. (1985). The relationship between syndrome and personality in DSM-III: Experience with 2,462 patients. *American Journal of Psychiatry* 142:207–12.

Kohut, H. (1971). *The Analysis of the Self*. New York: International Universities Press.

————. (1977). *The Restoration of the Self*. New York: International Universities Press.

Kohut, H., and Wolfe, E. S. (1978). The disorders of the self and their treatment. *International Journal of Psychoanalysis* 59:413–25.

Kosten, T. R. (1998). Addiction as a brain disease (editorial). *American Journal of Psychiatry* 155:711–12.

Krystal, H. (1988). *Integration and Self-Healing: Affect, Trauma, Alexithymia*. Hillsdale, NJ: Analytic Press.

Krystal, H., and Raskin, H. A. (1970). *Drug Dependence: Aspects of Ego Functions*. Detroit: Wayne State University Press.

Leshner, A. I. (1997). Addiction is a brain disease and it matters. *Science* 278:45–47.

Lichtenberg, J. D. (1983). *Psychoanalysis and Infant Research*. Hillsdale, NJ: Analytic Press.

Marlatt, G. A., and Gordon, J. R. (1980). Determinants of relapse: Implications for the maintenance of behavior change. In *Behavioral Medicine: Changing Health Lifestyles*, edited by P. O. Davidson and S. M. Davidson, 410–52. New York: Brunner/Mazel.

Mason, B. J., Kocsis, J. H., Ritvo, C. E., and Cutler, R. B. (1996). A double-blind, placebo-controlled trial of desipramine for primary alcohol dependence stratified on the presence or absence of major depression. *Journal of the American Medical Association* 275:761–767.

McDougall, J. (1984). The "disaffected" patient: reflections on affect pathology. *Psychoanalytic Quarterly* 53:386–409.

McGrath, P. J., Nunes, E. V., Stewart, J. W., Goldman, D., Agosti, V., Ocepek-Welikson, K., and Quitkin, F. M. (1996). Imipramine treatment of alcoholics with major depression: A placebo-controlled clinical trial. *Archives of General Psychiatry* 53:232–40.

McLellan, A. T., Lewis, D. C., O'Brien, C. P., Kleber, H. D. (2000). Drug dependence, a chronic medical illness: Implications for treatment, insurance, and outcome evaluation. *Journal of the American Medical Association.* 284:1689–95.

Menninger, K. (1938). *Man against Himself.* New York: Free Press.

Milkman, H., and Frosch, W. A. (1973). On the preferential abuse of heroin and amphetamine. *Journal of Nervous and Mental Disease* 156:242–48.

Miller, N. S. (1994). The interaction between co-existing disorders. In *Treating Co-existing Psychiatric and Addictive Disorders: A Practical Guide*, edited by N. S. Miller, 7–21. Center City, MN: Hazelden.

Moss, H. B., Mezzich, A., Yao, J. K., Gavaler, J., and Martin, C. S. (1995). Aggressivity among sons of substance-abusing fathers: Association with psychiatric disorder in the father and on, paternal personality, pubertal development and socioeconomic status. *American Journal of Drug and Alcohol Abuse* 21:195–208.

Nace, E. P., Davis, C., and Gaspari, J. D. (1991). Axis-II comorbidity in the substance abuse sample. *American Journal of Psychiatry* 148:118–20.

Nace, E. P., Saxon, J. J., and Shore, M. (1983). A comparison of borderline and non-borderline alcoholic patients. *Archives of General Psychiatry* 40:54–56.

Nemiah, J. C. (1970). The psychological management and treatment of patients with peptic ulcer. *Advances in Psychosomatic Medicine* 6:169–73.

Nesse, R. M. (2000). Is depression an adaptation? *Archives of General Psychiatry* 57:14–20.

Nunes, E. V., and Quitkin, F. M. (1997). Treatment of depression in drug dependent patients: Effects on mood and drug use. In *Treatment of Drug Dependent Individuals with Comorbid Mental Disorders*, edited by L. S. Onken, J. D. Blaine, and A. M. Horton, 61–85. NIDA Research Monograph 172. Rockville, MD: National Institute on Drug Abuse.

Nunes, E. V., Quitkin, F. M., Stewart, J. W., et al. (1996). Imipramine treatment of opiate-dependent patients with depressive disorders. *Archives of General Psychiatry* 55:153–60.

Ornstein, P. H., ed. (1978). *The Search for the Self: Selected Writings of Heinz Kohut.* Vols. 1 and 2. New York: International Universities Press.

Petrakis, I., Carroll, K. M., Nich, C., et al. (1998). Fluoxetine treatment of depressive disorders in methadone-maintained opioid addicts. *Drug and Alcohol Dependence* 50:221–26.

Prochaska, J. O., and DiClemente, C. C. (1985). Common processes of change in smoking, weight control, and psychological distress. In *Coping and Substance Abuse*, edited by S. Shiffman and T. A. Willis, 345–63. New York: Academic Press.

Regier, D. A., Farmer, M. D., Ral, D. S., Locke, B. Z., Keith, S. J., Judd, L. L., and Goodwin, F. K. (1990). Comorbidity of mental disorders with alcohol and other drugs: Results from the epidemiologic catchment area (ECA) study. *Journal of the American Medical Society* 264:2511–18.

Rosenfeld, H. A. (1965). The psychopathology of drug addiction and alcoholism: A critical review of the psychoanalytic literature. In *Psychotic States*. London: Hogarth Press.

Rounsaville, B. J., Weissman, M. M., Kleber, H., et al. (1982). Heterogeneity of psychiatric diagnosis in treated opiate addicts. *Archives of General Psychiatry* 39:161–66.

Roy, A. (1998). Placebo-controlled study of sertraline in depressed recently abstinent alcoholics. *Biological Psychiatry* 44:633–37.

Roy Byrne, P. P., Pages, K. P., Russo, J. E., et al. (2000). Nefazodone treatment of major depression in alcohol-dependent patients: A double-blind, placebo-controlled trial. *Journal of Clinical Psychopharmacology* 20:129–36.

Schiffer, F. (1988). Psychotherapy of nine successfully treated cocaine abusers: Techniques and Dynamics. *Journal of Substance Abuse Treatment* 5:131–37.

Schuckit, M. A. (1985). The clinical implications of primary diagnostic groups among alcoholics. *Archives of General Psychiatry* 42:1043–49.

———. (1986). Genetic and clinical implications of alcoholism and affective disorder. *American Journal of Psychiatry* 143:140–47.

Schuckit, M. A., and Hesselbrock, V. (1994). Alcohol dependence and anxiety disorders: What is the relationship? *American Journal of Psychiatry* 151:1723–24.

Schuckit, M. A., Irwin, M., and Brown, S. A. (1990). The history of anxiety symptoms among 171 primary alcoholics. *Journal of Studies on Alcohol* 51:34–41.

Shedler, J., and Block, J. (1990). Adolescent drug use and psychological health. *American Psychologist* 45:612–30.

Sifneos, P. E. (1967). Clinical observations on some patients suffering from a variety of psychosomatic diseases. In *Proceedings of the Seventh European Conference on Psychosomatic Research*. Basel: S. Karger.

Spotts, J. V., and Shontz, F. C. (1987). Drug-induced ego states: A trajectory theory of drug experience. *Society of Pharmacology* 1:19–51.

Stonequist, E. V. (1937). *The Marginal Man: A Study in Personality and Culture Conflict*. New York: Charles Scribner's Sons.

Vaillant, G. E. (1983). *The Natural History of Alcoholism*. Cambridge, MA: Harvard University Press.

Vaillant, G. E., and Milofsky, E. S. (1982). The etiology of alcoholism: A prospective viewpoint. *American Psychologist* 37:494–503.

Walant, K. B. (1995). *Creating the Capacity for Attachment: Treating Addictions and the Alienated Self*. Northvale, NJ: Jason Aronson.

Weiss, R. D., and Mirin, S. M. (1984). Drug, host and environmental factors in the development of chronic cocaine abuse. In *Substance Abuse and Psychotherapy*, edited by S. M. Mirin, 42–55. Washington, DC: American Psychiatric Association Press.

Weiss, R. D., Mirin, S. M., Griffin, M. L., and Michaels, J. L. (1988). Psychopathology in cocaine abusers: Changing trends. *Journal of Nervous and Mental Disease* 176 (12): 719–25.

Wieder, H., and Kaplan, E. (1969). Drug use in adolescents. *Psychoanalytic Study of the Child* 24:399–431.

Willens, T. E., Biederman, J., Millstein, R. B., Wozniak, J., Hahesy, A. L., and Spencer, T. J. (1999). Risk for substance use disorders in youths with child-adolescent onset bipolar disorders. *Journal of the American Academy of Child and Adolescent Psychiatry* 38:680–85.

Wilson, A., Passik, S. D., Faude, J., Abrams, J., and Gordon, E. (1989). A hierarchical model of opiate addiction: Failures of self-regulation as a central aspect of substance abuse. *Journal of Nervous and Mental Diseases* 177:390–93.

Woody, G. E., Luborsky, L., McLellan, A. T., et al. (1983). Psychotherapy for opiate addicts. *Archives of General Psychiatry* 40:639–45.

Woody, G. E., McLellan, A. T., Luborsky, L., et al. (1995). Psychotherapy in community methadone programs: A validation study. *American Journal of Psychiatry* 152:1302–8.

Wurmser, L. (1974). Psychoanalytic considerations of the etiology of compulsive drug use. *Journal of the American Psychoanalytic Association* 22:820–43.

Yorke, C. (1970). A critical review of some psychoanalytic literature on drug addiction. *British Journal of Medical Psychology* 43:141.

Zucker, R. A., and Gomberg, E.S. L. (1986). Etiology of alcoholism reconsidered: The case for a biopsychosocial process. *American Psychologist* 41:783–93.

CHAPTER 2

Questions of Substance

PSYCHODYNAMIC REFLECTIONS ON ADDICTIVE VULNERABILITY AND TREATMENT

With Martin Weegmann

This dialogue between two clinicians, who have each specialized in the treatment and psychodynamic research of addiction over many years, considers the continuing relevance of psychodynamic views and importance of a broadly self-medication and relational stance. We discuss the psychotherapy of addiction and those qualities required by the worker, particularly important in view of the tremendous chaos, suffering, and confusion our patients experience. In the final section, on change and recovery, we compare notes on how individuals move forward and surmount addictive problems and patterns, whether in group or individual work.

Relevance of the Psychoanalytic Perspective

Martin: Your "self-medication hypothesis" (SMH; Khantzian 1985, 1997) offers an adaptive, evidence-based and far less sweeping psychodynamic perspective than those prevailing in the past, which were highly speculative and theory-based. Is there a link between the SHM and contemporary attachment theory? I'm thinking of Bill Reading's (2002) ideas on misattachment to drugs and the pernicious replacement of "affectional bonds" by "addictional bonds." Secondly, is it true that all substance misusers exhibit serious psychopathology? Some other approaches (motivational interviewing, relapse prevention) de-emphasize pathology altogether and eschew labels.

Edward: For the readers who are not familiar with the SMH, I should briefly identify and define its key elements. In contrast to early psychoanalytic theories of addiction, and not insignificantly contemporary neuroscientific theory, that identify pleasure and reward as motivating addictions, the SMH places human psychological suffering at the heart of addictive disorders. There are two aspects of the SMH: first addictive drugs become compelling because they relieve or change a range of painful or intolerable feelings (affects), and secondly, there is a considerable degree of specificity or preference in a person drug-of-choice (Khantzian 1985, 1997).

Indeed, in my experience there is a preeminent link between the SMH and contemporary attachment theory. In individual and group psychotherapy, addicted patients tell and demonstrate a lot about not only how addictive drugs help to cope with a troubled inner emotional terrain, but they just as often are conveying how troublesome the interpersonal terrain is for them and how addictive substances help to deal with difficulties in relating to others. Bill Reading is correct in concluding that attachment to addictive drugs is a "mis-attachment," substituting for more ordinary and necessary affectional bonds. For individuals flooded with rage, for example, such affect is fragmenting within and threatening from without, making relationships unlikely or impossible; such individuals have the discovery that opiates re-hinge within and make connections to others less threatening and thus more possible. The enfeebled and deenergized find the activating properties of stimulants to be agents that mobilize them and make the negotiation of human relationships more likely and even enjoyable; otherwise they feel unattainable. Those who suffer with anxiety are deterred from the company of others either because their apprehension immobilizes them, or defensive restraint removes them from the company of others. Aside from these affective components precluding interpersonal connections, for which I give examples here, there are of course developmental precedents that heighten and are related to the difficulties with relationships. It is on this basis of disordered emotions and object relationships, perhaps, that Phil Flores (2004) has suggested that addiction is an attachment disorder.

With regard to your question about serious psychopathology in addicted individuals, in my early work with addictive disorders (mainly with opioid dependent individuals coming to a methadone program), I was lecturing and writing that addiction "was associated with severe and significant psychopathology unless proven otherwise." In retrospect, I believe this conclusion was more a reflection of the population that I was working with at that time where the patients that we were dealing with were coming from more impoverished and traumatizing backgrounds. It probably also reflected my beginning venture with early psychoanalytic thinking and theory, just being out of psychoanalytic training. In contrast to that quote which I now find embarrassing, if not extreme and offensive, I have come to a different conclusion, namely, that many of my patients in recovery are some of the most mature and admirable people that I have worked with. This evolution in my thinking is reflected in more contemporary psychodynamic voices as well, which would indicate that addiction is less a function of pervasive psychopathology, but more a reflection of dysfunction or vulnerability in sectors of personality organization.

I wonder, Martin, if your experience is similar to mine with regard to troubled object relation as an important determinant and predisposing factor in addictive disorders, and whether you can describe how you witness attachment issues play out in individual and group psychotherapy?

Martin: I agree with your view that it is unhelpful to generalize about those with substance misuse (SM).[1] Older psychoanalytic views about primitive fixation, pre-oedipal problems, oral dependency, and so on are woefully inadequate, so I think it wise to have a different kind of language of explanation (e.g., developmental deficits, sectors of vulnerability/distortion, retreats, psychosocial adversity/opportunity, affect dysregulation, etc.). Early theory was excessively drive-oriented, speculative and highly interpretive; by contrast, modern perspectives, such as the ones represented elsewhere in this special edition, are more collaborative, attuned to painful self- and affect-states and interpersonal deficits, and draw more on the here and now—what is generated in the relationship with the therapist. However, at an individual level, the relation of psychopathology and addiction presents a chicken-and-egg dilemma. Causes and correlations are frequently confused, and while many SMs have histories of serious developmental disadvantage, deprivation, and so on, not all do and some are difficult and troubled adults even when they have not been difficult and disadvantaged children. Drugs and drink cause extensive trauma in themselves (e.g., loss of control, reduced awareness, legal consequences, damage to "livers and lovers," as Jim Orford (1985) puts it); damage doubles up. Risk, resilience, chance, availability, metabolism, the presence of helpful or harmful others all play a part and, crucially, how does the individual construe experience? There is a useful anecdote about two brothers in therapy, each complaining about their alcoholic father: one says, "I drink a lot 'cause of my dad," and the other, "With a dad like mine, small wonder I'm teetotal." What can be de-stabilizing or shattering to one individual might have a steeling effect on another.

Beyond the individual level, analytic therapists have to appreciate cultural locations—as you did, when you referred to a particular constituency of opiate-dependent users from poor backgrounds. As a group analyst I'm fascinated by social unconscious reality as a component of psychic reality. So, from this point

---

1. Three abbreviations are used in this chapter, not to be confused with each other. "SMH" refers to the self-medication hypothesis; "SM" refers to substance misuse; and "SMs" refers to substance misusers.

of view, I don't think that widespread opium use, across the social classes, in 19th-century Britain, or in certain countries nowadays, can be reduced to individual pathology. Indeed, it can easily be argued that opium use was adaptive to those who were ill-fed, ill-housed and subject to abject labor conditions. De Quincey, in his famous confession, spoke about opium preparations as cheap, portable ecstasies. Likewise, when many Vietnam vets returned, most were able to cease the heroin use on which many had relied, to cope with fear, boredom, and so on. Of course, much depended on their life circumstances, resources and the ability to re-adapt to a purposeful civilian life.

Regarding attachment, I see Bill Reading's perspective as pragmatic—how are people's attachment needs sidetracked and how does the drug take over as object of security? Relapse is a re-seeking of proximity, to the familiar object. The Flores view is valuable, but I fear can become an over-generalization; for me, addiction is a "disorder of affect regulation," in the way you have described, rather than an "attachment disorder" universally based on childhood insecure attachment patterns. This is not to underestimate countless tragic histories of abuse and betrayal, nor to discount powerful internal processes of avoidance, counter-dependence, vengeance on self or the creation of all-purpose retreats.

Clinically, attachment to the drug is the obvious challenge. Just as children develop internal working models in which expectancies of care and response are envisaged, so too the drug user has an internal working model of the substance—what it can do, what is desired and so on. Correspondingly, in the initial stages, does the client see the therapist as a threat, coming between them and their drug, spoiling an affair, as it were, or do they see the therapist as an ally, a friend in the face of the addiction? Anna Freud made a similar point a longtime ago. I like to think in terms of a dynamic triangle—"therapist/client/drug"—and concentrate on the task, "how can I build upon my client's (even when minimal) interest in what they are doing to themselves?" Two cases come to mind. During an assessment, a young drug user bragged about his injecting ability, showing his veins defiantly. Tragically, he had lost a leg due to injecting. Here, maybe I was being told, "I've got the power, the drug, I can do what I like, and you can't stop me—I can turn tragedy into triumph." More to the point, he put two fingers up at the core values of the agency—harm reduction. Perhaps he was demonstrating a posture of "attack, so that I don't have to attach, to anyone or anything, other than my drug"? Second, in a group, a dry drinker always sat close to me, leaning closer still when others spoke about temptation and relapses. Perhaps she was expressing fear, clinging to me as authority in the group, for the strength she felt she did not have. This strikes me as proximity-seeking behavior and lack of security, or trust, in alternatives. Drugs erode structures, as Kohut (1977) put it, and life beyond drugs is uncertain, if not terrifying.

Psychotherapy of Addiction

Martin: What are optimal therapist qualities in this field?

Edward: I am inclined to begin my response by saying what they are not. Therapists doing this work best not be stiff, unfriendly, humorless, or doctrinaire. On the other hand, our patients need us to be accessible, engaging, and attuned to what psychological and painful environmental issues have made a reliance on substances of dependence seem so necessary. Recently, preparing for a lecture, I found myself considering what I thought were essential elements for effective treatment, regardless of theoretical orientation. Among the qualities that I thought about which are most important I would list *kindness, empathy*, and *comfort* as foremost in what we bring to our patient encounters. To that I would add *patience* (keeping in mind the problems with alexithymia, action, avoidance), being *instructive* (e.g., help patience to learn about emotions and self-care), *self-awareness, mutual respect* (i.e., the therapeutic alliance), and *balance* (talking and listening).

To start with *kindness* might seem too self-evident or trivial to mention. Nevertheless, it is an important quality for clinicians to cultivate for several reasons. First, the notion that "you can't trust an addict" still looms in our work, and if you harbor such an attitude—and, worse still, if you harbor it and are unaware—it is unlikely you will connect effectively (or kindly) to patients. A second reason to mention kindness stems from the fact that classical psychodynamic therapies fostered a climate of reserve growing out of the traditions of the "blank screen" and "therapeutic neutrality"; these traditions and influences die a slow death and still pervade and influence therapist of many different orientations more than one might admit or be aware of. These traditions are obviously distancing and not apt to foster a climate of acceptance and understanding. For similar reasons, if clinicians are not careful, they might be unwittingly weary of adopting *empathy* as an important quality to adopt in practice. Whether one has an addiction problem, or for that matter has any other source of distress or dysfunction, feeling heard and understood is one of the most liberating human experiences. In therapeutic relationships they are essential aspects of empathy. Having stressed the importance of kindness and empathy, I should hasten to add that these elements of therapy should be adopted with a dose of restraint and concerns for tolerability, given that patients can be made to feel very uncomfortable with an empathic approach if they feel undeserving, struggling with darker feelings of rage and resentment, or are not forthcoming. This could be a setup for a misalignment and feeling not understood. Such an approach might also be experienced as threatening for individuals who fear human closeness and/or severely traumatized individuals such as borderline patients. As someone once said, "You can empathize someone right out of the room." As for the quality of *comfort* we must bring to our patients, it is important to remember that they can be so discomforted about matters involving emotions, self-esteem, and relationships, and that their problems with self-care leave them disquietingly on the edge of harm. Any one or more of these might be operative in-patient encounters and appreciating and gently tuning into to these vulnerabilities will go far in providing and cultivating comfort. Of course, *self-awareness* must be a cornerstone of psychotherapy and we try to foster it in our patients, but more often we can forget the importance of it and we continuously must monitor for it in ourselves as well. Intersubjective theory has taught us well the importance of what the therapeutic encounter engenders in us as important clues for appreciating the inner terrain of what our patients' experience. How to elaborate on *mutual respect* but to relate it to the last bullet—namely, such respect grows out of the manner in which we listen to and speak with our patients, balancing listening with an ease and spontaneity in speaking, sounding like neither an oracle or a detached observer. Are these not the main and important ingredients of the therapeutic alliance?

Martin: That's a useful list, but it's hard to distinguish qualities suited to work in mental health in general from those associated with SM work. Being interested in the training and cultivation of capacities, I think that a basic commitment to this client group is essential—not everyone can work in this field or should. One specific counter-transference enigma is, how do we keep our faith in words, in understanding and in the power of human contact, when the person in front of us is seeking their solutions and power in the drug? It is important to know something about one's own "cultural" counter-transference, as Schoenewolf (1993) has put it—meaning one's attitudes toward drugs, alcohol, use and misuse, including the cultural connotation which they have in our particular upbringing. Everyone has a relationship to drugs and alcohol. Therapeutic commitment is essential, as SMs, like anyone else, will see through anyone just going through the motions. To add to the capacities, I'd say a good degree of stability—centeredness—as we have to witness chaotic worlds, escalating situations and reversals all the time. A similar point has been made by Wilson (1994) in relation to PTSD, and many a time we will simply have no real idea what it is like to live in the shoes of someone living on the edge, from crisis to drama, within a culture we can only imagine from a distance. Having clear values helps, although one does not wish to impose these on others. Being secure and supported in one's role is also crucial—so that one is not swept off one's feet by client demands to be rid of pain, magical expectations and so on. At a deep level, how do we respond to individuals who seem to have lost control and where moderation/regulation seems impossible?

Of course, one has to understand chronicity while maintaining a realistically hopeful stance. I'm interested in the strains of staying with the damage that surround SMs—how do we face it, without loss of nerve, complacency or cynicism? How do we help SMs face the damage they would prefer not to know about? One thing I've learned over the years is that SMs can and will take us to the very edges of human experience—when despondency sets in, when fear predominates, where acting is automatic and where thinking is sacrificed. The image of "psychic retreats" is helpful, but with SMs the real risk is that the person moves into the retreat full-time, it becoming a way of life. Consequently, it is very hard for addicted persons to believe they can return from drug exile, to live normally again. Addiction can be compared to the sort of "black sun" that Kristeva (1989) uses to characterize melancholia, with the user caught, as it were, in an "exitless personal vault." On the other hand, our clients always surprise us, so I'd hate to lose my capacity for realistic wonder, appreciation and enjoyment of the others' progress. Many SMs do recover and it is impossible to predict whom it will be in advance—the course of true therapy (and life) never did run smooth. The last thing, quality-wise, is, due acceptance of not knowing; unless one has had addiction problems—even so, which I have not, it is hard to comprehend the addictive process—the stranglehold of the drugs, the take-over and the tragic asset stripping of human qualities. So, I say, respect the disorder and our relative ignorance about addiction.

Edward: To comment on your compelling reference to the chaos, suffering, and confusion our patients experience, your observation about the plight of addicted individuals causes me to refer back to previous comments you made about not pathologizing addicted patients and appreciating the cultural and environmental influences on the development and course of addictive disorders. You rightfully used terms such as "developmental deficits, sectors of distortion, psychosocial adversity, affect dysregulation, etc." as opposed to psychopathology. I do not believe I did justice to your thoughtful and evocative remarks. Many critics of the SMH focus on looking for correlations between psychiatric disorders and SM factors. I have always insisted that individuals are self-medicating painful or bewildering affect states, ones that you elaborate upon. Such distress may or may not be associated with psychiatric conditions. Individuals could be said to be self-medicating depression, for example, but more likely they are trying to relieve agitation, lethargy, and/or states of anergia associated with depression, as are schizophrenic patients, for example, self-medicating negative symptoms such as anhedonia and asociality due to their illness.

I agree that my list makes one ponder if the qualities we bring to substance-dependent individuals are or should be that different than those required for individuals with other psychiatric conditions. You rightfully point out, however, that our work does require a special kind of commitment, centeredness and values. Where we are in our careers and when we are doing the work also makes a difference. Starting our methadone clinic early in my career in the 1970s, in the setting of a municipal hospital in a run-down building on remote hospital grounds, I recall a better-put-together (not addicted) patient commenting about the exposed pipes, dirty walls, and pealing paint in my office, saying, "Doc, I'm wondering whether you are a dedicated physician working in a dump like this, or whether you are on the skids." Needless to say, the work surrounds were neither accommodating nor pleasant—much like the surrounds of most of our patients coming to the methadone clinic. In contrast, my current private office is modestly appointed but comfortable and reasonably pleasant. The patients are also more stable and settled coming from more agreeable and less disrupted backgrounds than those of thirty or more years ago. Depending on the environment in which we find ourselves, our work locates us and our patients differently. I would add these background and foreground factors to your comments about the predisposing and consequential chaos associated with addictions and how they affect attitudes about hope and despair in our work. As you remind us, the elusive nature and the "not knowing" aspects of therapeutic work with addicted patients should instill a measure of humility about expectations for ourselves and our patients if we want to do this work.

Can you comment more on the models and means you draw upon to hold yourself therapeutically to the bedeviling and challenging difficulties our patients face?

Martin: I like that gestalt image of background/foreground. Clients react to buildings, waiting areas and services as much as to individual therapists and this is a reason why work with fellow workers is so important—supervision, work discussion, training. As for models and means, no one model is ever sufficient. As a result, I like to play with and travel between models, adapting what I do as much as I can to a client's needs; this is "traveling theory," to use a wonderful term of Edward Said's. But we need to understand the *clients'* model foremost. Models are to a degree self-objects, are they not? They provide therapists with a sense of coherence, predictability, confidence, etc. Psychoanalytically, I might move between ideas from self-psychology (e.g., the drug as self-object, soothing object and so on), attachment and *mentalization* models (e.g., building a safe base for exploration, expanding the capacity to "think about" inner states and cues) and the Kleinian (e.g., the idea of the psychic positions people oscillate between) and so on. Context counts for all—not only the life context of the addict, their supportive and harmful networks but also the context of treatment, its ethos, structure, governing principles; group analyst Barbara Elliot talks about the centrality of context, even over content, in substance misuse interventions

(Elliot 2003). I'm much influenced by one of America's finest pragmatists, John Dewey, who devoted his life to the idea that knowledge is linked to intervening, that we work on local problems and develop reflective thinking/inquiry; I try in my work to cultivate a parallel attitude of inquiry with and in my clients, daring them to think otherwise, to take that road "less travelled by" (Frost 1920). There is so much fear of change, the "solution" seemingly scarier than the drug.

In recent years, I've incorporated ideas from narrative approaches; it used to be said that the "superego is soluble in alcohol," true enough, but for me the *symbolic* is equally washed away by substances. Addiction spells the death of reflection, it is story-stopping. The power of ordinary stories and discourse cannot be overestimated (AA has known this for decades) and SMs desperately need support to change the way they think and talk about themselves and others. From a narrative viewpoint, addiction has romantic, ironic and tragic and clearly repetitive elements. So how do we enable story-change and release a different kind of author? For me, and for practitioners like Jonathan Diamond in the United States, the psychoanalytic and narrative fit very well together.

SMs need analytic understanding, as distinct from actual analytic therapy, at all stages—active using, early sobriety, controlled usage, medium-term recovery, relapse prevention and long-term abstinence. It is one reason why I find Kaufman's (1994) "three-stage model" of early-, medium- and long-term recovery useful as well as your "four 'c's'": control, containment, contact and comfort. A UK colleague has developed the "stepped care" model (Shamil Wanigaratne 2002), albeit using a different terminology. I find it essential to integrate my psychodynamic orientation with approaches such as MI, relapse prevention and Twelve-Step Facilitation.

In terms of inner means—strong, even-minded curiosity helps me and so does a humanist faith; it is important if very difficult to have enough empathy for the *addict* in the addict, as it were, as well as the person wanting—in theory—to get out or to change. Simply holding onto one's chair was an image used by Bion, which is essential at times, but I remind myself that as I grip mine, a person opposite may have a tenuous hold over his/her very life.

Do you think that time limited/focused or more open-ended psychodynamic work is best?

Edward: Before responding to your last question I wanted to comment that I appreciate your reference to flexibly adopting different models to accommodate to the needs of our patients. As Goldberg (1990) has suggested, we psychodynamic types can become imprisoned by our theories, thus running the risk of shoe horning our patients into the prevailing theories we adopt or prefer. I am also reminded of Richard Chessick's book (1989), in which he elegantly reminds us that patients respond best when we listen through different channels such as those of object relations, self-psychology, or interactional theory to best tune into the inner landscape of our patients' experiences. The key operative in how we access and tune into our patients should be that of "client needs."

As for your question what has worked best for me, in my private practice I have always been most comfortable with an open ended psychodynamic model in which the patient and I discover over time what is appropriate in terms of length and intensity of treatment. Actually doing long-term work, with many patients it turns out operationally that there are a series of therapies at different times, some of shorter and some of longer duration, often combing individual work with group therapy. I would also single out a growing conviction that I have come by about long-term group therapy, especially in terms of fostering and maintaining contact and comfort. Namely, that it is entirely appropriate and beneficial, finding this to be so even with well put together patients. Connection to trusted, admired, and caring people is an invaluable buffer against despair, anxiety, and discontent, key ingredients for relapse. In this way, group therapy works much the same way as individuals who draw such comfort from participating in twelve step programs for many years, albeit the latter is more cost efficient, and the former is more sustaining, intimate, and focused.

Recovery and Change

Edward: I wonder whether you might begin here by reflecting on what you think are some of the essential elements of treatment that stimulate recovery and change?

Martin: I like the old adage about why do drunks hang around lamp posts, is it for illumination or support? Joking aside, help for SMs will vary relative to a given point (e.g., active support, cognitive linking, emotional acceptance, etc.) for someone who during, say, a third detox, has a crashing realization of the damage done to self and others. How to help him face this, including irreversible damage, and encourage further recovery, so he does not go out to re-use the drug that caused the damage, that blocks awareness of the damage that led to the detox in the first place? Likewise, how does one support someone who, in the early months of recovery, experiences what I call "abstinence disappointment" or "recovery resentment"? She begins to feel cheated—why isn't life "better" now that she has stopped and why are others still mistrustful? Here one has to take on board the feelings of let down, escalating rage, resentment and the like. Bill W. (1967) had a good way of describing this, something like "When we harbored grudges and planned revenge for defeats. We were really beating ourselves with the club of anger we had." As we assist more solid progress, encouraging reflective self-capacities and self-care is central, is it not? Once again, you will glean my pragmatist, psychodynamic style at work—staying with the local, with goals that are attainable, starting from "where the client is at." I use your idea of "disuse atrophy" a lot—people, over years of misuse, lose their ordinary capacities, ability to plan, and so on. The therapist can act in part as a resource for building the self and also as kind of memory—holding the consequences of previous addiction, relapses in mind, so easily lost in seas of nostalgia, minimisation and efforts to recapture lost highs. Staying with difficult counter transference is essential—if we cannot, how do we expect our clients to tolerate the worse feelings that they can experience?

The mystery of recovery fascinates me. Why do some need extensive professional help and others stop, by other means? Some believe that Fellowship Groups (AA, NA, and so on) offer the strongest resource of social hope—an "I can't, we can" realism. Would you go so far as to say that AA (for example) and psychotherapy is the ideal marriage?

Edward: If not, they are at least compatible and kissing cousins. Referring back to your joke, they both offer elements of illumination and support—albeit AA more serendipitously and with less focus on specific vulnerabilities than our therapies attempt to orchestrate. John Mack (1981) in an important, seminal paper referred to the "we" aspect of AA by emphasizing how it fosters the required interdependence that the human condition dictates, an aspect of life that so often has eluded individuals suffering addictive disorders. He proposes that self-governance is not a solitary process, but that it occurs best in the context of involved and caring others. The presence of and connection to others more likely assures safety, comfort, and the sense of well-being. AA succeeds in my experience because it provides a necessary and immediate installation of these ingredients which in turn provides the structure and guides for promoting containment and abstinence. Although there is now more empirical evidence about the efficacy of AA (Project MATCH 1997), it does not work for everybody. It has been my experience that playing the role of a primary care therapist one can hold patients to additional treatments and programs, including AA, and the therapist can then monitor for acceptance and benefit (or the lack thereof) and broker alternative approaches when the recommended ones do not work (Khantzian 1988).

Your comments about the varying and variable needs that emerge in recovering individuals are more often better served by the individual and group therapies we employ. Our treatments provide opportunities to fine-tune and focus upon recurrent or idiosyncratic issues that our patients face or experience which have either predisposed them to or resulted as a consequence of their addictive illness. Nevertheless, I agree with you that it is so hard to predict how or to explain why some recover spontaneously without intervention of any kind, some flourish with AA alone, and others yet require and benefit from a full-court press combining elements of self-help, individual and group therapy. As previously mentioned, my adopting a role as a "primary care therapist" allows me to broker and monitor responses to the potentially helpful elements of different modalities we recommend to our patients. It often turns out, for example, that the situation of individual psychotherapy is bewilderingly uncomfortable for a person, but that the context of AA for that same individual is much more helpful in identifying and understanding the "people, places, and things" that contributes to addictive behaviour and relapse. I would finally offer here that if an individual can accept both AA and psychotherapy, they more often can be a powerful combination in providing the containing and transforming influences required for change and recovery, and indeed, in that respect they can make for an "ideal marriage."

Martin: Can you give a recent example of successful recovery? What helped them to take action, resolve dilemmas and move forward?

Edward: The case[2] that comes to mind is that of Hank, a married alcoholic dependent man in his mid-40s, with a four-year-old daughter when he first visited with me. He continued to see me in individual and group therapy for the next five years. Over that period there were a series of minor and major relapses, the main consequences of which were in his marriage. He was an admirably frank, thoughtful, and considerate man, who despite a background of early loss (his father died when he was eight years old, mother remained depressed all of his life, and his brother nine years older became alcoholic by his late teens) continued to be resilient in pursuing his college and graduate studies, albeit punctuated by the alcoholic setbacks. In his treatment he had the realization that the experience of relapse while in treatment with me was part of what ultimately helped to sustain his recovery.

When we first met a major source of distress was his work as an administrator in a not for profit agency serving youthful offenders, a position from which he had just resigned. Funding cutbacks and a menacing supervisor were interfering with his usual kind and supportive style in working with agency staff and clients. The combinations of the workplace stress, the layoffs which he had to process with his staff, and his escalating use of alcohol caused him to take a leave of absence and ultimately to resign his position. Because he had married into an affluent family, and because they were generously supported by her family, he enjoyed the "luxury" of taking an extended period of unemployment. Subsequently after about a year, his wife returned to previous employment as

2. Hank gave written permission to use his case in the disguised form in which it is presented here.

a corporate attorney and he took responsibility for being a stay-at-home dad which he effectively and admirably embraced. Admittedly the financial affluence he enjoyed was a significant advantage in pursuing treatment, but it was not the most important factor in his eventual recovery.

Much of his individual psychotherapy focused on his chronic sense of dysphoria, rooted in difficulties in identifying and giving voice to his feelings, a tendency to be isolative socially (he had few, if any, close friends), and a shaky self-esteem. Fortunately, a therapy group to which I introduced him turned out to be a group of men who were frank speaking, supportive, and earthy (I came to refer to them as a "salty bunch of characters"). The group provided a needed source for contact and comfort. An unanticipated benefit of the group was that most of the men, including Hank, were taking positively to AA and they frequently reminded each other of the containing and beneficial socializing influence of the program. Clearly the group was a powerful therapeutic factor in his ultimate recovery, but one of the most therapeutic aspects of the group experience for Hank was the group's tactful persistence in pointing out the isolating nature of his stay at home role and the erosion on any self-confidence that he might have. Despite the commitment of the members to abstinence, it happened that the group turned out to be one of "harm reduction," such that for most of them abstinence only gradually evolved, including for Hank. This is a group that we previously reported upon (Khantzian 2006) in which during a particular group session Hank articulated his appreciation for the group culture which, albeit somewhat permissive about relapses, had worked in such a way that the relapses were neither prolonged or devastating and that none of them needed frequent detoxifications as they had previously required.

Ultimately it was a major relapse for Hank that set in motion a total commitment to changing his relationship with alcohol, his career, and family. The group's increasing concern about his escalating regular drinking, his own resulting weariness from daily hangovers, and characteristic alarm, and final ultimatums from his wife, resulted in his acceptance of a popular detoxification and rehabilitation program. These converging elements solidified a plan and program for major alterations in family and career changes. Within a year after release from rehab, and after a year of complete abstinence from alcohol, he succeeded in negotiating admission to an institute for training as a mental health counselor. One of the beneficial aspects of this development was that he rediscovered his love for study and research. Writing assignments and papers were enjoyable challenges which he met with excitement and enthusiasm. Intern assignments with clients, including leading group counseling sessions himself, was similarly welcomed. I and the group witnessed the emergence of a different persona, one of an upbeat, confident and eager man, qualities that stood out in contrast to his previous more apathetic way of being.

To summarize, it was elements of individual therapy, the power of the group therapeutic experiences, chance (i.e., the unique composition of the group), the crises in his relationship with his wife, and a valuable rehabilitation experience that beneficially converged to allow a good and decent man to discover, rediscover and redefine himself. Finally, I would also single out the context of individual and group therapy wherein the therapist, patient, and other group members bear witness to the setbacks and successes that is invaluable in promoting the change and maturation we associate with recovery.

Edward: One of my favorite quotes regarding group therapy, not without significance, by two British analysts, is the following:

> *After a successful psychoanalytic treatment a patient is definitely less neurotic (or psychotic) but perhaps not necessarily more mature. On the other hand after a successful treatment by group methods the patient is not necessarily less neurotic but inevitably more mature.* (Enid and Michael Balint; Balint [1972])

Appreciating the importance of group experiences, whether of the self-help or therapeutic kind, do you agree with the Balints, and if so, might you elaborate on why you think it is so that group experiences foster maturation and how and why this is important for recovery?

Martin: I would need to qualify my keenness. Whilst group is often restorative, I'd want to advocate equally for the role of individual therapy. Some clients require the attention and transformative potential of a specific relationship with a therapist, whose detailed interest and acceptance of them is paramount. Underneath every couch (or chair) however is a group, so I actively keep the individual's "groupself" in mind (e.g., it might be a delinquent peer group, conflictual family group, supportive network, and so on). Rey (1988) wrote a valuable paper on the question of *who* the patient brings with them into therapy and I'd add to his list of "internal objects," a person's cultural locations and identity, which takes us back to the social unconscious; so, what models of drinking/using were there in her culture? How was intoxication and excess viewed? Was there a sober household? How were men supposed to act? What values fed responses to emotional distress, or developmental achievement, for that matter? The "storied self," to use a narrative term, is more than an assemblage of "internal objects," so called.

When a person joins or graduates into a group that is a good sign. We have both written extensively on how AA works as a remarkable "group therapy without the group therapist," how the Twelve Steps act as guides and metaphors for living and how group membership addresses isolation, grandiosity, counter-dependence and the like. To paraphrase my favorite playwright (Eugene O'Neil), if alcoholics are broken, the grace of AA groups is glue! I certainly testify to the maturing effects of group membership, whether mutual-help or professional groups. Just having one's "terminal uniqueness" (an AA saying) tempered, beliefs such as "no one else understands" disabused, more points of view to listen to than one's own and the inevitability that others have illuminations that one could not achieve alone . . . all these things help. "Kinship in suffering" was how Bill W. put it, whilst Foulkes spoke about 'being in the same boat." With group one has no option but to hear, contribute to, be part of a multi-dialogical reality and all the wisdom or growth can result from this "surplus of vision"; SMs need to re-learn *sober* dialogue, to be specific (Weegmann, submitted). In individual therapy, there are fewer voices to contend with, and many SMs require the intimacy—"into-me-see"—and the reliable, thoughtful presence of one other who can help still the clouded mind. Some require others in the plural, or both at different junctures. So, I believe that "maturity" and "less neurotic" don't have to be in competition.

Martin: I wonder about the "recovery" word in our field. Is it quite enough to capture all that might be involved in moving from the long shadow of addiction? Given I don't have an alternative word, how do you see the main processes of recovery?

Edward: Serendipitously, recently reviewing a report for a program for recovering physicians, I came on a wonderful quote that positioned me to think about my work with patients who have achieved solid recovery. The quote was "The world breaks everyone and afterward many are strong at the broken places" (Ernest Hemingway, *A Farewell to Arms*, 1929). For me this quote means that where addictions have broken a person, there is a reversal and attrition of mindless, repetitive self-defeating behavior, social isolation, shaky or absent self-esteem and restrictions in knowing, tolerating and expressing emotions. Or, put more positively, there is growing thoughtfulness about and monitoring of one's behavior, a greater capacity to relate and connect to others, a better evaluation and sense of self, and more ease in recognizing, tolerating and expressing feelings. To boil this down to a couple of words, successful recovery essentially involves *repair* and *maturation*.

Martin: I suspect you are more optimistic than me, at least on this day. I see recovery as provisional, based on a constant dialectic of overcoming and reversal, movement forward and steps backward. Inner reparation is difficult enough when the loss encountered or damage done is predominantly at the level of feelings and fantasy, but is still greater when that loss and damage is actual, in which case, one often has to significantly change one's life and make real amends, where this is still possible or desirable, a process deeply embedded in fellowship traditions but unaddressed in many of the psychotherapies. I suspect some can take shorter cuts than others, perhaps because they (and their loved ones) are just relieved that they no longer have to maintain a habit. Others benefit from a much more thorough-going reconstruction of self and commitments, in which case I would say that spiritual change is required. We know that Jung in his letter to Bill W. said, "*spiritus contra spiritum*" ("spirits drives out spirituality"). In this connection, I'd like to see a psychodynamic tradition that is more at home with concepts of forgiveness, compassion and value-change. That way, SMs can begin to construct a viable life, "after drugs" as it were. Ed, thanks for the pleasure of this exchange.

Acknowledgments

Thanks to Steve Ryan for suggestions.

References

Balint, E. (1972). Fair shares and mutual concerns. *International Journal of Psychoanalysis* 53:61–65.
Bill W. (1967). *As Bill Sees It: The AA Way of Life*. New York: Alcoholics Anonymous World Services Inc.
Burton, N. (2005). Finding the lost girls: Multiplicity and dissociation in the treatment of addictions. *Psychoanalytic Dialogues* 15 (4): 587–612.
Chessick, R. (1989). *The Technique & Practice of Listening in Intensive Psychotherapy*. New York: Jason Aronson.
Director, L. (2005). Encounters with omnipotence in the psychoanalysis of substance users. *Psychoanalytic Dialogues* 15 (4): 567–86.
Elliot, B. (2003). *Containing the Uncontainable: Alcohol Misuse and the Personal Choice Community Programme*. Chichester: Wiley.
Flores, P. J. (2004). *Addiction as an Attachment Disorder*. New York: Jason Aronson.
Frost, R. (1920). The road less travelled. Poem.
Goldberg, A. (1990). *The Prisonhouse of Psychoanalysis*. Hillsdale, NJ: Analytic Press.
Kaufman, E. (1996). *Psychotherapy of Addicted Persons*. New York: Guildford Press.
Khantzian, E. J. (1985). The self-medication hypothesis of addictive disorders: Focus on heroin and cocaine dependence. *American Journal Psychiatry* 142:1259–64.
———. (1988). The primary care therapist and patient needs in substance abuse treatment. *American Journal of Drug and Alcohol Abuse* 14 (2): 159–67.

————. (1997). The self-medication hypothesis of substance use disorders: A reconsideration and recent applications. *Harvard Review Psychiatry* 4:231–44.

————. (2006). Group therapy, abstinence, harm reduction: The real and honest word. *Journal of Groups in Addiction & Recovery* 1 (2): 5–13.

Kohut, H. (1977). Preface to *The Psychodynamics of Drug Dependence*, edited by J. Blaine and D. Julius. NIDA Monograph. Washington, DC: Government Printing Office.

Kristeva, J. (1989). *Black Sun: Depression and Melancholia.* Translated by Leon Roudiez. New York: Columbia University Press.

Mack, J. E. (1981). Alcoholism, AA and the governance of the self. In *Dynamic Approaches to the Understanding and Treatment of Alcoholism*, edited by M. H. Bean and N. E. Zinberg, 128–62. New York: Free Press.

Orford, J. (1985). *Excessive Appetites: A Psychological View of Addictions.* Chichester: Wiley.

Project MATCH Research Group. (1997). Matching alcoholism treatment to client heterogeneity: Project MATCH Posttreatment Drinking Outcomes. *Journal of Studies on Alcohol* 58:7–29.

Reading, B. (2002). The application of Bowlby's attachment theory to the psychotherapy of addictions, In *Psychodynamics of Addiction*, edited by M. Weegmann and R. Cohen. Chichester: Wiley.

Rey, H. (1988). That which patients bring to analysis. *International Journal of Psychoanalysis* 69:457–70.

Schoenewolf, G. (1993). *Counterresistance: The Therapist's Interference with the Therapeutic Process.* New York: Jason Aronson.

Wanigaratne, S., and Kearney. F. (2002). Psychodynamic aspects of relapse prevention in the treatment of addictive disorders. In *Psychodynamics of Addiction*, edited by M. Weegmann and R. Cohen. Chichester: Wiley.

Weegmann, M. Beyond the shadow of drugs: Group therapy for substance misusers. (Submitted to *Group Analysis*.)

Wilson, J., and Lindy, J., eds. (1994). *Countertransference in the Treatment of PTSD.* New York: Guilford Press.

CHAPTER 3

Addiction: Why Are Some of Us More Vulnerable Than Others?

Although neuroscientists have made major contributions over the past several decades in elucidating the brain mechanisms and underlying neurotransmitter systems involved with addictive drugs, there has been insufficient attention paid to what some of the psychological mechanisms and vulnerabilities might be to explain why addictive substances can be so seductive, consuming, and destructive. Clearly, regular use of addictive substances cause changes in the brain, produce physical dependence, and when an addicted person's drug is removed or cut off symptoms of withdrawal ensue. A wide range of distressing symptoms occur characteristic of the drug upon which the person has become dependent. Many argue that it is the acute and prolonged withdrawal symptoms and distress that cause addicted individuals to revert back to their use of addictive substances. In this chapter, we will present evidence and a point of view that there are other compelling reasons having to do with the ability of addictive drugs to relieve a range of distressful states that make them so appealing. Such a perspective does not and should not compete with the neurobiological aspects of addictive problems. In addition to emphasizing the general pain removing effects of addictive substances, we will sample a number of distressful clinical conditions where the co-occurrence of addiction is particularly high and causes individuals so affected to discover the pain-relieving properties of addictive drugs associated with their co-occurring disorders.

This chapter is based on three premises:

- We are all more or less susceptible to becoming drug dependent.
- Some of us are more susceptible for special reasons.
- Addictive drugs are not universally appealing.

The observations in this chapter are based on in-depth clinical evaluation and treatment of substance dependent individuals spanning a period of five decades, and they are complemented by empirical findings from recent psychiatric studies.

Addictive Vulnerability

Human nature dictates that challenges involving emotions, relationships, self-esteem, and behavior are inescapable. Addictive drugs have appeal because they relieve distress associated with these challenges. As I will elaborate, certain life conditions or disorders make addictive behavior more likely. Although I will emphasize certain conditions and types of addiction, I want to stress that it is the human condition that leaves us susceptible to substance use disorders (SUDs). In my experience human psychological suffering is at the root of addictive disorders; it is not primarily pleasure seeking, reward, or self-destruction as is often suggested. In recent years a metaphor has become popular to capture how addictive drugs captivate a person—namely, that the drugs "hijack" the brain pleasure centers. There is just as much evidence that the drugs hijack the mind—namely, the centers in the brain that regulate emotions and psychological pain. Individuals who succumb to addictive disorders are more often self-medicating psychological distress or suffering associated with psychiatric disorders.

Many of the observations in this chapter derive from the "self-medication hypothesis" (SMH) of addictive disorders, first articulated in 1985 and subsequently updated in 1997 (Khantzian 1985, 1997). Not infrequently it is referred as one of the "most intuitively appealing theories" of addiction (Glass 1990). There are two basic aspects of the SMH: (a) Individuals use, abuse, and become dependent upon addictive drugs because they relieve psychological distress; and (b) there is a considerable degree of specificity involved in an individual's drug preference. Although patients and others may refer to getting "high" or experiencing euphoria on addictive drug, when further questioned about how the drugs make them feel, individuals describe how addictive drugs relieve dysphoria associated with a range of uncomfortable feelings or painful emotions. The following are some of the distressful states relieved by the main classes of addictive drugs:

- *Opiates* help a person to feel "calm, mellow or normal"; they counter agitation, aggression, and violent feelings.
- *Stimulants* counter states of low energy, sense of weakness, and feeling unloved, often associated with depression; they also boost hyperenergized fast-lane people and they calm hyperactive individuals who have ADHD.

- *Alcohol/depressants*, depending on dose, drown out negative, unwelcome feelings (high doses), or can allow feeling of closeness and warmth (low doses) for those who cannot ordinarily allow such reactions (e.g., "I can feel like one of the guys . . . I can join the human race").

The above reactions can commonly be elicited by asking the simple question "what did the drug do for you when you first used it?" It turns out the question is not so simple in that patients will respond with such reactions that "it made me feel normal . . . calm . . . mellow for the first time." Individuals overwhelmed with rage and a sense of falling apart describe how opiates help them to feel more integrated and re-hinged; de-energized and de-activated individuals who are down on themselves say they are able to get going and feel better about themselves with the use of stimulants such as cocaine or crystal meth, and expansive bipolar types indicate they feel even better about themselves on stimulants; and restricted people say they can allow, otherwise unallowable, expression of affectionate (and aggressive) feelings and accept them with the loosening effects of alcohol. It is worth emphasizing that a person does not set out to become dependent on opiates, stimulants, or depressants. Rather individuals have a "discovery," in the process of experimentation, that one of these drugs best suits them because it relieves, changes, or makes more bearable particular feelings and dysphoria unique to them that are relieved by their drug of choice. As I indicated at the beginning of this chapter, addictive drugs are not universally appealing. In my experience, a person discovers that one drug or another is or becomes appealing because that person suffers with certain emotions, or distress associated with a psychiatric disorder, a state or condition in which the effect of the drug produces a welcome change or relief.

Based on the above observations I have concluded that addictions are a self-regulation disorder (Khantzian 1995). Substance users suffer because they have difficulties regulating their emotions, self-esteem, relationships, and behavior-especially self-care. A main feature of psychiatric illness is difficulties in self-regulation. Individuals discover, short term, that substances relieve, ameliorate, or help control emotional dysregulation associated with psychiatric illness.

Vulnerable Populations: A Sample

There is a significantly high co-occurrence of SUDs in patients with psychiatric disorders (Kessler et al. 1997). For the most part, studies documenting this high co-occurrence rate indicate that the psychiatric disorder preceded the SUD. With the pressure for clinicians to document and classify symptoms associated with psychiatric conditions to meet diagnostic criteria for third-party payers as specified in DSM-IVR, what is often lost site of is the enormous suffering associated with psychiatric illness. In this section, I will review several conditions in which there is a significant psychological distress linked to the need to revert to addictive drugs to deal with the associated suffering these conditions entail.

SCHIZOPHRENIA

Over the past several decades there has been an important development in elucidating the different types of symptoms associated with schizophrenia. Investigators distinguish between *positive* and *negative* symptoms, referring to the more florid symptoms of the disorder in the former case, and the more subtle, lingering symptoms in the latter. They are distinguished as follows:

Positive Symptoms	Negative Symptoms
Hallucinations	Alogia (paucity of words)
Delusions	Affective flattening
Paranoia	Anhedonia (inability to feel pleasure)
Agitation	Asociality
Aggression	Apathy
	Attentional impairments

These symptoms are painful, disruptive, and debilitating, each in their own way. The positive symptoms are frightening, unsettling, and often dramatic, threatening to those experiencing them and to those witnessing them. The positive symptoms are disturbing and painful enough, but negative symptoms are especially crippling in their persistence, and isolating in ways that interfere with necessary human relationships and interactions, giving such patients their indifferent, listless, withdrawn qualities. Although a schizophrenic patient, for example, might indicate that the voices they hear can be drowned out or that they can ignore them with heavy doses of alcohol, experiences which are distressing enough, it has been my experience that it is the pain and suffering associated with negative symptoms which schizophrenic individuals mainly try to overcome with their use of addictive substances. They are at least as painful, if not more so, because the negative symptoms are vague, confusing, and inaccessible.

Not surprisingly, addictive drugs ameliorate or change the distress associated with negative symptoms. There is a disproportionately very high co-occurrence of *nicotine dependence*, a stimulant, among schizophrenic patients. Whereas the occurrence of nicotine dependence is about 24 percent in the general population, it ranges between 70–90 percent in schizophrenic populations (Ziedonis et al. 1994). There is a surprisingly high incidence of cocaine dependence in this population as well. It is surprising with a drug such as cocaine, which can precipitate psychosis, one would wonder why a person with schizophrenia would be attracted to it. We and others (Brady et al. 1990) have concluded that such patients are self-medicating painful negative symptoms, more often protected from the drug's disorganizing effect when they are taking their antipsychotic medications. In fact, in one study, the investigators observed that schizophrenic patients admitted to an acute psychiatric unit who were using cocaine had significantly lower scores on negative symptom scales compared to schizophrenic patients admitted to the same unit who were not using cocaine (Serper et al. 1995). Yet when evaluated several weeks later on the same unit the cocaine-using schizophrenic patients had the same high rates of negative symptoms as the patients who had not been using cocaine on admission. This suggests that the patients using cocaine had experienced temporary relief from their negative symptoms, only for its "benefits" to wane during their hospital stay removed from the cocaine.

Theoretically, *opiates* would be a calming agent for schizophrenic patients given its calming effects on the agitation and states of anger and rage which so often is associated with schizophrenia. With the exception of areas where heroin is endemic and easily attainable, the impaired coping skills of schizophrenic patients makes it unlikely they would be able to survive the hazards of acquiring the drug which might relieve the enormous distress and disorganization involved with schizophrenia. There is evidence that opiates would quiet and contain the disorganization and agitation such patients experience. In fact, in 1981 the New York Academy of Science convened a conference in which the role of opiates was considered in mental illness and their possible use in treatment of schizophrenia and other severe psychiatric conditions (Vereby 1982). One possibility being considered was the use of the long-acting opiate, methadone, in the treatment of refractory cases of schizophrenia. This consideration was entirely consistent with the emphasis in my previous work on the ant-aggression, anti-disorganization action of opiates upon which I was asked to elaborate in that conference. It is also consistent with an earlier European and more recent American experience when opiates have been used for psychotic, agitated patients refractory to conventional antipsychotic medication. This option has been less necessary with the advent of second-generation antipsychotic drugs such as clozapine.

Alcohol is the main depressants preferred by schizophrenic individuals. As we have indicated, in heavy doses they can drown out or obliterate unwelcome hallucinations, delusions, and to a lesser extent paranoia, that is, the positive symptoms. In low to moderate doses negative symptoms such as the inability to socialize, apathy, and the inability to experience pleasure are ameliorated. As a patient once reminded me, "Doc, they tell me to go to the social club and mix with the other patients or to go to their dances, but I can't get there unless I stop by the liquor store and get my pint of rum, and then I feel like I can join the human race and try and have some fun."

POSTTRAUMATIC STRESS DISORDER (PTSD)

Nowhere is the association between the suffering involved in a psychiatric condition and substance use disorders more evident than in patients who suffer with PTSD. The odds ratio for SUDs in individuals with PTSD is three to four times greater than individuals without PTSD (Ouimette and Brown 2004). The suffering is endless and unrelenting with multiple manifestations. The following is a summary of the main reactions described in DSM-IVR:

- Re-experiencing the trauma including recurrent memories, dreams, and related psychological distress
- Persistent avoidance or numbing
- Decreased interest in important activities; feeling of detachment; restricted emotions
- Hyperarousal including sleep disturbance, irritability/anger, poor concentration, hypervigilance, and increased startle response

As an esteemed colleague, Bessel Van der Kolk, has noted, it is a condition in which there is a failure for time to heal all wounds. Little wonder that such individuals are so prone to turn to the feeling altering properties of addictive drugs. The drugs counter or change the disrupted emotions, self-esteem, relationships, and behaviors that result from PTSD—that is, they experience relief with addictive drugs from their immense problems with self-regulation. Obliterating doses of alcohol counter emotional flooding, and low to moderate doses release them from the affective numbing associated with PTSD. Opiates quell or contain the rage and violent feelings experienced by PTSD sufferers, one of the most disquieting and disruptive reactions for self and others for those who have endured such trauma. Early in our experience, working with traumatized Vietnam veterans, we were most struck with how they reported the calming down of their enduring rage, a result of their combat experiences, when they first used heroin. And finally, is it any surprise that individuals with PTSD report how stimulants such as cocaine and methamphetamine act as powerful antidotes to the social withdrawal and anhedonia of PTSD, and thus drawn to it and captivated by it.

ATTENTION-DEFICIT HYPERACTIVITY DISORDER (ADHD)

It is estimated that 25–50 percent of adolescents with SUDs have ADHD as estimated by Wilens and Biederman, prominent investigators in the treatment and prevention of ADHD (Wilens and Biederman 2006). These investigators consider ADHD as a developmental disorder and, in their experience, consider it an important antecedent to SUDs. They have evidence that early treatment of ADHD with psychostimulants significantly decreases SUDs and cigarette smoking. There is a significant old and more recent literature that documents that there is a significant co-occurrence of anger, anxiety, mood disorders, and behavioral problems associated with ADHD. In our opinion and experience, a perspective which Wilens and Biederman endorse, there is heightened self-regulation difficulties in adolescents with ADHD which predisposes them to SUDs and the need to self-medicate the distress associated with their ADHD.

Referring back to the three main classes of addictive drugs and their main action or effects which we reviewed previously, it is understandable how individuals with ADHD would be drawn to these addictive drugs as well as marijuana and nicotine. Given the significant levels of anxiety, anger, depression, and behavioral problems with which such individuals struggle, one would correctly expect that stimulants, including nicotine, could paradoxically calm the restlessness or serve as an activating agent for associated depressive symptoms, that the stimulating and sedating properties of cannabis could serve a similar purpose, that alcohol would be disproportionately misused, and that opiates would calm and sooth the angry feelings and irritability with which such individuals struggle.

In the early 1980s, I was beginning to suspect that some of my patients were self-medicating their ADHD symptoms and the related distress associated with the condition. In 1982, a 30-year-old female patient with an enormous dependence on cocaine (using intravenously, about a $250,000-a-year habit and able to do so because she had a connection high in the distribution chain) was referred to me for evaluation. After taking a detailed history, I diagnosed that she suffered with co-occurring ADHD. After consulting with several respected colleagues, I decided to treat her underlying ADHD with methylphenidate (Ritalin®), to my knowledge not previously tried in such a case. On a high pediatric dose (20 mg three times per day) she reported feeling calm, able to take a normal nap (usually a coma-like sleep follows acute withdrawal from cocaine), and that she felt she had a choice for the first time to not use the cocaine. I reported this case in 1983 as an extreme case that had marked improvement with the methylphenidate treatment (Khantzian 1983). With now 25 years of follow-up with this remarkable case, there has not been a reversion to stimulant dependence despite her previous exclusive dependence on stimulants prior to her treatment dating back more than 10 years. Her treatment with the methylphenidate was considered controversial at the time by some, but was mostly ignored until the past several years when Dr. Frances Levin and associates at Columbia University Medical Center have begun preliminary studies on the efficacy of stimulant substitution for cocaine and methamphetamine dependence and demonstrated preliminary encouraging results with stimulant medication substitution (Mariana and Levin 2006). (Recently I collaborated with this group, publishing follow-up clinical findings and formulations to support this perspective.[1])

NICOTINE DEPENDENCE

There is evidence that smoking and nicotine dependence are associated with a range of distressful states (Hughes 2001, 2005; Breslau, Kilbey, and Andreski 1993). Although nicotine has traditionally been considered a stimulant, the evidence suggests that it has a range of different actions or effects explainable by the fact that there are subsystems of nicotinic receptor sites in the brain to account for this difference. In this respect, it is somewhat at odds with the premise of the SMH that there is a considerable degree of specificity in a person's drug-of-choice. On this basis, Dr. John Hughes, a distinguished researcher on nicotine dependence, has referred to nicotine as a "renaissance drug." For example, he lists the different actions of nicotine as follows:

- Improves concentration
- Relieves anxiety and depression
- Relieves anger
- Decreases appetite

He then challenges the reader to consider what the problems of 16-year-olds are. He offers the following:

- Concentrating on school work
- Controlling their mood
- Aggression (especially boys)
- Weight gain (especially girls)

Little wonder that the hook is so often set in adolescence for lifetime dependency on nicotine and why it is one of the most difficult addictions to overcome. To paraphrase Tom Lehrer, from his song, "The Old Dope Peddlar," the kids of today are the customers of tomorrow.

There are several large epidemiological studies showing a strong association between depressive conditions and major depression and nicotine dependence, and how the presence of either make quitting more difficult. In one study, drawing on a large national data base, the investigators found that smoking rates

---

1. Mariani, J. J., Khantzian, E. J., and Levin, F. R. (2014). The self-medication hypothesis and psychostimulant treatment of cocaine dependence: An update. *American Journal on Addiction* 23:189–93.

increased and quit rates decreased as depressive symptoms increased (Anda et al. 1990). With a nine-year follow-up in this same study, there was an 18 percent quit rate in smokers who were not depressed, but only a 10 percent quit rate for the depressed smokers, nearly twice the quit rate for non-depressed smokers. In another large epidemiological based study investigators found a strong association between cigarette smoking and major depression (Glassman et al. 1990). Strikingly, the lead author of the article described how he observed recent quitters develop a gradual onset (over weeks) of severe depression and almost immediate relief within hours of smoking. In an editorial accompanying these two articles, the associate editor of the journal (*Journal of the American Medical Association*) concluded that the data was consistent with and endorsed the self-medication hypothesis (3).

Conclusion

As humans we face lifelong challenges to regulate our emotions, self-esteem, relationships, and behaviors. Addictive drugs interact with the pain and distress these challenges can produce. For some these challenges are greater than for others. Because of extreme distress, or susceptibility to psychiatric illness and behavioral disorders, certain individuals suffer in the extreme with self-regulation difficulties. Individuals self-medicate with addictive drugs because in the short term they relieve or make more tolerable psychological pain or the distress associated with psychiatric disorders.

References

Anda, R. F., Williamson, D. F., Escobedo, L. G., Mast, E. E., Giovino, G. A., and Remington, P. L. (1990). Depression and the dynamics of smoking: A national perspective. *Journal of the American Medical Association* 264:1541–45.

Brady, K., Anton, R., Ballenger, J. C., et al. (1990) Cocaine abuse among schizophrenic patients. *American Journal of Psychiatry* 147:1164–67.

Glass, R. (1990). Blue mood, blackened lungs: Depression and smoking. *Journal of the American Medical Association* 264:1583–84.

Glassman, A. H., Helzer, J. E., Covey, L. S., Cottler, L. B., Steiner, F., Tipp, J. S., et al. (1990). Smoking, smoking cessation, and major depression. *Journal of the American Medical Association* 264:1546–49.

Hughes, J. R. (2001). Why does smoking so often produce dependence? A somewhat different view. *Tobacco Control* 10:62–64.

Hughes, J. Gambling and Addiction Conference: Finding Common Ground on Prevention, Treatment, and Policy. Las Vegas, Nevada, December 7, 2005.

Kessler, R. C., Crum, R. M., Warner, L. A., Nelson, C. B., et al. (1997). Lifetime co-occurrence of DSM-III-R alcohol abuse and dependence with other psychiatric disorders in the nation comorbidity survey. *Archives of General Psychiatry* 54:313–21.

Khantzian, E. J. (1983). An extreme case of cocaine dependence and marked improvement with methylphenidate treatment. *American Journal of Psychiatry* 140:784–85.

———. (November 1985). The self-medication hypothesis of addictive disorders: Focus on heroin and cocaine dependence. *American Journal of Psychiatry* 142 (11): 1259–64.

———. (1995). Self-regulation vulnerabilities in substance abusers: Treatment implications. In *The psychology and treatment of addictive behavior*, edited by S. Dowling, 17–41. New York: International University Press.

———. (January–February 1997). The self-medication hypothesis of substance use disorders: Reconsideration and recent applications. *Harvard Review of Psychiatry* 4 (5): 231–44.

Mariana, J., and Levin, F. Workshop: Stimulant Pharmacotherapy in Patients with Substance Use Disorders. American Academy of Addiction Psychiatry Annual Scientific Conference, St. Petersburg, Florida, December 2006.

Ouimette, P., and Brown, P. J., eds. (2004). *Trauma and Substance Abuse: Causes, Consequences, and Treatment of Comorbid Disorders*. Washington, DC: American Psychological Association.

Serper, M. R., Albert, M., Richardson, N. A., Dickson, S., Allen, M., and Werner, A. (1995). Clinical effects of recent cocaine use on patients with acute schizophrenia. *American Journal of Psychiatry* 152:1464–69.

Vereby, K., ed. (1982). *Opioids in Mental Illness: Theories, Clinical Observations, and Treatment Possibilities*. Vol. 398. New York: Annals of the New York Academy of Sciences.

Wilens, T., and Biederman, J. (2006). Alcohol, drugs, and attention-deficit/hyperactivity disorder: A model for the study of addiction in youth. *Journal of Psychopharmacology* 20:580–88.

Ziedonis, D. M., Kosten, T. R., Glazer, W. M., and Frances, R. J. (1994). Nicotine dependence and schizophrenia. *Hospital & Community Psychiatry* 54:204–6.

CHAPTER 4

The Capacity for Self-Care and Addiction

The behaviors of addicted individuals persistently suggest that they are self-destructive (Khantzian 1995). That is, the well-known deadly effects of addictive drugs and behaviors and all the associated dangers do not seem to deter susceptible individuals from the "compulsion" to use them. Such individuals seem oblivious or not caring about the dangers of addictive drug use and behaviors and suggest the presence of conscious or unconscious self-destructive or suicidal motives. So much so that some have cynically referred to addictive behavior as "suicide on the installment" and psychoanalysts of an era past have invoked "death instincts" (Meninger 1938; Tabachnik 1976) to explain the deadly consequences of addictions.

Based on four decades of clinical work with addicted individuals, and drawing on a developmental/psychodynamic perspective, I have concluded that the seemingly dangerous and deadly consequences of addictive behavior are not primarily a statement about suicidal motives or human self-destructiveness. Admittedly there is a strong occurrence of suicide associated with addictions, but this more likely is a consequence of the deterioration and emotional and physical debilitation associated with advanced drug/alcohol dependence. Rather such behaviors are a condition or a statement about the underdevelopment or absence of a *capacity for self-care*. We have elaborated upon or referred to self-care problems in a number of publications over the past several decades (Khantzian and Mack 1983; Khantzian 1995, 1999, 2008) as a major etiologic factor in the development of addictions. In this chapter, I will draw on some of the background factors and clinical observations that have caused me and others to consider how impairments in the capacity for self-care are central in the development of addictive behavior, what the main features are of the capacity for self-care and its deficits, and then briefly consider the implications in the treatment of addicted individuals. We believe this focus is important because it is not sufficiently appreciated how self-care deficits, in combinations with other psychological vulnerabilities combine to make susceptibility to addiction tragically likely. Furthermore, the concept of self-care deficits as a major contributory factor to the development of addiction is a testable hypothesis that has heuristic values in further understanding and treating addictive vulnerability.

Background

At the outset it is important to distinguish self-care deficiencies from "addictive drives" and the compulsion to use and revert to addictive drugs and behaviors. Addictive drives and compulsive use, to a considerable degree, is rooted in motives to self-medicate unendurable painful feeling states for which addictive substances and behaviors provide temporary relief or control (Khantzian 1999; Khantzian and Albanese 2008). Before physical dependence is established a significant reason for the compulsion to use drugs is that individuals remember that the drugs provide control over and relief from intolerable emotional distress. Once physical tolerance and dependence is established a major and obvious drive to revert and use drugs is determined by the physical and emotional distress associated with withdrawal which is relieved by resumption of the drug that caused the dependency. *This drivenness to use drugs is to be distinguished from self-care deficits which refer more to the failure to control or contain behavior in the face of risky or dangerous situations* (italics for emphasis).

Much has also been written about the impulsive and compulsive (see Dodes 1996) aspects of addiction rooted in the personality makeup of individuals who become addicted, which some would argue is an essential aspect of becoming addicted. Clearly such factors play a role. However, most individuals struggle more or less with impulses and compulsive tendencies, but have juxtaposed to them responses of restraint, caution, or worry about such tendencies which protect. We elaborate on self-care deficits here because insufficient consideration is given to how such deficits are important in the development and maintenance of addictive behavior.

We came to formulate self-care as a developed system of ego functions in the context of considering "survival instincts" as a means of assuring human safety and existence, and what the dynamics were in addictive vulnerability wherein they seemed to be so deficient in individuals using addictive substances (Khantzian and Mack 1983). Working as a liaison psychiatrist consulting to the medical and surgical services, I wondered about and was impressed how so many patients I was seeing seemed so oblivious to the consequences of careless behaviors that seemed related to preventable medical and surgical conditions that landed them in the hospital. Subsequently, dating back to the "heroin epidemic" of the 1970s, I became aware of the seeming obliviousness to the dangers of intravenous drug use with patients coming to our methadone maintenance program. Interviewing many intravenous using heroin-addicted individuals, I again found myself wondering about and reacting to how individuals transitioned from ingesting drugs orally or nasally to using drugs intravenously. I was aware of my own strong subjective reaction to the idea of sticking a needle into my own veins—namely, how repugnant it felt, that is, a powerful countertransference response (modern theory would say a strong intersubjective reaction). I decided that such a reaction tactfully shared with patients might be revealing and they were. I shared how as a doctor I was used to using needles, but the idea of putting a needle in my own veins felt very uncomfortable. The patients' responses were monotonously the same, in tone and content in their response. Such reactions as "No doc, I didn't give it much thought . . . [or] . . . No, I didn't feel anything like that . . . [or] . . . No, I didn't feel nervous" were remarkably consistent and common.

It could be argued that such responses were a function of regressed, careless reactions secondary to immersion in a drug lifestyle. However, working in long-term psychotherapy with formerly drug-dependent individuals who were abstinent and in stable recovery, I was subsequently impressed that similar lack of concerns about requirements for daily living was cropping up repeatedly as a function of a lack of worry or anticipation of negative consequences. Unbalanced checkbooks, unpaid insurance bills, and lapsed licenses causing embarrassment and life complications, or preventable medical/dental and surgical problems were recurrent or not uncommon. It was in this context of patients jeopardizing their well-being that we began to explore existent explanation and alternative formulations as to what assured human survival, or what factors might account for unintended self-harm and self-destruction.

Psychodynamics of Self-Preservation and Self-Harm

EARLY FORMULATIONS

Early psychoanalytic investigators interpreted problems such as accident proneness, violent or impulsive behavior, eating disorders, addiction, and other forms of self-neglect as pleasure seeking or the result of unconscious self-destructive motives. Not without significance, these early formulations still prevail and continue to influence every-day thinking, and even scientific explanations, to account for such behaviors. Examples include when a person accidentally incurs a mishap or a slip of the tongue we are quick to wonder about unconscious intentions or what was really on their minds; or the countless instances in media and scientific articles of invoking of pleasure and reward motives for a wide range of errant or troublesome behaviors. In a review of early psychodynamic theories of such behaviors we concluded that such explanations failed to adequately consider how such behaviors are more prevalent and thrive when self-protective functions and capacities for self-restraint are less well developed and fail to counter impulsive and self-destructive tendencies (Khantzian and Mack 1983).

CONTEMPORARY FORMULATIONS

In contrast to the early explanations that placed emphasis on unconscious pleasure of self-destructive motives, current dynamic formulations place greater emphasis on developmental and structural deficits wherein individuals fail to acquire from their caretaking/growing up environment ego capacities which assure adequate self-protection from and concern about harmful situations and behaviors. In some instances, the caretaking has been too protective such that there is insufficient opportunity for exploration and experimentation to learn how to be careful; consider the toddler who bumps into the coffee table and the mother says, "Bad table," as opposed to the mother who comforts the bruised child and cautions and teaches her/him to be careful. And clearly children who are overwhelmed by grossly depriving or abusive environments are more often sufficiently overwhelmed or disorganized such that internalizing self-care functions are unlikely. Viewed from such a perspective, it becomes not so much what drives destructive behaviors, but rather what factors fail to constrain, contain, and control them. Susceptible individuals are not so much simply driven or compelled in their behavior, as they are impaired or deficient in self-care functions that are otherwise present in the more mature personality organization or ego of an individual.

Self-Care as a Developed (Ego) System

Early psychoanalytic investigators referred to "survival instincts" to describe what capacities assured human safety. From the perspective we emphasize here, it is less a matter of instincts but more one of ego functions and capacities that assure safety and well-being. In the 1983 referenced paper by me and Dr. Mack we considered and listed what a well-developed system of ego functions consisted of that assured self-care. They are as follows:

1. An investment in caring about or valuing oneself—sufficient self-esteem to feel oneself to be worth protecting

2. The capacity to anticipate dangerous situations and to respond to the cues which anxiety provides
3. The ability to control impulses and renounce pleasures whose consequences are harmful
4. Pleasure in mastering inevitable situations of risk, or in which dangers are appropriately measured
5. Knowledge about the outside world and oneself sufficient for survival in it
6. The ability to be sufficiently self-assertive or aggressive enough to protect oneself
7. Certain skills in relationship, especially the ability to choose others who, ideally, will enhance one's protection, or at least will not jeopardize one's existence (Khantzian and Mack 1983, 210–11)

Recognizing Self-Care Deficits in Practice

Working in long-term psychotherapy with substance-use-disordered individuals, clinicians and patients are afforded the opportunity to observe and understand how deficits in the capacity for self-care play out in the predisposition to addiction, relapse, and recovery. Patients repeatedly display how they think and react differently to a host of dangerous or hazardous situations, especially those involved with but not limited to addictive behaviors. Whereas individuals who have well-developed self-care functions ordinarily experience worry or have apprehension in the face of a dangerous situation, addictively prone individuals fail to think about the hazards they face or do not experience appropriate fear or anxiety that might guide them away or protect them from harm. The following case of Carl reported in a recent publication (Khantzian and Albanese 2008) is illustrative of how insufficiently developed self-care capacities constantly left him susceptible to mishaps, embarrassment, and injury.

Careless Carl

Carl was a skilled carpenter. The care he took in his craft contrasted sharply with how he took care of himself. His clients were consistently pleased with the care and attention he devoted to his work, whether it was in fashioning a special cabinet or completing the finish-work in a redesigned room. Yet when it came to billing for his projects he often lost his receipts or the accounting for the hours he and his workmen put into a job. He often also misplaced the keys to his pickup truck when starting out in the morning, leading to endless turmoil in his family in helping him to get organized and out the door for his day's work. Carl also caused himself havoc in his personal finances, not balancing his checking account and overdrawing, missing insurance payments, or losing important financial documents. He also was subject to accidental falls and scrapes because he often moved and jumped ahead of himself before checking his surroundings.

Carl was not dependent on alcohol, but he overused and abused it, often causing him embarrassments when he was with family or friends. Despite knowing his tendencies, he repeatedly behaved in silly or inappropriate ways, more often, when he drank. Though often bemoaning his fate as a "loser" after such occurrences, he seemed incapable of anticipating trouble associated with situations, people, and things that would cause him embarrassment and remorse when he either drank too much and/or was excessive in his behaviors. Some of his excesses were a function of his need to be super-friendly and likeable. But the main difficulty seemed to be obliviousness to cues and warnings that a given situation or relationships could lead to problematic behavior which he only seemed to have a hint of after the fact. (Khantzian and Albanese 2008, 18)

As Carl's case demonstrates his inability to sufficiently worry or think enough about the details and actions necessary to support his work as a craftsman constantly left him in a state of disorganization and upset. In a sense, discomfort, worry, and upset was more apt to occur after the fact than before, as did shame and embarrassment follow his silly and impulsive behavior rather than guide him in an anticipatory way before acting inappropriately.

The following vignette is taken from an earlier publication (Khantzian 1995) demonstrating how self-care vulnerabilities are evident and played out in a group therapy session.

A CASE VIGNETTE: FEARLESS FRED

A group therapy meeting with a group of drug-dependent individuals typifies problems with self-care and their confusion about and inability to deal with feeling as a guide in the face of dangerous or threatening circumstances. Admittedly the extra-group event that gave rise to the group interaction was rather dramatic and traumatic for one of its members, but it nevertheless demonstrates how addictively prone individuals are more prone to become involved with the details and logistics of an evocative event or to react with anger and impulsive action rather than to use their thoughts and feelings as a guide to act or not act in a dangerous situation.

The member, Fred, who related the experience, was a recovering physician. He began the group by describing an incident in his clinic in which the boyfriend of a pregnant patient whipped out a knife and slashed her across her shoulder and chest when he misunderstood from the doctor's estimation of gestation that she might have been impregnated by someone else.

Fred first described his shock and his maneuvers to position himself next to the door of the examining room while the boyfriend was angrily screaming and threatening her. The doctor debated leaving until his nurse-assistant (who had called the police) handed him his softball bat and convinced him that the patient's life was in danger. With the boyfriend's back to him, and without further reflection, Fred hit the man's arm with the bat, releasing his knife, and as he swung around, the doctor then hit him across the abdomen and thereby immobilized him until the police arrived.

Immediately after completing his story, a lawyer-cocaine addict who was a hyperactive, restless character launched into an animated monologue on the doctor's potential liability to assault charges by having interceded. As the leader, I tried to slow him down, to point out his tendency to be legalistic, and to get more to his feelings. Instead, he and another group member, also a physician, began to argue whether going to the legal aspects of the situation was reasonable. I made several attempts to interrupt by asking them to try and focus on how the story made them feel. Mostly a tone of irritability pervaded the group interaction, with the lawyer and the other physician returning to their argument about the suitability of the lawyer's concerns about the legal implications of the event. The other three members seemed uncharacteristically willing to tolerate this exchange. Fred, who told the story, responded to my inquiry about his reactions by telling me and the group how almost immediately after the episode he arranged a "three-day break" in Florida, without his family, to visit a trusted confidant-uncle and ex-marine whom he knew would provide sanctuary, advice, and wise counsel on what had happened. I pointed out to him that he seemed bewildered about and unable to describe his feelings but instead described what he had done. A third physician in the group, in a detached and characteristically analytic manner, commented on the argument between the other two members and then went on to suggest that the doctor had perhaps endangered himself by interceding but also allowed that if he had been involved he might have considered a more devastating blow to the head.

It was only toward the end of the meeting that the fifth member of the group, also a lawyer (the youngest member of the group, who was working as a planner and counselor in a drug treatment program as part of his recovery efforts), forcefully interrupted the proceedings and expressed his shock over the event, his anger and sadness, and his worry for the threat that Fred had been forced to endure. He also allowed that he might have unnecessarily jeopardized himself had he not been as successful in immobilizing the assailant. The young lawyer also correctly reminded the group that they could usually do better with each other's distress and feelings. I pointed out that it was easier for the group members to pick a fight with each other than to stay with the feelings that had been stirred by the story. By the end of the meeting it had become clear that both Fred, who had experienced the episode, and the lawyer who first reacted were the least able to describe their feelings. With some defensiveness the lawyer was able to consider that his preoccupation with the legal aspects of the situation served to avoid his confusion about his feelings, and that the doctor had similarly acted on his own by going to Florida. (Khantzian 1995)

Adequately established self-care functions assure well-being, safety, and the ability to adopt avoidance or appropriate action in the face of danger or threat. Feeling of fear, apprehension, and emotional recoil are just some of the emotions that serve to warn or protect against danger, including those involved in addictive behavior. The ability to draw cause-consequence relationships and to be thoughtful, or to use a more contemporary term, "mindful," about one's circumstance are essential aspects of the capacity for self-care. Individuals who lack for self-care functions feel and think differently, if they feel or think at all, around self-harmful or dangerous events and situations. In the case of Carl, his inability to think about the details of managing his behavior at home and at work caused him and his family much consternation. Lapses in paper work, timely management of his checking account or payment of bills jeopardized his reputation as a business man, and mindless and thoughtless behavior complicated by periodic excessive drinking caused him considerable shame and embarrassment. Admittedly in the case of Fred, he had acted heroically, but in the group interaction what was most evident was the tendency for Fred and most of the other group members to become circumstantial, argumentative, and confused around the drama and danger that Fred had experienced and described. Except for the last member's more appropriate and thoughtful expression of alarm, fear, and sadness for what Fred had experienced, such considerations and reflections were missing and overridden by the members pension for action, irritability, and confusion.

Evaluating and treating thousands of patients with addictive disorders over a period of four decades I have been impressed that the capacity for self-care has been more or less absent or deficient. That is, deficits in self-care are on a continuum in addictively prone individuals and that such deficits have been an important factor in succumbing to addiction and behaviors associated with addiction. For some, partially developed concerns for well-being and safety become overridden by powerful emotions or impulses produced by stressful or traumatic experiences; under such circumstances people with shaky self-care capacities react in ways they might not otherwise, and for example, might agree to experiment with smoking free-base cocaine. Should such a person be struggling with depressive feelings and inertia the hook might be set to discover the activating and euphorogenic properties of the drug. Given that self-care deficits play a role in succumbing to addiction, it is also noteworthy that to whatever degree self-care functions are present they are subject to erosion as a person's addiction advances. It might be argued that self-care problems are function of other co-occurring problems such as depression, psychosis, anxiety, and ADHD.

In working with patients, it has been my experience that indeed such conditions might interfere with self-care. More often, however, as previously indicated self-care deficits untreated remain an enduring problem and persist when these co-existing conditions have been properly treated and ameliorated.

Finally, a word is in order about "denial" that is so often invoked (both rightfully and unfortunately) to explain addictive behavior. From what I have developed here it should go without saying that so much of what goes into addictive disorders is not so much simply a denial or unwillingness to acknowledge that one has a problem. Problems with self-care are not only involved in the day-to-day failures to avoid mishaps associated with addiction, but such deficits play a big part in a person's inability to see the big picture of how consuming and destructive their addictions are for themselves and others. It is in respect to the recurrent failure to be unaware and unalarmed about daily mishaps and catastrophes as well as the inability to acknowledge awareness of the disease that self-care problems warrant therapeutic attention in working with addicted patients.

Some Treatment Implications

Problems with self-care are best addressed therapeutically in a broader context of considering addiction as a self-regulation disorder (Khantzian 1995). Beyond difficulties with self-care that fail to protect against danger and harm, problems with regulating emotions, self-esteem, and relationships are involved in the predisposition for, maintenance of, and relapse to addiction. Feelings that can guide behavior are often elusive, confusing, or absent in addictively prone individuals, as is compromised self-esteem and poor interpersonal relationships where matters of self-respect are unavailable, and/or where choice of relationships are not based on a person's best interests. These self-regulations problems interact and conspire with self-care difficulties to make addiction and relapse likely. Treatments that are effective focus on these areas of self-regulation difficulties.

Witnessing and working with self-care problems can feel bewildering and maddening. An exhaustive exploration in how to deal with such vulnerabilities goes beyond the scope of this chapter. I will only highlight some considerations from a psychodynamic perspective how a clinician can work with self-care vulnerabilities in an understanding and helpful way. Subjective reactions such as "how could they have been so oblivious . . . [or] . . . that was stupid behavior . . . [or] . . . couldn't they see disaster coming when they went into the bar with their friends" are but a few of the powerful reactions of shock and dismay patients can evoke in a therapist. The temptation to tell (or worse still, to lecture) people, albeit tempting, are countertransference or "intersubjective reactions" (Stolorow 1995) that should not be ignored, but they should not be indulged either. Instead, such reactions should be an indication as to how tragically clueless patients can feel about themselves and their own behavior. Such reactions can help the therapist focus on the void or developmental deficits with which such patients suffer and what therapeutically needs attention. As is the case with other psychological vulnerabilities and deficits, character traits and defenses compensate for at the same time they reveal such vulnerabilities. In the case of self-care deficits, defenses of bravado, counterphobia, or passive resignation are common. As with most characterologic defenses or traits, they play out in the treatment relationships, and more often counterproductively cause problems in their interpersonal relationships. Although such responses can become problematic to deal with, they can gently and gradually be dealt with by helping patients understand the underlying self-care problems that fuel their defensiveness in and out of treatment.

Mainstays of effective psychotherapy such as empathy, developing a positive relationship with the patient (i.e., the therapeutic alliance), a balance of listening and speaking, patience, and a readiness to develop and maintain a focus on addicted patients' self-regulation problems go far in helping individuals to become aware of their self-care deficits and to begin to modify their behaviors. Therapists should feel unapologetically ready to be instructive, to share reactions of alarm when potential or actual harmful situations arise and are absent in the patient, and to actively clarify and explain to patients' their recurrent tendency to not anticipate harm or danger.

References

Dodes, L. (1996). Compulsion and addiction. *Journal of the American Psychoanalytic Association* 44:815–35.

Khantzian, E. J. (1995). Self-regulation vulnerabilities in substance abusers: Treatment implications. In *The Psychology and Treatment of Addictive Behavior*, edited by S. Dowling, 17–41. New York: International Universities Press.

Khantzian, E. J. (1999). *Treating Addiction as a Human Process*. Northvale, NJ: Jason Aronson.

Khantzian, E. J., and Albanese, M. J. (2008). *Understanding Addiction as Self-Medication: Finding Hope behind the Pain*. Lanham, MD: Rowman & Littlefield.

Khantzian, E. J., and Mack, J. (1983). Self-preservation and the care of the self. *Psychoanalytic Study of the Child* 38: 209–32.

Menninger, K. A. (1938). *Man against Himself*. New York: Harcourt, Brace.

Stolorow, R. D. (1995). an intersubjective view of self psychology. *Psychoanalytic Dialogues* 5:393–99.

Tabachnick, N. (1976). Death trend and adaptation. *Journal of the American Academy of Psychoanalysis* 41:49–62.

CHAPTER 5

The Self-Medication Hypothesis and Attachment Theory

PATHWAYS FOR UNDERSTANDING AND AMELIORATING ADDICTIVE SUFFERING

The 20th John Bowlby Memorial Lecture (2013)

Our pejorative and unempathic attitude toward individuals labeled as having "Substance Use Disorders" (SUDs) in part derives from early psychoanalytic drive theory. Dual instinct theory suggested that addictive behavior is driven by pleasure seeking or self-destructive motives, so much so that in the latter instance Menninger (1935) stated that addiction was a form of chronic suicide. What a misunderstanding. Our patients with "addictive disorders" are in need of being understood not so much as pleasure seekers or self-destructive characters, but more as individuals who are in pain and seek and need contact and comfort.

The self-medication hypothesis (SMH) derives from persistent clinical observation and inquiry about how individuals who depend on addictive substances do so because they have had the powerful discovery that what they suffer with is relieved temporarily by addictive substances. This is so whether it is a vague sense of dysphoria because feelings are confusing or elusive, or because affects are overwhelming and unbearable. Depending on the substance used, the psychoactive actions of the drugs of abuse provide short-term surcease for a wide range of painful and confusing feeling states.

In this chapter, I will briefly describe basic aspects of the self-medication hypothesis. I will then review how it has stimulated a consideration of addiction as a self-regulation disorder, and to further consider how the suffering associated with addiction, especially traumatic suffering, disrupts the human capacity for secure attachments. I will use case material to provide examples of how these themes play out and are enacted in patients' lives and in the therapeutic relationship. Finally I will review how the self-medication hypothesis and attachment paradigms provide a basis to empathically and intersubjectively attune to and ameliorate the distress and suffering that drives addictive behavior and relationships.

THE SELF-MEDICATION HYPOTHESIS
OF ADDICTIVE DISORDERS

A fundamental premise of the SMH is that addiction behavior is grounded in the human penchant (especially in the infant, but persisting into adulthood) for seeking comfort and contact, not pleasure. In this section I will review the elements of the SMH as first articulated (Khantzian 1985), and subsequently elaborated upon (Khantzian 1997). In the following section I will explain how my thinking evolved about the SMH to consider addiction as a self-regulation disorder (Khantzian 2003).

In my early focus on self-medication factors in addictive disorders the main emphasis was on painful affect states which individuals were attempting to alleviate with addictive substances. My thinking at that time reflected the intersection of my psychodynamic/psychoanalytic training, which I was in the middle of, with the then evolving terminology for psychoactive drugs in general. Namely, starting in the early 1960s, we changed our terms for psychiatric medications from "tranquilizers" (i.e., major and minor tranquilizers) to designating them by their specific action (i.e., anti-psychotic, anti-anxiety, anti-depressant). My first systematic involvement with treating the addictions began with the initiation of the Methadone Maintenance Program at the Cambridge Hospital in 1970. Almost immediately I began to wonder what motivated the dependence on heroin. My thinking initially and subsequently reflected an evolution much like that with the change in nomenclature for prescribed psychotropic medications. I first speculated that heroin was a powerful opiate analgesic (i.e., a "pain killer") and that the appeal of the opiates resided in their ability to relieve emotional pain in general. Once I began evaluating each patient coming to the program, almost immediately I started to change my thinking—namely, I began to consider that the effect of opiates had a more specific appeal. This change in thinking stimulated embryonic thinking about the SMH, as did the contributions of other psychodynamic investigators who coined the terms "drug of choice" (Weider and Kaplan 1969) and "preferential use of drugs" (Milkman and Frosch 1973).

The SMH proposes that addictive drugs have their appeal and become compelling principally for two reasons: first, they relieve human psychological suffering and, second, there is a considerable degree of specificity in a person's drug-of-choice. With regard to specificity, clinical experience reveals that individuals resort to more than one class of drugs, often a function of availability wherein they will juggle doses of other drugs to simulate their drug of choice, but when pursued more closely an individual will indicate a drug preference. The following is the description of the appeal of the main class of addictive drugs taken from the 1997 update of the SMH:

- *Opiates.* Besides their general calming and "normalizing" effect, opiates attenuate intense, rageful, and violent affect. They counter the internally fragmenting and disorganizing effects of rage and the externally threatening and disruptive effects of such affects on interpersonal relations.
- *Central nervous system depressants (including alcohol).* Alcohol's appeal may reside in its properties as a "superego solvent." However, in my own experience, and based on observations by Krystal, short-acting depressants with rapid onset of action (e.g., alcohol, barbiturates, benzodiazepines) have their appeal because they are good "ego solvents." That is, they act on those parts of the self that are cut off from self and others by rigid defenses that produce feelings of isolation and emptiness and related tense/anxious states and mask fears of closeness and dependency. Although they are not good antidepressants, alcohol and related drugs create the illusion of relief because they temporarily soften rigid defenses and ameliorate states of isolation and emptiness that predispose to depression.
- *Stimulants.* Stimulants act as augmenters for hypomanic, high-energy individuals as well as persons with atypical bipolar disorder. They also appeal to people who are de-energized and bored, and to those who suffer from depression. In addition, stimulants, including cocaine, can act paradoxically to calm and counteract hyperactivity, emotional lability, and inattention in persons with attention-deficit/hyperactivity disorder (Khantzian 1983, 1985). (Khantzian 1997, 232–33)

Space consideration does not allow me to go into great detail here, but there are aspects of the SMH that are disputed and considered controversial. In the following section I will address some of these criticisms of and possible inconsistencies in the SMH. For example, some investigators support the concept of self-medication in addictive disorders, but questions the need for, or the validity of, the specificity issue (Darke 2013), and others outright dismiss the SMH as dangerously false and misleading (DuPont and Gold 2007).

I would mention here that the way I have garnered the specific appeal that patients experience with their drug-of-choice derives from a basic inquiry that I make and have made with each patient over the past four decades—namely, "What did the [preferred] drug do for you when you first used the drug?" Also, given the confusion and inaccessibility of feelings with which so many addicted individuals struggle, the specificity issues often become less clear. I have speculated elsewhere, how frequently the elusiveness and absence of feelings contributes to the repetitious, compulsive nature of addictive behavior where the operative changes from the relief of suffering to the control of the suffering (Khantzian 1995, 1997, 2003).

ADDICTION AS A SELF-REGULATION DISORDER: TRAUMA, ATTACHMENT AND SURVIVAL INSTINCTS

Criticisms of and seeming inconsistencies in the SMH stimulated me to begin to think about what else beyond painful or unmanageable affects are dysregulated in addictive behavior and to consider addiction as a self-regulation disorder. However, before I get to those considerations, I would nevertheless emphasize the primary importance to affect life in relation to the addictions. Affects play an extremely important role in the development of addiction and cut across all other aspects of self-regulation.

- Affects are the organizing basis for self-experience (Stolorow, Brandchaft, and Atwood 1995),
- The foundation for a sense of wellbeing and self-esteem (Kohut 1971, 1977),
- The currency for human connection and attachment (Bowlby 1973), and,
- A primary ingredient for guiding behavior, especially self-care. (Khantzian and Mack 1983)

Major trauma and neglect greatly heighten and worsen the self-regulation deficits that are so commonly and persistently associated with addictive disorders.

At least three factors stirred my consideration of addiction as a self-regulation disorder: First, many individuals suffer with painful emotional states and feelings but they do not necessarily become addicted; second, more often there are added painful affects that result as a consequence of addiction; and third, if the SMH suggests that addiction is an attempt at self-repair, how can all the associated self-harm, danger, and threat to life be explained? Because of space requirements I can only briefly summarize here how the deficits in self-regulation interact with each other and with addictive substances to make dependence more likely or compelling. The interested reader can find more detailed explanations elsewhere (Khantzian 1985, 1995, 1997, 2003, 2012).

Addicted individuals suffer because they cannot regulate their emotions, self-other relations, and self-care. They self-medicate the pain and suffering associated with these self-regulation difficulties. Patients with addictive disorders suffer in the extreme with their emotions. Feelings are cut-off, absent, or confusing, or they are intense and overwhelming. In the former case stimulating drugs can be enlivening or activating. If feelings are defensively restricted and cut off, as they so often are in addicted people, the releasing properties of sedative-hypnotics in low to moderate doses can allow the experience and expression of feelings of warmth and closeness that they cannot otherwise allow. When feelings are threatening, or overwhelming, opiates can become captivating in their ability to powerfully contain intense, disorganizing, and dysphoric affects, especially rage and associated agitation. Similarly, but not as effectively, high doses of depressants such as alcohol can contain such intense affect.

Shaky or poor sense of self/self-esteem and interpersonal relationships leave addictively prone individuals subject to discover the ameliorating effects of addictive substances and behaviors. Feelings of poor self-cohesion and fragmentation are relieved by the calming action of opiates or sedatives in such individuals. The chronic absence of a sense of well-being and the inability to satisfactorily connect to others makes the soothing and comforting actions of opiates and depressants alluringly welcome. Narcissistic defenses of disdain and self-sufficiency related to poor self-esteem, which lead to feelings of isolation, are temporarily lifted in such individuals with stimulants or low to moderate doses of alcohol, and allow connection to others that otherwise would feel unallowable or undoable. For those who more passively resign themselves to withdraw with a sense of injured self, such a retreat is made easier with obliterating doses of alcohol.

Survival instincts in patients with addictive disorders are too often woefully underdeveloped or absent. In fact, they are not instincts so much as developmental deficits in an (ego) capacity for self-care that assure survival. We have explored in more detail elsewhere (Khantzian and Mack 1983; Khantzian 1995, 1997, 2003, 2012) how in the absence or diminished capacities for self-care, addicted individuals fail to experience fear, worry, anticipatory shame, or alarm in the face of potential harm and danger, especially those associated with addiction. This deficit interacts malignantly with the pain and suffering involved with regulating emotions, self-esteem, and relationships to make addictive behavior and attachment more likely. Furthermore, one has to feel worthy in order to take care of oneself, but meaningful and caring connections also help to assure well-being and safety.

I will be presenting three cases in this chapter.[1] In two of the three cases, addiction was not one of the looming issues, but as I indicate, it could have been. I use these cases, however, because they are most recent to the time of writing this chapter, and they robustly highlight the relational, intersubjective, and attachment themes central to this chapter and this conference. Furthermore, I hope it demonstrates how I try to attune and empathically work with the dysregulation and attachment issues with which my patients struggle.

---

1. Individuals' identities have been disguised to preserve patient anonymity.

The case that follows here highlights how major trauma and neglect in a person's early life can endlessly and repeatedly effect a person's sense of worthiness, self-esteem, and the inability to establish and maintain stable and comforting long-term relationships. Although the patient gives an indication how he might have become addictively attached to gambling, he was not addicted, but he could have been (subsequent to writing up this case I learned that both paternal grandparents were compulsive gamblers). His case also demonstrates an important corollary of the SMH—namely, that addictive substances, albeit potentially and powerfully seductive, are not universally appealing for the majority of humans, and how and why this is so.

Jake

Jake is a 57-year-old admirable and dear person, despite extraordinary abuse and abandonment at the hands of a cruel and alcoholic father and traumatic withdrawal by his mother for a period when he was around five years old. He says that his mother withdrew from him at that time because she was a loving but misguided mother who worried that Jake would become a "momma's boy" after she divorced Jake's father. Walant (2002) would consider this kind of attitude "normative abuse" wherein the need of the child for comfort and contact is subordinated to cultural norms. (In her 2002 publication she focused on how the child's needs are subordinated to separation and individuation consideration. More recently, she stresses how the child's needs are subordinated to a range of cultural assumptions because society holds those views as correct—personal communication.) Jake's trauma history was further compounded when, at the age of nine, he was sodomized, beaten, and threatened with his life if he told anyone. Significantly, and likely shaping an aspect of his personality organization, he recalls that in that episode he survived by passively resigning to the beating and challenging the rapist to go ahead and beat him. Notwithstanding the trauma and neglect, he has experienced extraordinary accomplishments academically and professionally in his adult life, not without some painful setbacks. He is another one of the people with whom I have worked who could have become addicted but he had not, although in what follows he hinted that he could have succumbed to a behavioral or "process addiction." An unexpected developmental blessing and protection in this respect was the immersion in a rigorous academic program in secondary school that initiated a life-long interest in the classics. It is likely that it contributed to and resonated with his intelligence which stimulated an enduring capacity to cerebrally and emotionally "mentalize" (Allen, Fonagy, and Bateman 2008) about life, factors all too often absent in addictively prone people.

After a manic episode in his mid-thirties wherein he erroneously mismanaged a client's fund as a certified public accountant (CPA), he reinvented himself as an IT specialist working for various individuals and businesses as a very gifted and valued problem solver for all his clients. Married for about five years to a person that he felt was needy and whom he felt he could never satisfy, he divorced, but remained steadfastly devoted to his daughter. Subsequent to his divorce he periodically became involved in a number of relationships with women wherein he invariably promised and delivered more than he received, and, more often, the relationships ended unsatisfactorily. In his business, he constantly displayed a tendency to undercharge and to overextend himself in his dealings with his clients. A constant theme in his individual and group psychotherapy with me was the repetition to act as undeserving and in ways not in his best interest. When pointed out, especially in group therapy, he would passively shrug his shoulders and say, "Whatever."

In a recent psychotherapy visit he was lamenting that another IT person was vying for the business of one of his most valued and lucrative clients, a situation that was occurring at a time of decline in his business. He was complaining once again, as often happens, of feeling underappreciated and undervalued for the devotion he dedicated to his clients, not unlike how he often feels in his relations with his family. In this context he also shared a recent experience where he had similarly and mistakenly assumed his daughter was mad with him about a recent exchange. I said to him, "You feel like people who are supposed to love and take care of you keep fucking you over—that's your trauma experience speaking." He responded by reminding me that he has spent his whole life trying to please others at his own expense. Jake agreed with me when I said he was feeling it again with his client who might be unappreciatively switching the business to the new competitor. As he was thinking out loud about some unsatisfactory alternatives of how to make up for lost income if he lost the client, I chose to address how I thought his trauma history was affecting his inability to renegotiate with the client. Namely, to remind the client how diligently and conscientiously he did and could serve them and that he was in a better bargaining position than he could appreciate. I was subjectively responding to his feelings of under entitlement when he was describing his impulse to accede to the competitor when I somewhat playfully offered that I was having a "brilliant" insight (he had a wonderful sense of humor)—namely, I said, "What gets most damaged with a trauma history is survival instincts." He quickly affirmed my observation, saying he's always put the interest of others ahead of his own.

After a pause I decided to ask him how come he had never become addicted. He explained he had tried a lot of drugs but thought his need to "keep [his] wits" about things and because of control issues had prevented his continued use. He said that was why he did not like marijuana. I also suspected that his otherwise dysfunctional and characteristic defense of passive resignation, in this respect, protected him from the more commonly observed risk taking associated with addictive behavior. He added that he tried cocaine but that it did not do much for him and certainly it "was not a magical elixir." Jake also clarified that coming off cocaine he would get terribly depressed and weepy. Interestingly and significantly, he told me that when he was manic many years ago he drank two bottles of wine at a time to calm himself. At the end of the hour he thought out loud that he could have been an addictive gambler because he "could feel the rush" when he did gamble.

Jake was clear with me over the course of his therapy about how deeply he had suffered with his trauma. I was also aware how the consequences of the traumatic neglect and abuse weaved their way into the fabric of his personality organization and profoundly played out around his self-care and interpersonal dealings. I was repeatedly impressed with how he had a tendency to get into numerous jams with promises that he made which he often could not adequately deliver on because he could be so overextended by them. I often felt he was extending to others what he wished had been extended to him during his traumatically damaging and depriving childhood. In this interview I thought the mini-crisis around losing a client evoked characteristic inhibitions and self-denial about his own needs. As I was experiencing his under entitlement it prompted me to respond by linking it to his trauma history. I believe that same subjective, or intersubjective, if you will, reaction was involved in my pursuing with him the almost invariable association that I and others have observed between posttraumatic stress disorder (PTSD) and addictive vulnerability. In this context with my addicted patients, I often light heartedly warn them about my "mother-hen instincts" when I wonder and worry with them about their behaviors; but I suspect it is an intersubjective response to the absent or inadequate hovering issues that they experienced when they were very young. It is also fair to say in Jake's case that he had a special "protection" against addictive vulnerability working for him—namely, to think and feel about the consequences of his drug experiences (i.e., "mentalize") and at least in this way, assured better self-care and welfare than he customarily allowed for himself. His reactions to my enquiry about addiction vulnerability was revealing and significant in that it affirmed once again that addictive substances for various reasons are not always captivating or universally appealing and that they can even be experienced as aversive. Whether it was intervening control issues or his passive resignation that protected him, or that he lacked a biological/genetic susceptibility, or other factors, was interesting and striking. Perhaps it was an indication that his keen intelligence and the capacity to make cause-consequence connections (invariably deficient in addictively prone individuals) served him to avoid the pitfall of addiction. Not insignificantly, he did self-medicate his dysphoria with large amounts of wine when he was manic, one more condition in which there is intense affect and agitation and a disproportionate association with substance dependence.

FRUSTRATED ATTACHMENT AND SELF-MEDICATION

Attachment issues as Bowlby (1973) indicates persist from infancy through adult life. If humans are secure they proceed with a sense that they can engage and interact with others with a sense of comfort and confidence. When early attachments have been compromised, disrupted, traumatic, and neglectful, the human tendency is one of relational retreat and isolation and to attach to the inanimate dependencies of addictive substances and behaviors. One can relate to some of this to the aphorisms that addicted patients adopt, which reflect their conflict and ambivalence about their attachments:

"We are relief-seeking missiles."
"We don't have relationships—we take hostages."
Or, as one patient put it, "I'm a born-again isolationist."

Persuasive arguments have been advanced in the United States and the United Kingdom for conceptualizing addiction as an attachment disorder. Walant (2002) places attachment issues at the root of addictive behavior. She emphasizes how parents place cultural norms for autonomy and individuation (and depending on the times, other cultural norms) ahead of the child's needs for closeness and dependency and thus there is a failure in empathic attunement to the child's attachment needs. For example, a chronically relapsing alcoholic patient recently recalled how when she was about eleven years old she remembers her mother insisting that they not hold her one-year-old brother when he cried because they would "spoil him." From Walant's perspective, substance dependent individuals need help psychotherapeutically in cultivating the capacity for attachment to counter the disengagement they have developed and adopted in childhood to avoid the pain of their interpersonal difficulties extending into adulthood. She describes necessary empathic, relational, and interactive approaches to psychotherapeutically achieve this end. Flores (2004) persuasively contends that establishing and maintaining solid attachment assures safety, human comfort, and well-being. He argues this is not just a good idea; it is the law. In the absence of solid attachments, alcoholism and addiction can result. On this basis he proposes that treatments targeting attachment dynamics through individual and group therapies are needed to challenge the counter dependency and interpersonal avoidances associated with substance use disorders.

In the United Kingdom, Reading (2002) has explored how the tenets of attachment theory are fundamental for understanding the relational deficits of people with an addiction and for unravelling the connections to their drug of choice. He places addiction in an interpersonal context and considers how individuals who might be addictively prone adopt the inanimate attachment to drugs to substitute for their inconsistent and insecure attachment issues that date back to their childhood. Reading (2002) elegantly proposes that client and therapist need to appreciate and understand together how "addictional bonds" (23) replace affectional bonds.

The following case vignette illustrates how the problem of emotional reserve and inhibition dating back to childhood, interacting with contemporary issues of emotional disconnect with a spouse, fueled a growing dependency on alcohol. It also illustrates how the therapeutic relationship can attune to and intersubjectively activate the issues of disconnection that compel addictive behavior.

John

John is a 51-year-old manager of a very successful family business (not his own) who can take much of the credit for its current achievements. He is a tall and proud man, and his bearing reflects his staunch, somewhat reserved puritanical heritage and values, although he is not without a sense of humor. His demeanor also reflected the family tendency to be reserved and unexpressive with emotions. I have been following him for about two-and-a-half years. He came under pressure from his wife, who was experiencing his progressive heavy drinking as increasingly intolerable. He initially consented to weekly visits, but shortly after achieving significant reduction in the amount and frequency of his drinking he indicated a preference to see me on a more intermittent but regular basis. Nevertheless, he said the visits were important because he felt I was an important "governing influence" in controlling his consumption of alcohol (a term he picked up from me upon which I will comment subsequently). Our relationship was supportive and friendly (at times even playful around our mutual interests in sports), but the visits were more in the nature of checkups on how he was controlling his use of alcohol, and how things were progressing at work and at home. We enjoyed a mutually respectful and admiring relationship. I appreciated his reluctance and inability to explore in more depth matters involving feelings and relationships, only periodically touching upon conflicts involving work-related personnel encounters or issues in his family (his wife, Jane, tended to be socially isolated and recently was exhibiting some signs of depression). With the exception of a few relapses wherein his drinking was excessive and out of control, he was succeeding in limiting his drinking to one or two drinks or on rare occasions three drinks a day. I am generally dogged with my patients in pursuing the issue of what their drug of choice does for them—that is, what are they self-medicating? It is an avenue to therapeutically access the distress that governs their use and overuse of substances, but it also plays an important part in establishing an empathic alliance. Namely, the approach shifts from a typical one in which the patient can feel scolded about what the drugs are doing *to* (italicized for emphasis) them to one where an understanding is offered as to what the drug is doing *for* them. This is especially so given the harsh judgments that are placed on people with an addiction for their drug use, not the least of which is the harsh judgments and shame patients place on themselves. I had only peripherally touched on the matter in my initial encounter with John and the best I could surmise with him was that it served the purpose of releasing him from his emotional and interpersonal reserve given his cultural background and moral rectitude.

When we met this particular morning it was after my August break, and after several stops and starts working around his and my schedule. After reviewing a tense business negotiation that had caused him to miss our first scheduled visit after my vacation break, we touched on how things had been with his family. He spoke glowingly of how his daughter and son were doing at college, but then more glumly spoke about how things were with him and his wife. Strikingly, I found a variation of a line from a Cole Porter tune going through my head: "I get a kick out of champagne." (Of course, and not insignificantly, in the song he doesn't get the kick out of champagne but he does get it with his woman.) At that point I thought to say, "So there's no spark there with Jane?" referring to her depressive anergia. He agreed and quickly acknowledged, when I suggested it, that it did explain how he could get the spark out of alcohol. After a pause, I asked him about their sexual life. He said there wasn't any, and furthermore, there hadn't been any for at least the past five years; in fact, it had waned dating back to the time after the children were born. John shared that his libido remained high but Jane seemed to have lost her sexual desire and they didn't talk about it. We quickly ascertained together that his excessive drinking and increasing time out of the house corresponded to the period of Jane's waning and absent interest in sexual contact. We continued with the "spark" metaphor, John indicating that lingering later at work or at the pub provided the spark he was missing at home. I wondered aloud if he had thought of getting the spark elsewhere, that is, relationally. He reminded me of his puritanical heritage and said that that would produce a crisis of conscience. I then somewhat cryptically asked him if he knew about oxytocin. I explained that it was the human hormone that is released with childbirth as well as with lovemaking, that it assures human bonding and intimacy. He quickly caught on that I was suggesting he was missing not only the spark that comes from relating sexually but also the spark that comes with intimate human connection and comfort. I wondered with him how he was dealing with less spark coming from "champagne" and might he be subject to relapse with alcohol excess or some other excess. As the end of the hour neared, he rather sheepishly shared with me that he enjoyed the company of a very attractive, single woman, Susan, on the occasion of business meetings and social functions, quickly inserting that it was a friendship he much enjoyed, but that it was not sexual. When asked if keeping a secret like that was not a source of conflict and guilt, he assured me that his wife Jane knew Susan and more often John would mention that he would be attending a meeting or event with her to which she did not object. He ended by saying, "So how could I feel guilty if Jane knew?"

Speaking intersubjectively, from somewhere in my psyche and that of John's and with the help of Cole Porter, the word "spark" jumped into my consciousness and into our interaction. It stimulated an inroad into and a better understanding of the emotional and relational vacuum with which John lived at home. It also gave me insight into what he was actually self-medicating. Given his reserve and Jane's depressive anergia, disconnection, and disinterest in their relationship, it provided John and me with a basis to appreciate how and why these factors had interacted such that he had progressively depended on alcohol and found its effect increasingly appealing. That appreciation also provided us with a basis to explore an aspect of his personal life that was close, meaningful, and enriching, which he had not shared with anybody. I felt, and he gave some indication going out the door, that he felt similarly—namely, that he and I were now better connected around what alcohol did for him, as well as understanding the very important relationship with Susan. It provided us with a better relational vehicle to continue to monitor what his use of alcohol meant, and for he and I to better appreciate his need for human warmth and connection. Finally, we have reviewed elsewhere how "self-governance," alluded to earlier by John and me in our session, is not a one-person psychology—that alcohol problems, and life problems in general, are best not solved alone but in a self-other, interpersonal context (Khantzian and Mack 1989).

DISORDERED SELF-REGULATION, TRAUMA, AND THE INCAPACITY FOR SECURE ATTACHMENTS

In what follows I will, from a self-medication and attachment perspective, review how traumatic life experiences, whether they be abusive or neglectful, profoundly affect the human capacity for self-regulation. I will in particular stress how developmental disturbances affect life and the impact on sense of self and self-esteem powerfully interact to derail the capacity for secure, trusting, and comforting relationships and thus make it more likely that individuals will turn to and find comfort and relief in addictive substances. As Reading (2002) and others have stressed, and as a central tenet of this chapter, when attachments are troubled, individuals often substitute chemical connections for human ones.

Substance-dependent individuals become powerfully attached to their drugs because they have discovered that short-term addictive drugs work. They can relieve the suffering associated with feelings that are confusing or absent, or feelings that are intense and overwhelming. If feelings are on shutdown, there's no impetus to connect; if feelings are too intense and overwhelming, they threaten self and relationships with others. These basic problems with affect regulation are important because, from the earliest phases of development, affects are the principal organizers of self-experience throughout life (Stolorow, Brandchaft, and Atwood 1995). It is the view of Stolorow and his colleagues that the function of "self-objects" fundamentally refers "to the integration of affect into the organization of self-experience" (Stolorow, Brandchaft, and Atwood 1995, 66). This idea underscores the importance of the need for attuned responsiveness to affect states in all stages of life, attunement that tragically has been insufficient or absent in individuals with insecure attachment patterns that may lead to addictive behaviors. This perspective has obvious clinical implications for empathic attunement to the developmental incapacities we encounter and for us as therapists to know, experience, and verbalize feelings with which addictively prone individuals suffer.

Discussing the role of affects in the development of our sense of self, Stolorow and associates emphasize the role of parental responsiveness and when it has not been steady and attuned, self-fragmentation results. "Defenses against affect then become necessary to preserve the integrity of a brittle self-structure" (Stolorow, Brandchaft, and Atwood 1995, 67). Substance use is not considered by Stolorow and colleagues here, but it could have been—namely, substance-dependent individuals suffer because they lack in experiences of inner comfort, coherence and constancy, and addictive substances, especially the more calming and soothing ones, serve that purpose. The impoverished sense of self, so commonly evident with individuals who have an addiction, also significantly contributes to poor self-esteem and lack of mature self-love such as self-respect and pride. In their absence, meaningful and trusting connections to others are unlikely. In this respect, the activating and stimulating action of drugs such as cocaine or crystal meth help such individuals break through their impoverished or diminished sense of self to "connect to others," otherwise they are unable to. However, stimulant users speak of the pseudo-intimacy the drug provides, referring to such interactions as "speed talk."

The following two vignettes involving a patient I shall call Kate embody how growing up in a traumatizing and neglectful home environment left her with a lifelong sense of feeling undervalued, lonely, and unimportant. The vignettes also provide a chance to see how these dynamics can become activated, enacted in the treatment relationship, and therapeutically joined in treatment.

Kate, October 18, 2012

Before I get to Kate, I share a vignette a supervisor shared with me a long time ago. It goes something like this: Patient comes into the psychiatrist's office feeling awful; the psychotherapist feels okay. The session ends, the patient walks out the door feeling better; the psychiatrist feels awful. Something went wrong. It worked differently with Kate and me when we met today for her weekly psychotherapy which I will explain shortly. Kate has suffered unimaginable painful, crippling and disfiguring arthritis affecting all her joints, extremities, hips, and her spine. She is not addicted, but she is drug dependent. I will explain the difference subsequently. Her high doses of opiate analgesics for her pain have likely kept her chronic anger, if not rage, at tolerable levels intrapsychically and interpersonally. She has had a series of therapies with me dating back over 30 years. When I first met her, she reminded me of a beautiful variation of Barbara Streisand. Needless to say, she appears quite differently now. Her life and pain have been further complicated and compounded by a life-threatening condition her daughter has suffered since childhood; it involves a rare circulatory condition wherein any injury or infection to her upper extremities could become a catastrophic event. Kate is a physician assistant and to her credit and dismay she more often knows what is in her daughter's best interest, better than the clinicians who encounter her when there is one of the many and recurrent crises with her condition.

Kate's mother suffered from the consequences of both parents being alcoholics rendering Kate's mother unempathic and emotionally unavailable to Kate in her years of growing up. In addition to the effects of witnessing violent and abusive interactions between her parents, and painful spankings when mother or father were in a bad mood, the main effect of the traumatic neglect in Kate's life has been to make her adapt by becoming a selfless person, subordinating her needs in general, but particularly to the needs and care of her chronically ill daughter, an athletic son, and an anxious husband. In the case of her husband Tom, his anxiety drove him to succeed in his career as a trial lawyer but to be seemingly oblivious to Kate's suffering and all the challenges she faces in managing their home, to say nothing of all the additional burdens of their daughter's medical conditions. The central theme for our current psychotherapeutic work has involved helping Kate to feel validated and supported around the deep bitter resentment and rage that has accumulated over the years toward her husband's unavailability, at the same time trying to help her appreciate how the intensity of her reactions is fueled and amplified because of painful, enduring feelings of abandonment and neglect by her mother.

I say Kate could have become addicted because the intensity of her physical and emotional pain is so profound, affecting all aspects of her life and in particular, her self-esteem and relationships. Had she experimented with addictive drugs she might have become hooked on one of them. It could have been the ameliorating action of an opiate, especially the potentially calming and muting effect of heroin on her bitter resentment and rage; or it could have been the stimulating/activating action of cocaine that might have countered her despair and anhedonia. Is this not the flip-flop of affective numbing and flooding of PTSD? I offer a snippet of an interaction between us today that typifies, notwithstanding her husband's neglect, how unworthy she feels in general and acts around any source of comfort and acceptance of her distress and pain.

> On this particular day I was no less awed by how deep and pervasive her suffering is as she was characteristically reviewing past and present hurts and resentments, as usual, mostly targeting her husband. Then at one point as the end of the hour neared, she in passing mentioned that she had experienced a new pain this past week in her left groin area. When I asked her to elaborate about it she brushed me off with in effect an "oh well" reaction, almost as if I wouldn't be interested. I quickly pointed out, "As soon as you told me about your pain you dismissed me." Somewhat sarcastically she replied, "What about my pain do you want me to talk about?" I simply suggested she should talk with me more about her pain, reminding her that with her background as a child she had never developed that kind of a voice or felt worthy of attention. Welling up with bitter tears she said, "It's a lot . . . it keeps me from feeling I have a purpose in life . . . it limits me, I can't go out and do what I want to do." I told her that that's what she should be talking about. She again reverted to directing her resentment toward her husband, but this time with a different and, literally, a louder voice: "I want him to feel, he doesn't feel, [and even more loudly] . . . just feel!" As we were both standing, and as she was about to go out of the door, with bitter deep sadness and crying, I thought to re-remind her that she had almost dismissed me today about her groin pain. I offered, "Maybe today going out the door, hopefully with less pain, you might let me feel it." She thanked me as she opened the door and left.

We often at times like those, when we witness compounding tragedy and loss such as Kate's, find ourselves thinking, "This is like pages out of Job (the old testament prophet)." There has been no exception for me with Kate in this respect. Her life has involved tragic developmental traumatic neglect and abuse culminating in the marriage to an anxious man who could not get beyond his own problems to properly respond to those of his wife, and then the major near-unbearable medical conditions that she and her daughter have endured. Working and staying with the intensity and depth of her suffering has been one of the most difficult clinical challenges in my career. To my understanding, what has mattered the most in her case has been staying with her pain. Some might wonder, as my opening vignette suggests, that Kate was dumping her emotions on me. An intersubjective perspective would suggest otherwise. Our work together suggested to me the need for more corrective and, hopefully, transformative interactions. Such interactions, as she evoked with me this day, might over time allow for the lessening of Kate's suffering through processes of empathic acceptance of her pain and to help her to feel freer of the toxic resentments. At the same time gentle forays into Kate's characteristic defenses can help her better appreciate how she unwittingly fosters her worst dilemma of feeling no one can accept or understand how she feels, a dilemma that fuels and heightens her bitterness and rage. As the mentalizing and intersubjective theorists suggest (Allen, Fonagy, and Bateman 2008; Stolorow, Brandchaft, and Atwood 1995), a secure therapeutic attachment can serve to reignite, activate, and promote hope and trust that was lost or absent in childhood. I can concur with them that human relationships, starting with me as her therapist and her first experience of a secure enough base, can supplant conscious and unconscious defenses and resistances against meaningful and comforting relationships.

Kate, November 15, 2012

> This morning I was reminded about the difference between being "addicted" and being "drug dependent"—namely, in the case of the former, addicted means a person is drug dependent, but additionally they are continuously drug seeking, using without medical supervision, and using in a way that is harmful and dangerous, and use is continued despite all the negative consequences. Drug dependent simply means that one is physiologically dependent and if drug use is stopped abruptly the individual experiences painful physical withdrawal symptom.
>
> This morning in the context of my being interrupted by a call about another patient needing Suboxone to detoxify from opiates, a brief exchange followed with Kate about how she is prescribed a moderately high dose of long-acting oxycodone four times per day to manage the crippling arthritic pain. So she is drug dependent. She admits she experiences withdrawal symptoms and pain if she cuts back or does not take the oxycodone. But that's not what was significant about this morning's visit. Or was it? Because it was about pain—her pain and mine. Shortly after the interruption with my call and our exchange about her dependence on the pain medication, and one more diatribe about how disconnected her husband is about her needs and isolation, we were again interrupted when her daughter rang her twice on her mobile phone and she chose to take the call on the second ring. It was absolutely striking to me the marked change in her demeanor and her animated and affectionate and loving tone with her daughter. After she hung up, in a rather loud and impassioned way I exclaimed, "My God Kate! You so much need to be in a loving place . . . it might be a Herculean challenge, but you need to find a way to love Tom."
>
> After stressing to her how much more comfortable she appeared as she lovingly spoke with her daughter, I emphatically affirmed, "Kate, please

appreciate that although I am raising my voice, know that I am on your side." She responded impassively, "That is very astute." "Are you being sarcastic?" I asked. The answer was "Yes." I was enraged and wanted to say, "How dare you!" Instead, I protested loudly, candidly indicating to her that I experienced and was with her pain more than I had ever been with any patient. But then I added that she can't fix Tom's abominable and disappointing ways but she needs to see how she thrives when feeling loving, but dies emotionally when she remains bitterly cynical and cut-off. To my total surprise, going out of the door she responded, saying that she had an "attitude problem."

From an intersubjective perspective, I realize my anger/rage with her (not acted out, but acted on and expressed) kept me in the room with her, and her reactions to me came together to benefit her therapeutically. Maybe it was materially important for her to gather in my reaction subjectively and it played a part in examining and better appreciating her "attitude problem."

THERAPEUTIC IMPLICATIONS[2]

As I have emphasized, individuals who have become dependent on addictive drugs suffer because they are overwhelmed by or cut-off from their feelings, their sense of self and self-esteem is precarious, their capacity for secure attachments and comfortable relationships are elusive, and self-care is underdeveloped. Therapists and patients need to work together to access and understand how these vulnerabilities are intimately involved in the development of a dependency on addictive substances and other repetitive self-defeating behaviors. In this concluding section I will highlight some of the necessary elements and therapeutic modes of relating for effective psychotherapeutic action.

Psychoanalytic approaches of passivity, therapeutic detachment, and strictly interpretive techniques are not best suited for individuals with addictive disorders, if they are suited at all, and more likely such approaches perpetuate the confusion, shame, sense of alienation, and disconnection with which patients with an addiction suffer. In my work I have emphasized the need to be more interactive (balance talking and listening) and incorporate attitudes of kindness, support, empathy, respect, patience, and instruction in the service of building and maintaining a strong therapeutic alliance and attachment. These elements are essential in order to deal with and overcome the problems with self-regulation and attachments, which we have previously reviewed in this chapter, that become so powerfully linked to addictive behaviors (Khantzian 2012–2013).

---

2. This final section is based on two recent publications (Khantzian 2012, 2013).

When patients seem confused and say they do not know what they are feeling, therapists can help by evoking, identifying, and putting into words, feelings as they surface or become apparent in the therapeutic interactions. Instruction is often a necessary mode in this respect and entirely consistent with a psychodynamic approach. This is where the emphasis on "mentalizing" is so germane to work with people who have problems with an addiction. For those who suffer with intense and unbearable affect, it is worth remembering how the therapeutic relationship itself is a containing influence when such intense emotions are met with patience, forbearance, and respect for the origins of such distressful states. Otherwise patient and therapist withdraw from each other and the connection and attachment problems are repeated in the therapy relationship. Clearly such intensity of affect is one of the main and most troubling consequences of PTSD. The legitimacy of such reactions needs to be appreciated and acknowledged and the process of linking such rage and anger to the person's need to resort to addictive substances helps patients to feel understood and validated. Gentle explorations of the experiences that engender such emotions can gradually diminish or resolve such intense affect. In this context, judicious use of legitimate psychotropic medications targeting these affects can significantly attenuate the intensity to make the working through of these affects in psychotherapy more possible.

It is in the realm of a shaky sense of self and the relational difficulties of patients with an addiction that the importance of kindness, empathy, and support provide effective attunement to their needs for appreciation and validation, and how their injured sense of self and their relational distrusts and dis-ease leave them so susceptible to the inanimate attachment to addictive substances. Individuals with an addiction feel undeserving of the care and connection to others. Being interactive, engaging, and empathic are important elements in responding to patients' ambivalence about relationships. Impassivity and detached interpretations can be counter-therapeutic and retraumatizing. Careful exploration of the ambivalence about relationships can materially stimulate possibilities of beneficial connections to others. It is in this respect that the connections stimulated by individual and group therapy, and 12-step programs are extraordinarily helpful in addressing and ameliorating the attachment difficulties and sense of alienation with which substance dependent individuals struggle (Khantzian 2013).

The unthinking and unfeeling behaviors of patients who are substance dependent that are characteristic of deficits in self-care become evident in the therapeutic relationship through the alarm stirred up in the therapist by a patient's risky or dangerous behavior. Such reactions and interactions can alert the therapist and patient to how such deficits are major factors in relapse. As we have indicated, patients benefit from realizing how more often such deficits derive from traumatic and neglectful environments that leave them ill-prepared in assuring their well-being and safety. When therapists witness these deficits, they should be unhesitant in using their reactions of alarm and concern that patients stir to identify the lack of such responses in the patient. Constant attention to patients' poor self-care can help to instill a growing awareness of how their self-care deficits continuously leave those so affected continuously in harm's way, especially those involved with the harm and dangers associated with addictive substances. Long-term therapy often helps in reaching and understanding the developmental and environmental roots of these deficits, but a here-and-now, active, instructive approach is essential in order to stimulate and enable a better capacity to recognize, anticipate, and avoid self-harm, particularly related to addictive substances. "We need to help patients use self-respect, feelings of apprehension/worry, relationships with others, and thoughtfulness as a guide for safe behavior and self-preservation" (Khantzian 2012, 278).

In conclusion, a contemporary psychoanalytic understanding of addiction has generated and documented observable, developmental, structural, ego/self, and relational disturbances that predispose a person to maintain addictive behaviors and the accompanying insecure attachment relationships. These findings provide a basis to guide therapists in focusing on the self-regulation problems of patients with an addiction psychotherapeutically. Impassive and strictly interpretive approaches are contraindicated if not outright damaging. Modern psychotherapeutic practice employs more relational, interactive, supportive, and empathic attitudes and approaches to help patients and therapists to focus on the vulnerabilities and dysfunction that perpetuate addictive suffering and pain. This contemporary attachment and relational perspective provides understanding, hope, and more effective means to overcome the compelling, self-defeating, and tragic causes and consequences of addiction (Khantzian 2013).

References

Allen, J. G., Fonagy, P., and Bateman, A. W. (2008). *Mentalizing in Clinical Practice*. Washington, DC: American Psychiatric Publishing.

Bowlby, J. (1973). *Attachment and Loss*. Vol. 2, *Separation: Anxiety and Anger*. New York: Basic Books.

Darke, S. (2013). Pathways to heroin dependence: Time to reappraise self-medication. *Addiction* 108:659–67.

DuPont, R. L., and Gold, M. S. (2007). Comorbidity and "self-medication." *Journal of Addictive Disorders* 26 (1): 13–23.

Flores, P. J. (2004). *Addiction as an Attachment Disorder*. New York: Jason Aronson.

Khantzian, E. J. (1985). The self-medication hypothesis of addictive disorders. *American Journal of Psychiatry* 142:1259–64.

————. (1995). Self-regulation vulnerabilities in substance abusers: Treatment implications. In *The Psychology and Treatment of Addictive Behavior*, edited by S. Dowling, 17–41. New York: International Universities Press.

————. (1997). The self-medication hypothesis of substance use disorders: A reconsideration and recent applications. *Harvard Review of Psychiatry* 4:231–44.

————. (2003). Understanding addictive vulnerability: An evolving psychodynamic perspective. *Neuro-Psychoanalysis* 5:5–21.

————. (2012). Reflections on treating addictive disorders: A psychodynamic perspective. *American Journal on Addictions* 21:274–79.

————. (2013). Psychodynamic psychotherapy for the treatment of substance use disorders. In *The Textbook of Addiction Treatment: International Perspectives*, edited by N. El-Guebaly, M. Galanter, and G. Carra. New York: Springer, in press.

Khantzian, E. J., and Mack, J. E. (1983). Self-preservation and the care of the self: Ego instincts reconsidered. *Psychoanalytic Study of the Child* 38:209–32.

————. (1989). Alcoholics Anonymous and contemporary psychodynamic theory. In *Recent Developments in Alcoholism*, edited by M. Galanter, 67–89. New York: Plenum.

Kohut, H. (1971). *The Analysis of the Self*. New York: International Universities Press.

————. (1977). *The Restoration of the Self*. New York: International Universities Press.

Menninger, K. (1938). *Man against Himself*. New York: Free Press.

Milkman, H., and Frosch, W. A. (1973). On the preferential abuse of heroin and amphetamine. *Journal of Nervous and Mental Disease* 156:242–48.

Reading, B. (2002). The application of Bowlby's attachment theory to the psychotherapy of the addictions. In *The Psychodynamics of Addiction*, edited by M. Weegmann and R. Cohen, 13–30. London: Whurr.

Stolorow, R. D., Brandchaft, B., and Atwood, G. E. (1995). *Psychoanalytic Treatment: An Intersubjective Approach*. London: Routledge.

Walant, K. B. (2002). *Creating the Capacity for Attachment: Treating Addictions and the Alienated Self*. New York: Jason Aronson.

Weider, H., and Kaplan, E. (1969). Drug use in adolescents. *Psychoanalytic Study of the Child* 24:399–431.

Part II

THE SELF-MEDICATION HYPOTHESIS REVISITED

My background for and articulation of the self-medication hypothesis (SMH) had its origins in the development of a methadone maintenance program for opiate dependent individuals at the Cambridge Hospital in 1970, then one of the first such programs in the country. (At that time, there were only a few programs—several in New York City, one in California, and one in Boston at the Boston City Hospital.) Most studies of opiate dependence up until that time were based on research conducted with individuals in the federal prison and hospital system in the state of Kentucky. Methadone programs allowed students and clinicians such as me to study opiate-dependent individuals in their communities of origin at the same time we were treating them. Not insignificantly, I was in the middle of my psychoanalytic training and I and my department chairman, John E. Mack, saw this as an opportunity to bring to bear a contemporary psychoanalytic perspective for a better understanding of addiction.

The need for such a program was in response to alarm about a heroin "epidemic" at that time, much like we are witnessing now, but unlike the current alarm, the focus was about a significantly different population. Namely, the then target group coming for treatment was primarily from ethnic and racial minorities and the underprivileged, whereas the heroin epidemic of recent times has cut a much wider swath socioeconomically throughout society. Nevertheless, in my experience, and based on the literature, the psychodynamic and psychiatric findings strikingly and tragically appear to be remarkably the same.

In the beginnings of the methadone maintenance program—after overcoming my initial trepidation and bias of heroin-addicted individuals as menacing and dangerous (i.e., counter-transference), and after beginning to take detailed psychiatric histories for all patients coming for treatment—I quickly came to appreciate the extraordinary life stories of childhood trauma, neglect and oppression, and tough, depriving environments. I was soon persuaded that the patients we were treating were an extremely vulnerable population who suffered immensely as a consequence of their adverse and harsh developmental backgrounds. At first, I thought that opiates had their appeal because of the general pain-relieving action of opiates, but as I continued these evaluations, I began to better appreciate that the patients were experiencing a more specific "benefit" from the action of opiates—namely, the relief of powerful and threating affects involving rage, intense anger, and associated agitation and dysphoria. That is, opiates acted as antiaggression, anti-violence, anti-agitation agents, providing temporary relief for such disorganizing and threatening feelings. Thus were the early beginnings or anlage for the SMH.

In 1985, I published the first articulation of the SMH with a focus on heroin and cocaine. Subsequently, in 1997, I further reviewed its application to areas not previously considered. As emphasized in those and numerous other reports, the SMH proposes that addictive drugs have appeal because (a) they relieve human psychological suffering, and (b) there is considerable degree of preference or self-selection in a person's drug of choice. In my work, I have inferred or stated some fundamental premises on which the SMH rests. First, addiction is grounded in the human penchant (especially in the infant, but persisting into adulthood) for seeking comfort and contact, not pleasure. Second, addictive drugs, despite their powerful effects, are not universally appealing, and third, the SMH supplies valuable clues and understanding of the nature of predisposing conditions and painful affect states, and why and how these drugs are more captivating for some and not for others.

The SMH has been much trivialized, demonized, and endorsed, the latter especially by clinicians. That people "self-medicate" with addictive drugs has become a household expression and is often used in everyday language and in media accounts referring to why people take addictive drugs, with little appreciation of the study that has gone into such behavior and the intricacies about affects, self-esteem, relationships, and self-care issues involved when people self-medicate. Ironically, in the case of demonization of a theory, we often joke that the measure of a good idea is the extent of the criticism and attack it draws. The SMH has been no exception. For example, two prominent investigators (DuPont and Gold 2007) have suggested that the SMH is a "dangerously false and misleading" idea. In another context, an institutional review board (IRB) advised a doctoral candidate not to pursue self-medication factors in her study of a population of addicted individuals because it could be dangerous by stirring cravings, and cause relapse. More positively, there have been and continue to be many endorsements of the SMH and numerous and frequent citations of it in the literature as evidenced in Google Scholar, Research Gate, and academia.edu websites. In 1990, shortly after the first publication of the SMH, the associate editor of the *Journal of the American Medi-*

cal Association, Richard Glass, in an editorial titled "Blue Mood, Blackened Lungs" in response to papers in that issue on nicotine dependence associated with depression, wrote as follows:

> The notion of "self-medication" is one of the most intuitively ap-
> pealing theories about drug abuse. According to this hypothesis
> (Khantzian 1990), drug abuse begins as a partially successful attempt
> to assuage painful feelings. This does not mean seeking "pleasure"
> from the use of drugs. Rather, individuals predisposed by biological
> or psychological vulnerabilities find that drug effects corresponding
> to their particular problems are powerfully reinforcing.

In chapters 6–10 in this section, I have included a number of publications that demonstrate the range of issues and thinking that the SMH has spawned. I explore and underscore fundamentals about the SMH, including, in chapter 6, the importance of understanding addiction as a self-regulation disorder and how addictive substances relieve a range of painful feelings associated with the inability to regulate emotions, self-esteem, relationships, and self-care. In chapter 7, I draw out with dually diagnosed patients and how, more than anything, their psychiatric conditions profoundly affect their inability to self-regulate all the emotional suffering that entails. I stress the importance of targeting and treating the psychiatric problems as pivotal for recovering. In chapter 8, Dr. Jesse Suh, his associates, and I present empirical data supporting the centrality of affective experience in addictive processes and the evidence that supports the phenomena of drug preference, or what is commonly referred to as drug of choice. The chapter, for which Dr. Suh was the lead author, was based on his doctoral dissertation testing the validity of the SMH. His dissertation was one of the most recent among a dozen or so dissertations adopted by doctoral candidates investigating the validity and various aspects of the SMH. Needless to say, it was a most gratifying process providing empirical evidence supporting self-medication theory. On a somewhat different course from most of my publications, with my esteemed colleagues from Columbia Medical Center, Dr. John Mariana and Dr. Frances Levin, in chapter 9 I present clinical case material in which the SMH guided the effective medication-assisted treatment (MAT) of heavily stimulant-dependent patients. Chapter 10 was the result of an interview with the editors of a publication originating in Johannesburg, South Africa, *New Therapist*. As I considered the stimulating inquiries posed by the editors with their invitation, I decided to accept their request and respond to the broad range of issues they raised, giving me an opportunity to reflect on much of my life's work, as well as to address some of the existent controversies and debates that are so much a part of addiction studies and treatment approaches. Frankly, they and I were pleased with the outcome.

References

DuPont, R. L., and Gold, M. S. (2007). Comorbidity and "self-medication." *Journal of Addictive Disorders* 26 (1):13–23.

Glass, R. (1990). Blue mood, blackened lungs: Depression and smoking. *Journal of the American Medical Association* 264:1583–84.

CHAPTER 6

The SMH and Addiction as a Problem in Self-Regulation

With Mark J. Albanese

As we have been saying, suffering is at the heart of addictions. People who become addicted suffer because they have difficulty regulating their (1) emotions; (2) sense of self-worth; (3) relationships; and (4) behaviors, especially self-care. While much has been written about how the widespread availability of addictive drugs, their pleasure-producing effects, and the human proclivity for self-destruction make addiction likely, our clinical experience convincingly demonstrates that the short-term ability of addictive substances to relieve, change, or make more tolerable the distress associated with the problems of dysregulated emotions, self-worth, relationships, and behaviors powerfully reinforces dependence on the substance. People who know and are comfortable about their feelings, like themselves, get along easily with others, and are careful about their behaviors are not apt to become addicted, not withstanding an overwhelming genetic predisposition.

Tony the Barber—Not Knowing
Tony has been in recovery from alcohol and cocaine dependence for 15 years. He is proud of how far he has come with the help of AA and counseling. He's a talkative and jovial man, but he wasn't always that way. He says that during the days he was addicted, he was an angry, wild man who was reckless and unpredictable about where he went, what he did, and the people with whom he associated. In looking back on that time he says he was lost when it came to knowing his feelings and how important a part of life they were. He says that early in recovery his counselor would ask him what he felt about important events in his life, such as his mother's death, and repeatedly he would say, "I don't know, I don't know, I don't know!" He says it was always hard for him to be in touch with his feelings, and when upsetting events would happen he was likely to do something impulsive, get angry, or run away. Working with

his counselor over a long period of time he evolved from saying, "Maybe I feel . . . [to] . . . I think I feel . . . [to] I feel." When he talks about this he stammers and stumbles and is embarrassed to realize how out of touch and confused he was about his emotional life. He says that as he got better, his challenge was to stick with feeling his feelings, especially those that were painful and uncomfortable. He says his counseling and AA meetings in particular have helped him to recognize his emotions better and to realize that he is not unique in being confused and avoidant when it comes to dealing with and accepting distress.

Although one might be surprised that such basic aspects of life as being aware of and in touch with feelings could be as confusing and as intolerable as they were for Tony, those who treat addicted people commonly encounter these issues. The appeal of addictive drugs, depending on the drug and a person's reaction to it, is that they can blot out feelings, intensify them, or simply change them. When people are not as emotionally dysregulated as Tony, they can recognize and distinguish among emotions like anxiety and depression, and can accept that such emotions are an unavoidable part of life. In Tony's case, he not only could not come up with words for what he was feeling but often tended to experience and express his distress through impulsive actions and in vague bodily symptoms and discomfort, again not an unusual response for individuals who suffer with addictive problems. While the way individuals use addictive drugs to cope with emotions is initially helpful and the benefits short term, the effect is powerful enticement and what often sets the hook for vulnerable individuals. The problem is that using more and more drugs to achieve emotional regulation deepens the dependency, leading to atrophy of any self-regulatory skills, and physical dependence in which withdrawal—that is, coming off the drug—further reinforces the addiction. In the end, the difficulties dealing with feelings are made worse, compounded by the pain of withdrawal. In this way, addictions take on a life of their own, drug use begetting more drug use in an endless spiral.

A generation of psychoanalysts and psychodynamic psychiatrists in the mid- to late 20th century have discovered that feelings are neither a given nor uniformly the same for all individuals. Where Freud in the late 19th century and early 20th century stressed the role of drives, the unconscious, and the repression of feelings and thoughts, contemporary researchers have discovered that feelings, like other aspects of psychological development, progress in more or less predictable ways. When there is major damaging or neglectful experiences either growing up or later in life, the capacity to experience and know one's emotions can be damaged. Thus, someone like Tony is not so much blocking out or denying feelings, which early Freudian theory would suggest, but instead displaying a deficit in psychological development. In other words, there is a problem or disorder in knowing, naming, and feeling feelings. Peter Sifneos, an American psychoanalyst of Greek lineage, drawing on his ethnic heritage with John Nemiah, coined the term "alexithymia" to capture this deficit: the prefix, "a," referring to the absence of; "lex" referring to words; and "thymia" referring to feelings (Sifneos 1967). Literally translated, it means "no words for feelings." In our own work we have referred to this distressful, confusing, and vague experience of feelings as "dysphoria." The SMH emphasizes that addictive drugs and behaviors relieve this dysphoria associated with painful or confusing feelings, from which patients like Tony suffer, thus reinforcing the appeal of those substances and behaviors.

In contrast to Tony's constricted expression of emotion, others are overwhelmed with emotions, and resort to action, activity, and drugs to relieve their intensity and make them more tolerable. We will elaborate more on this aspect of how individuals self-medicate the distress of overwhelming or unbearable emotions in the next chapter.

Unlovable Carol

Carol is an accomplished pediatrician who had to overcome many obstacles to become a physician. When Carol first came for treatment she was colorfully dressed in black leather pants and a bright red jacket. She smiled frequently and was animated in her manner of speaking. Despite her attractive appearance and likeable manner, as her treatment progressed she revealed a deep insecurity and lack of confidence. She had become dependent on narcotic pain medications prescribed for her sister, for whom she cared while she suffered with terminal cancer. Her sister suggested that Carol try one of her pain pills after a root canal procedure. Carol had a dramatic discovery that the medication not only relieved her physical pain but also gave her a fantastic emotional lift and sense of well-being.

Carol and her sister both experienced a very troubled upbringing with an alcoholic father who overwhelmed the entire household. Carol had to provide some of the parenting for both herself and her sister. Both of them became overachievers, Carol as a physician and her sister as a business executive.

One of the main effects on her of those early years was a reservoir of anger and resentment which she said could easily erupt with the slightest provocation. She indicated, "Anger is very tough for me . . . it feels unsafe and at all costs I have to squelch it." In spite of her upbeat and appealing image, she described how insecure she felt and how she always had to project an image of perfection and lovability. Carol explained, "I mustn't let any one know about that [angry] part of me; they might not approve . . . they might not love me. I must be lovable—absolutely lovable, I have to be absolutely loveable!" The narcotic pain relievers calmed her and would cause her concerns about here lovability to recede.

Our sense of ourselves and how we want others to appreciate us is important enough, but someone like Carol is unsure about her basic lovability. This is a setup for chronic low self-esteem which can affect many aspects of life. Carol's words give ample indication of how such concerns can overtake a person. People such as Carol have experienced how addictive drugs like opioid analgesics calm the rage and anger that shake her confidence in herself. On another day or for another person, a stimulating drug could bolster self-esteem by energizing or helping to initiate contact with someone in order to feel better. For a person who struggling with self-confidence problems who is tightly wrapped and defensive about his needs for affection and approval, a low to moderate dose of alcohol could soften him up to accept or invite affection when ordinarily unable to do so.

The psychology of self-love or self-regard is an important aspect of understanding the vulnerability for addiction. Much psychological distress derives from not liking ourselves enough, as Carol's case testifies. The self-psychologist Heinz Kohut and his followers were pioneering in the last part of the 20th century in helping to articulate how problems with self-love can be detrimental to healthy mental life, and contribute to a range of troubling behaviors, including addiction (Kohut and Wolfe 1978). Some try to compensate for their poor self-regard by making too much of themselves and we unflatteringly characterize such individuals as "narcissists." In contrast, certain individuals make too much of others and derive their sense of well-being from them. In the case of the addiction-prone who struggle with such issues of self-regard, addictive substances become the object of their love and provide a means to feel better about themselves.

Reserved Jeff

Jeff is an appealing 47-year-old production manager who had a long history of alcohol and cocaine dependence. He recalls that in high school he was shy and reserved, until he discovered the lubricating effects of alcohol. Jeff said, "Alcohol allowed me to get outside myself . . . to put aside my reserved character." Without it he said he was "retiring and quiet . . . drinking I could express myself better and I was better company."

During his twenties he cut back significantly, drinking only occasionally and moderately. He describes himself reverting to a drab, grey existence during this period. In his 30s he discovered cocaine. Jeff said, "It allowed me to be a lot of things I had been in the past . . . my energy returned, I had a sense of humor and felt like a worthy companion again." He said previously he had been isolated, cut off, and avoiding social situations. Although the cocaine worked for awhile, as his use escalated he started to drink heavily again, all leading up to admitting himself for detoxification and rehabilitation. After his rehab stay, although he did not drink or use drugs, he found himself reverting to his old uncommunicative and isolative habits, not speaking with his wife, and cutting himself off socially, not reaching out to the few friends he had. Not insignificantly, he started taking the antidepressant Prozac® around five years out of rehab. Subsequently, he has been able to communicate

better, "the words now come out unfiltered . . . I even look forward to
going home from work to see my wife."

Relationships can be some of the most satisfying and bedeviling aspects of our existence as human beings. As much as we are social creatures, we can also be avoidant of relationships, even when we most need them. Some of us are better than others at relationships. For those less able to connect to others, life can be dreary, lonely, and depressing, as Jeff's life was for long stretches of time. Unfortunately, individuals such as Jeff are susceptible to the discovery that alcohol can temporarily fix their relationship difficulties. One view of addiction is that it is an "attachment disorder" (Flores 2004). Establishing and maintaining meaningful relationships, an essential aspect of life, provide a sense of comfort, safety, and security. As with so many personality components, the capacity to connect to others reflects back to matters of temperament and early parental relationships. Starting with the earliest phases of development, a lifelong challenge for human beings is to work out relationships in a satisfactory and satisfying way. Unfortunately for some, the capacity to relate to others gets derailed early in life, and addictions can be substituted for the comfort and well-being that relationships can provide.

Careless Carl

Carl was a skilled carpenter. The care he took in his craft contrasted sharply with how he took care of himself. His clients were consistently pleased with the care and attention he devoted to his work, whether it was in fashioning a special cabinet or completing the finish-work in a redesigned room. Yet when it came to billing for his projects he often lost his receipts or the accounting for the hours he and his workmen put into a job. He often also misplaced the keys to his pickup truck when starting out in the morning, leading to endless turmoil in his family as they helped him to get organized and out the door for his day's work. Carl also caused havoc in his personal finances, not balancing his checking account and overdrawing, missing insurance payments, and losing important financial documents. He also was subject to accidental falls and scrapes because he often moved and jumped ahead of himself before checking his surroundings.

Carl was not dependent on alcohol, but he overused and abused it, often causing him embarrassment when he was with family or friends. Despite knowing his tendencies, he repeatedly behaved in silly or inappropriate ways, especially when he drank. Though often bemoaning his fate as a "loser" after such occurrences, he seemed incapable of anticipating trouble associated with situations, people, and things that would cause him embarrassment and remorse when he drank too much /or was excessive in his behaviors. Some of his excesses were a function of his need to be super-friendly and likeable. But the main difficulty seemed to be obliviousness to cues and warnings that a given situation or relationships could lead to problematic behavior which he only seemed to have a hint of after the fact.

Anxiety and worry are inescapable in life. When excessive, they can be paralyzing; when absent, they can leave individuals in harm's way, as seems to be the case with Carl. In several decades of trying to understand the bases of addictive vulnerability we have been impressed repeatedly with how vital functions which insure our existence and safety, such as appropriate concern and worry, are often deficient or absent in people like Carl. Some theorists, including early psychoanalysts, believe survival reactions are instinctive and that accidents reflect unconscious drives. In our experience, such survival mechanisms are neither instinctive nor necessarily reflect unconscious motives, but rather develop out of the early environment in which the child gradually learns from her parents to be vigilant and aware of harm and danger, and to take action or to avoid situations that might be harmful or dangerous. In damaging or neglectful growing up environments such capacities are more often compromised. We have designated these functions as the "capacity for self-care" (Khantzian and Mack 1983). Not insignificantly, neuroscientists using neuroimaging techniques have documented how methamphetamine abusers who relapsed showed less activation in regions of the brain (prefrontal and temporal cortex and the insula) involving choice and action than did abusers who did not relapse (Paulus, Tapert, and Schuckit 2005). This is one more example of how findings from neuroscience can and do complement and support what we learn from clinical experience People like Carl are vulnerable to excessive and aberrant behaviors, including addictive behaviors with all their unwanted results, because their underdeveloped capacity for self-care causes them to not be anxious or worried enough about hazards in potential and actual dangerous situations. While we cannot deny unconscious self-destructive motives and instincts, we have found, from our developmental perspective that self-harm is frequently the result of an underdeveloped or absent capacity for self-care.

* * *

Individuals who succumb to addictions are often referred to as having an "addictive personality." Aside from being an unflattering and unempathic portrayal, such a description detracts from the preeminently human vulnerabilities involved in addictive problems. We do not subscribe to the notion of an addictive personality. Rather it is our experience and conviction that addictions involve conditions in which problems with regulating emotions, self-love, relationships, and self-care interact in varying degrees with each other, genetic vulnerability, and the environment, depending on the individual, to make addiction more likely. For Tony the barber it was the bewildering nature of emotions which, in combination with reckless and careless behavior, led to his involvement with and addiction to cocaine. In the case of Carol, her need to be loved and accepted at all times made narcotic pain killers enticing. In Jeff's case, the difficulty in connecting to others, and related problems with isolation and depression, made alcohol and cocaine all too attractive a means to relate to others when it was otherwise impossible. And finally, is it surprising that someone like Carl, so out of touch with hazards and dangers, should be prone to the risks of alcohol and other misadventures that result from not being careful? Addictive drugs, including alcohol, are not universally appealing. A particular drug becomes appealing when a person discovers that the short-term "benefits" of a particular drug become necessary to overcome some facet of or problem with regulating emotions, self-esteem, and relationships. In turn, the pain and distress associated with these vulnerabilities interact with deficits in self-care to make addiction more probable. Addiction problems are less a statement about pleasure seeking, reward, or self-destructiveness, than they are about human psychological vulnerabilities.

References

Flores, P. J. (2004). *Addiction as an Attachment Disorder*. New York: Jason Aronson.

Khantzian, E. J., and Mack, J. E. (1983). Self-preservation and the care of the self: Ego instincts reconsidered. *Psychoanalytic Study of the Child* 38:209–32.

Kohut, H., and Wolfe, E. S. (1978). The disorders of the self and their treatment. *International Journal of Psychoanalysis* 59:413–25.

Paulus, M. P., Tapert, S. F., and Schuckit, M. A. (2005). Neural activation patterns of methamphetamines-dependent subjects during decision making predict relapse. *Archives of General Psychiatry* 62:761–68.

Sifneos, P. E. (1967). Clinical observations on some patients suffering from a variety of psychosomatic diseases. In *Proceedings of the Seventh European Conference on Psychosomatic Research*. Basel: S. Karger.

CHAPTER 7

The Self-Medication Hypothesis Revisited

THE DUALLY DIAGNOSED PATIENT

The self-medication hypothesis (SMH) is derived from clinical work with patients who have substance use disorders (SUDs). There are two core aspects of the SMH— namely, that substances of abuse relieve human psychological suffering in susceptible individuals and that there is a considerable degree of psychopharmacologic specificity in an individual's preferred drug. Substances of abuse can relieve a wide range of painful feelings associated with psychiatric illness, thus making patients with a psychiatric disorder more susceptible to SUDs. Those patients who are dually diagnosed with psychiatric illness and SUDs become dependent on a particular class of drugs to relieve the painful affects that predominate with their psychiatric disorder. An appreciation of self-medication factors in dually diagnosed patients has important implications for targeting and treating the distress these patients experience.

Addictive vulnerability is intimately tied to human psychological distress. The self-medication hypothesis (SMH) suggests that at the heart of addictive disorders is suffering, not the seeking of pleasure, reward, or self-destruction, as prominent theories have proposed (Khantzian 1999). Nowhere is this more evident than in the patient who endures a comorbid psychiatric disorder, the so-called dually diagnosed patient. There is a growing body of evidence from clinical and epidemiologic studies indicating that a significant relationship exists between substance use disorders (SUDs) and psychiatric disorders, and there is a growing preponderance of evidence suggesting that co-occurring psychiatric disorders are etiologically related to and predate SUDs (Khantzian, Dodes, and Brehm 2005; Albanese 2003a, 2003b; Regier, Farmer, and Ral, et al. 1990; Kessler, Crum, and Warner, et al. 1997). This chapter reviews basic aspects of the SMH of SUDs and considers how it applies to the dilemmas of patients who suffer with psychiatric disorders.

The Self-Medication Hypothesis: Definition

There are two important aspects of the SMH: (1) individuals use, abuse, and become dependent upon substances because they relieve states of distress; and (2) there is a considerable degree of psychopharmacologic specificity in an individual's preferred drug. Individuals do not choose to become alcoholic or dependent on opiates, cocaine, or other drugs. Rather, in the course of experimenting with different drugs, a person susceptible to addiction discovers that a particular drug relieves, ameliorates, or changes different painful affect (i.e., feeling) states and becomes a favored drug. This second aspect of the SMH has been more difficult to prove empirically (Albanese 2003), but it is uncanny how often patients will verify it by responding when asked, "What is King Drug for you?" A corollary to this "discovery," depending upon varying feelings which might predominate in the person, is that a drug may be experienced as aversive. For example, an agitated or enraged person will experience cocaine as disorganizing and threatening. An important point here is that addictive drugs are not universally appealing.

Commonly Abused Drugs

The SMH is based primarily on clinical observations derived from a psychodynamic perspective utilized by investigators dating to the early 1970s. Terms such as "drug of choice" (Weider and Kaplan 1969), "preferential use of drugs" (Milkman and Frosch 1973), and "self-selection" (Khantzian 1975) were coined to describe how individuals found certain drugs appealing, contributing to the articulation of the SMH (Khantzian 1985). As summarized in a recent update of the SMH (Khantzian 1997), the following outlines the main action and appeal of the most commonly abused drugs.

OPIATES

Besides their general calming and "normalizing" effect, opiates attenuate intense, rageful, and violent affect. They counter the internally fragmenting and disorganizing effects of rage and the externally threatening and disruptive aspects of such effects on interpersonal relations.

CENTRAL NERVOUS SYSTEM DEPRESSANTS

Short-acting depressants with rapid onset of action (e.g., alcohol, barbiturates, benzodiazepines) have their appeal because they are good "ego solvents." That is, they act on those parts of the self that are cut off from self and others by rigid defenses. These are defenses which produce feelings of isolation, emptiness and related tense/anxious states, and mask fears of closeness and dependency. Although they are not good antidepressants, alcohol and related drugs create the illusion of relief because they temporarily soften the rigid defenses and ameliorate states of isolation and emptiness that predispose to depression.

STIMULANTS

Stimulants act as augmenters for hypomanic, high-energy individuals as well as those with atypical bipolar disorder. They also appeal to people who are de-energized and bored, and to those who suffer from depression, often of a subclinical variety. In addition, stimulants, including cocaine, can act paradoxically to calm and counteract hyperactivity, emotional lability, and inattention in persons with attention-deficit/hyperactivity disorder (ADHD) (Khantzian 1985). In the case of dually diagnosed patients, individuals employ stimulants to counter the cognitive dulling and sedating effects of neuroleptics.

MARIJUANA

Marijuana has both stimulating and sedating properties. There is relatively little in the literature to describe how and why this drug becomes compelling. Presumably, either the sedating or stimulating properties can be the basis of its appeal. Ned Hallowell, MD, an authority on ADHD, has indicated that marijuana is very appealing to patients with this condition (verbal communication). It would appear that both the sedating and stimulating (acting paradoxically) actions help to counter the restlessness and emotional lability associated with ADHD.

SUDs and Self-Regulation: Relationship to the SMH

Beyond enduring pain and distress, which addictive drugs initially relieve, substance abusers suffer because they have difficulties regulating their self-esteem, relationships, and, especially, their self-care. Adopting an overarching concept of SUDs as self-regulation disorder is necessary because it helps address some of the main criticisms of the SMH—namely, that many individuals suffer with distress but do not become addicted and that there is likely more suffering as a consequence of substance use and abuse as there is relief.

A detailed review of this aspect of the SMH is beyond the scope of this chapter. More detailed descriptions of self-regulation vulnerabilities in SUDs (Khantzian 1990, 1995, 1997, 1999) indicate that it is the combination of contributing factors, such as self-esteem and interpersonal issues, interacting with necessary factors, such as affect and self-care deficits that makes it more likely that an individual will succumb to addictive disorders. The concept of SUDs as self-regulation disorder also helps to explain how wittingly and unwittingly substance abusers perpetuate their suffering as a means to understand and control it. That is, the operative changes from the relief of suffering to the control of suffering. Another unfortunate consequence of continued substance abuse is that it further exacerbates and perpetuates self-regulation deficits.

Psychiatric Disorders, Self-Regulation, and Human Psychological Suffering

As with SUDs, it can be debated whether psychiatric illness is adaptive or maladaptive. There is an old basic psychodynamic assumption that every psychological problem represents a solution. That is, such problems represent ways to cope with troublesome feelings and external reality. In fact, a recent review of depression bears modern testimony to the persistent usefulness of this paradigm (Nesse 2000). Depression can serve as a coping device just as much as reliance on substances can.

Much of what is presented in this review is based on clinical narrative material—an approach that is more dimensional, dynamic, and derived from a process method of understanding patients' problems. The *Diagnostic and Statistical Manual of Mental Disorders*, 4th ed., revised (American Psychiatric Association 2000) adopts a categorical and symptom approach to organize symptoms and diagnose psychiatric illness. Each approach has advantages and disadvantages. For the purposes of this review, it can be argued that a diagnostic/categorical approach runs the risk of missing the considerable human suffering associated with psychiatric illness. More particularly, each psychiatric illness we encounter is associated with specific painful affect states that predominate.

Psychiatric disorders, like SUDs, are associated with considerable pain and dysfunction due to problems entailing regulation of emotions, self-esteem, relationships, and self-care. It is little wonder then that there is a disproportionately greater degree of substance abuse and dependence among patients with psychiatric illness (Regier et al. 1990; Kessler et al. 1997). Patients who are dually diagnosed discover that in the short-term, substances relieve, ameliorate, or help control emotional and behavioral dysregulation associated with their psychiatric disorder.

A Case Study

The following case vignette demonstrates a person's discovery that substances of abuse can serve to counter or relieve painful emotional states rooted in traumatic life experiences. It also detail the often-immense suffering that results, some of which may not so readily lend itself to psychiatric classification:

> Donald is a 35-year-old recently unemployed, divorced father of three. He was admitted to a public psychiatric hospital after several suicide attempts and after a failure to respond to treatment for long-standing depression. Divorce and the loss of his job loomed large as precipitants for his depression and the persistence of suicidal ideation and attempts. The patient had a history of heavy substance abuse starting in his mid-adolescent years until he received a medical discharge from the Army in his early 20s. Subsequent to leaving the military, he had achieved a protracted period of controlled alcohol use but resumed heavy drinking after discovering his wife's infidelity four years prior. The recent progressive and heavy use of alcohol became a major factor in deteriorating work performance and, ultimately, termination of his employment.
>
> Consultation was requested for the patient to determine if alcohol use was his only substance abuse problem. The interviewer was able to establish sufficiently good contact and trust to consider the information obtained in his evaluation to be credible and believable. Donald reported a remarkable background in terms of a significant abuse history (physical, sexual, and verbal) dating back to infancy and continuing into early adolescence. There was an uncanny interweaving of his personal traumatic abuse history with his use and misuse of addictive substances, wherein with little prompting he revealed how various substances acted as antidotes to the suffering his trauma had engendered. His history was also remarkable in that his substance abuse also dated back to early childhood. The description of his personal abuse experience was impressive for the brutal content, but chilling in the matter-of-fact way he recounted it. He claimed remembering that his biological father, also an alcoholic, regularly fondled him and sexually forced himself on him. He said it stopped only with father's sudden death when he was three years of age. His

lot was not much better (from age five into his teens) at the hands of his stepfather who constantly demeaned him and regularly beat him with his belt buckle, sometimes to discipline him, but at other times, seemingly for no apparent reason.

At the time of his evaluation Donald was receiving oxycodone 60 milligrams/day for degenerative arthritis of his right hip. A detailed inquiry into his use of substances revealed that his parents laughed when he accidentally became intoxicated at three years of age after consuming an alcoholic beverage that had been left lying around the house. He began to experiment with alcohol, marijuana, psychedelics, and psychostimulants by 15 years of age. By his late teens he was using alcohol heavily and had been using heroin intermittently for several years. He recalled feeling "exhilarated" when he first tried free-base cocaine; heroin had a calming and soothing effect, especially on his irritability and rage, which he vividly recalled. He said it made all of his constant inner discomfort disappear. Surprisingly, he made little or no connection to the observed analgesic and calming effect he had obtained from the oxycodone that had recently been prescribed for his hip pain during his current admission to the hospital. Alcohol, in obliterating doses, was used in a similar fashion to the heroin as a less expensive alternative to calm inner states of apprehension, dysphoria, and feelings of violence. His continuous inner distress, which he admittedly linked to his traumatic history, was expressed endlessly in both physical and emotional ways. He had experienced more than the average young man's share of somatic symptoms and reactions. The extent of his hip pain was both verified and questioned by several orthopedic consultants. Prior to his hospitalization, atrial fibrillation, which was precipitated when feeling stressed, required cardioversion. A range of gastrointestinal complaints was not uncommon.

As extreme and unbelievable as Donald's case sounds, it is not uncommon and typifies the lifelong dilemmas of patients with psychiatric illness and SUDs. The patient meets criteria for personality disorder with borderline and narcissistic features, major depression, posttraumatic stress disorder, and somatoform disorder. He made it clear that psychological and physical pain and suffering were constants in his life, taking subtle and overt forms. As with other trauma patients, his sleep hours were also invaded by distressing flashbacks and reenactments of his life of traumatic experiences. Such experience associated with infantile trauma has been referred to as "endless suffering" (Henry Krystal, MD, personal communication). Unfortunately, the persistent and extreme suffering Krystal refers to is often missed in individuals like Donald as a consequence of off-putting personality characteristics.

As was the case with Donald, it is not uncommon to hear how the stories of substance use and abuse interact with patients' inner emotional suffering and provide temporary surcease from their distress. This case also typifies the tragic repetitions that occur into adulthood in disrupted relationships and work history. The human tragedy of cases like Donald's gets lost on the terrain of debates about diagnoses, their believability, and the stigmatization of "drug abuse." In fact, what is begged here is a measure of empathy for the patients' suffering and their need to resort to drug solutions and other misbehaviors that are too often confusing, off-putting, and self-defeating.

Psychopathology, Affect States, and Self-Medication: A Sampling

DEPRESSION

It is important to stress once again that the SMH is about self-medicating painful affects, and not necessarily disorders/diagnoses, which may be subsyndromal. As Donald's case exemplifies, depression has many faces. There are depressions in which anger predominates; in other cases, agitations, anxiety, or psychomotor retardation are the most prominent features of a person's depression. Substances of abuse and their actions interact with a range of affects that can be associated with depression (Khantzian 1997).

Analgesic Opiates

Analgesic opiates calm, mute, and contain angry rageful affects. This is especially evident with bipolar mood disorders and its variants. In fact, it is probably true that subclinical variants of bipolar conditions and the dysphoria associated with them are frequently driving forces compelling the reliance on addictive drugs to relieve associated distress.

Depressants

Depressant drugs, such as benzodiazepines, barbiturates, and the lead candidate alcohol, have a biphasic action depending on dose. In high or obliterating doses, alcohol attenuates a range of intense feelings that often accompany depression, including agitation, anger, and irritability. In low to moderate (i.e., releasing) doses, depressants can relieve states of anxiety or tension associated with depression.

Stimulants

Stimulant drugs are activating and energizing and more often are experienced as a magical elixir countering the debilitating anhedonia of depression. They are also welcomed by many hypomanic individuals as augmenting drugs that heighten the euphoria such patients enjoy (Khantzian 1985).

ANXIETY DISORDERS

As with so many psychiatric disorders, anxiety disorders are more often related or linked to the personality organization of the person who suffers from them. Individuals subject to anxiety disorders tend to be tense, "tightly wrapped," isolative, and cut-off from others.

Depressants

In low to moderate doses, depressants act as unwrapping and connecting agents—an effect that helps people truly experience their feelings and connect to others in ways which they ordinarily cannot.

Stimulants

Stimulants can have a similar effect but on a different basis; in other words, the activating properties of a drug such as cocaine can help such individuals break through their inhibitions where they ordinarily would not.

Opiates

Presumably, the general muting action of opiates can quiet anxiety, but based on clinical experience, most such individuals do not become hooked on opiates.

SCHIZOPHRENIC DISORDERS

In the case of schizophrenic disorders, an individual's drug of choice and the way they use the drug is more complex. Each class of drugs is adopted differentially, depending on the particular symptoms that dominate or alternate in these conditions. In reviewing the appeal of various addictive drugs for patients who suffer with schizophrenic disorders, it is important to distinguish between positive and negative symptoms associated with schizophrenia. Positive symptoms (paranoia, delusions, aggression, hallucinations, agitation, etc.) are usually appeased by drugs that have a calming effect. However, negative symptoms (alogia, affective flattening, anhedonia, asociality, apathy, attentional impairments) are probably significantly more important in determining reliance on addictive substances among schizophrenic patients than positive symptoms, especially if dependence on nicotine is taken into account (Khantzian 1997). This is partially the result of the fact that negative symptoms are the residual aftermath of the more acute phase of schizophrenia when the patient is apt to be too disorganized to obtain or use substances of abuse. It also is the case that there is enormous suffering associated with negative symptoms, often not immediately apparent, that causes patients to resort to substances for relief of their suffering, even if it is only transient.

Analgesic Opiates

Positive symptoms presumably would be attenuated by analgesic opiates because of the drugs' calming and organizing action, especially with the accompanying rage and aggressivity associated with schizophrenia. However, with some rare exceptions where heroin is readily and easily available, schizophrenic patients are unable to obtain opiates because their disorganized condition in most instances makes them unable to negotiate the hazards to obtain opiates. However, alcohol is readily attainable by such patients, and is extensively abused by schizophrenic patients.

Depressants

In obliterating doses, alcohol attenuates the voices, delusions, agitation, and anger for schizophrenic patients. As one patient put it, "I can dismiss them (the voices) and not be so distressed by them." Low to moderate doses of alcohol counter the negative symptoms of asociality in such patients. A case in point, Albanese and colleagues (Albanese et al. 1994) published case material showing that when negative symptoms of patients, especially their inability to express their feelings and socialize, were relieved by the atypical neuroleptic clozapine, there was a corresponding decrease in patients' unrelenting reversion to alcohol use.

Stimulants

There is a disproportionate abuse of stimulants among patients suffering with schizophrenia (Brady et al. 1990; Schneier and Siris 1987). This might be surprising given the psychotogenic properties of stimulants. However, there is evidence indicating that schizophrenic patients find relief from their anhedonia and other negative symptoms through the activating properties of stimulants, including nicotine (Khantzian 1997). They also use stimulants to alleviate the sedating properties of neuroleptics.

POSTTRAUMATIC STRESS DISORDER

There is a complex biphasic nature to affect experience in patients suffering with posttraumatic stress disorder (PTSD); they are subject to either emotional flooding and thus overwhelmed with painful affect, or they experience affective numbing which is deadening or confusing. Both extremes are painful and debilitating. Not surprisingly, there is a disproportionate incidence of SUDs among individuals suffering with PTSD (Khantzian 1997, 1999). When flooded with intense emotions such as rage, agitation, or fragmentation, PTSD victims might experience opiates or obliterating doses of alcohol as potent antidotes to such unsettling and powerful affects. This is not an uncommon reaction in Vietnam veterans or borderline patients, for example. Conversely, in the case of affective numbing when PTSD patients feel closed down or emotionally dead, low to moderate doses of alcohol often provide release from the sense of restriction and being "cut off" from the rest of the world. Finally, PTSD patients likely discover marked relief from the negative symptoms of anhedonia, apathy, and affective flattening accompanying PTSD when they experiment with or use cocaine. This is just one more example of how the hook gets set with addictive drugs in the context of emotional distress and suffering.

Conclusion

A patient's drug of choice can be a meaningful clue to the painful emotions with which he or she suffers and can compel drug dependence in susceptible individuals. In the case of dually diagnosed patients, the patient's psychiatric illness might signal the particular drug with which they might be self-medicating. Such a perspective might also guide the clinician to identify and target what painful feelings might predominate, and how and why such affects might make a particular drug compelling. Finally, a self-medication perspective on substance use and abuse among dually-diagnosed patients can serve as a preeminent guide to treatment, psychotherapeutically and psychopharmacologically.

References

Albanese, M. J. (2003a). The self-medication hypothesis: Theory and content. *Psychiatric Times* 3:42–44.
———. (2003b). The self-medication hypothesis: Epidemiology, clinical findings and implications. *Psychiatric Times* 4:57–64.

Albanese, M. J., Khantzian, E. J., Murphy, S. I., and Green, A. I. (1994). Decreased substance use in chronically psychotic patients treated with clozapine. *American Journal of Psychiatry* 151:780–81.

American Psychiatric Association. (2000). *Diagnostic and Statistical Manual of Mental Disorders*. 4th ed. rev. Washington, DC: American Psychiatric Association.

Brady, K., Anton, R., Ballenger, J. C., Lydiard, R. B., Adinoff, B., and Selander, J. (1990). Cocaine abuse among schizophrenic patients. *American Journal of Psychiatry* 147:1164–67.

Kessler, R. C., Crum, R. M., Warner, L.A., et al. (1997). Lifetime co-occurrence of *DSM-III-R* alcohol abuse and dependence with other psychiatric disorders in the nation comorbidity survey. *Archives of General Psychiatry* 54:313–21.

Khantzian, E. J. (1975). Self-selection and progression in drug dependence. *Psychiatry Digest* 10:19–22.

———. (1985). The self-medication hypothesis of addictive disorders: Focus on heroin and cocaine dependence. *American Journal of Psychiatry* 142:1259–64.

———. (1990). Self-regulation and self-medication factors in alcoholism and the addictions: Similarities and differences. In *Recent Developments in Alcoholism*, edited by M. Galanter, 255–71. New York: Plenum.

———. (1995). Self-regulation vulnerabilities in substance abusers: Treatment implications. In *The Psychology and Treatment of Addictive Behaviors*, edited by S. Dowling, 17–41. Madison, CT: International Universities Press.

———. (1997). The self-medication hypothesis of substance use disorders: A reconsideration and recent applications. *Harvard Review of Psychiatry* 4:231–44.

———. (1999). *Treating Addiction as a Human Process*. Northvale, NJ: Jason Aronson.

Khantzian, E. J., Dodes, L., and Brehm, N. (2005). Determinants and perpetuators of substance abuse: Psychodynamics. In *Substance Abuse: A Comprehensive Textbook*, 4th ed., edited by J. H. Lowinson, P. Ruiz, R. B. Millman, and J. G. Langrod, 97–107. Baltimore, MD: Williams and Wilkins.

Milkman, H., and Frosch, W. A. (1973). On the preferential abuse of heroin and amphetamine. *Journal of Nervous and Mental Disease* 156:242–48.

Nesse, R. M. (2000). Is depression an adaptation? *Archives of General Psychiatry* 57:14–20.

Regier, D. A., Farmer, M. D., Ral, D.S., et al. (1990). Comorbidity of mental disorders with alcohol and other drugs: Results from the epidemiologic catchment area (ECA) study. *Journal of the American Medical Association* 264:2511–18.

Schneier. F. R., and Siris, S. G. (1987). A review of psychoactive substance use and abuse in schizophrenia: Patterns of drug choice. *Journal of Nervous Mental Disease* 175:641–52.

Weider, H., and Kaplan, E. (1969). Drug use in adolescents. *Psychoanalytic Study of the Child* 24:399–431.

CHAPTER 8

Self-Medication Hypothesis
CONNECTING AFFECTIVE EXPERIENCE AND DRUG CHOICE

With Jesse J. Suh, Stephen Ruffins, C. Edward Robins, and Mark J. Albanese

According to E. J. Khantzian's (2003) self-medication hypothesis (SMH), a psycho-analytically informed theory of substance addiction that considers emotional and psychological dimensions, substance addiction functions as a compensatory means to modulate affects and self-soothe from the distressful psychological states. To manage emotional pain, dysphoria, and anxiety, substance abusers use the drug actions, both physiological and psychological effects, to achieve emotional stability. The SMH was retrospectively tested using six Minnesota Multiphasic Personality Inventory–2 special scales with 402 non-drug users and drug users to capture the psychological elements relevant to the SMH. Three logistic regression models were formed to predict alcohol, cocaine, and heroin "drug-of-choice" groups. Predicting variables were the Repression, Overcontrolled Hostility, Psychomotor Acceleration, Depression, Posttraumatic Stress Disorder, and Cynicism scales. Repression and, inversely, Depression scales significantly predicted the alcohol group. Psychomotor Acceleration was the only significant predictor of the cocaine group. Cynicism significantly predicted heroin preference. The results are partially consistent with the SMH. Implications of these results for understanding the relationship between affect regulation and addiction and treatment interventions are discussed.

Since the introduction of Freud's (1923/1961) "Civilization and Its Discontents" and Rado's (1933) "Psychoanalysis of Pharmacothymia (Drug Addiction)," both of which held a view that the etiology of substance addiction is explained by severe, preexisting psychopathological conditions, subsequent psychoanalytic contributions in substance addiction have considered affect regulation and disturbance in relationships as the central focus (Khantzian 1999, 2003; Khantzian, Halliday, and McAuliffe 1990; Morgenstern and Leeds 1993). According to the self-medication hypothesis (SMH) (Khantzian 2003), substance addiction functions as a compensatory means to modulate distressful affects and self-soothe from unmanageable psychological states. Khantzian (1997, 2003) asserted that substance users experience dysphoric emotions as intolerable and overwhelming and cannot manage these emotional states on their own. Instead, substance abusers use drug actions, both physiological and psychological effects, to regulate distressful emotions and achieve an emotional stability (Khantzian 1997).

The SMH considers the effects of drugs (e.g., opiates, cocaine, and alcohol) that interact with the inner states of psychological suffering and personality organization (Khantzian 1997, 2003). Opiates (e.g., heroin, codeine, and oxycodone), in both natural and synthetic forms, have been widely used medically for their pain-reducing properties (Dodgen and Shea 2000). Khantzian (1985) has observed that the difficulties in management of rage and aggression are often linked back to earlier traumatic exposure to violence and aggression. His patients' experiences of traumas at various severity levels reportedly elicited aggression within the individuals, and they often had not established defensive and adaptive psychological mechanisms to regulate the feelings of rage and aggression (Khantzian, Mack, and Schatzberg 1974). According to Khantzian, opiate abuse functions as a temporarily adaptive response that mutes and attenuates the rage and aggression (Khantzian 1985, 1999).

The acute psychological effects of cocaine use include elevation of mood, increased self-confidence and self-esteem, improved mental performance, a decrease in fatigue, and increased energy and productivity (Dodgen and Shea 2000). Clinical findings (Khantzian 1985; Khantzian et al. 1990) demonstrate that cocaine is used by "low-energy" and "high-energy" type individuals. Low-energy individuals use cocaine because they do not possess an adequate degree of psychological capacity to relieve themselves from the feelings of boredom, emptiness, and fatigue state, whereas high-energy individuals use cocaine because of their magnified need for elated sensations. Cocaine users' need to regulate inner emptiness, boredom, and depressive states or to maintain restlessness draws them to the powerful, energizing effects of cocaine (Khantzian et al. 1990).

Alcohol, the most widely abused substance in the United States, is a central nervous system depressant and features relaxing and sedating effects (Dodgen and Shea 2000). According to Khantzian (1997), alcohol abusers often maintain rigidly overcontained, constricted emotions. To avoid distressful affects, emotions are isolated and "cut off" from abusers' awareness through the use of rigid defenses, leaving the feelings of emptiness and isolation (Khantzian et al. 1990). Alcohol abusers use rigid defenses to constrict or to cut off emotions from awareness, resulting in feelingless or disaffected states (Khantzian 1999). Alcohol use softens their rigid defensive structure and allows them to relieve these constricted emotions (Khantzian 1999).

Previously, empirical investigations of the SMH have shown a less than impressive relationship between drug choice and psychological variables (Castaneda, Lifshutz, Galanter, and Franco 1994; Craig 1988; Greene, Adyanthaya, Morse, and Davis 1993; Schinka, Curtiss, and Mulloy 1994). These studies used assessment tools based on major psychiatric symptom categories to assess the psychological dimensions. Given that the SMH involves underlying affects and psychological defenses, and their link to addiction, the SMH might not have been supported empirically because these studies used assessment tools that could not validly measure the psychological constructs relevant to the SMH (Khantzian 1997).

To examine the SMH, Aharonovich, Nguyen, and Nunes (2001) used the State–Trait Anger Expression Inventory (Spielberger 1996) and the Beck Depression Inventory–II (Beck, Steer, and Brown 1996), which are appropriate psychological measures because they measure the severity of affect-related constructs. Although the results confirmed that substance abusers experience higher levels of psychological distress, Khantzian's claim of drug specificity (i.e., the relationship between drug of choice and specific psychological variables) was not supported. Aharonovich et al.'s study had several methodological limitations. For example, the study had a small sample size (20 participants in each opiate, cocaine, and cannabis group), and the participants were in various stages of active drug use, such that their mood symptoms might have been substance induced or withdrawal symptom related (Aharonovich et al. 2001).

With the development of assessment tools that measure affect-related psychological constructs, the uniqueness of each substance group may be examined at an investigative level more sensitive to measuring those constructs indicated in the SMH. At this time, no other research has examined the SMH using affect-related variables in abstinent patients with substance use disorders. In this retrospective study, we hypothesized that the individuals in each drug class would share unique emotional states, demonstrating the relationship between the subjective affects and drug of choice: (a) higher levels of repression and emotional inhibition would predict one's preference for alcohol; (b) higher levels of depressive affect or the need for elated psychological state would predict one's preference for cocaine; and (c) higher levels of anger or trauma would predict one's preference for heroin.

Method

This is a secondary data analysis study. The database from a vocational program in New York City included demographic information, drug use and abuse history, and psychological assessments. The 16-week program provides a comprehensive array of services, including education, vocational training, individual and group counseling, job placement, and subsequent follow-up supports for low-income adults. The prospective clients are recruited from local shelters, drug treatment facilities, and various social service agencies. Clients with substance abuse history must maintain abstinence for three months before their enrollment and participate in ongoing random urine drug screening.

MEASURE

Minnesota Multiphasic Personality Inventory–2 (MMPI-2). The MMPI-2 has been the most widely used personality assessment tool in both clinical and research settings because of its high validity and reliability (Butcher and Williams 2000; Graham 2000; Greene 2000). The validity of the MMPI-2 standard scales is reportedly solid in identifying diagnoses (Wetzler, Khadivi, and Moser 1998) and classifying psychiatric inpatients (Archer, Griffin, and Aiduk 1995). The MMPI-2 is considered an adequate tool to assess psychoanalytic constructs (Ganellen 1996). However, these scales constitute an empirically derived measurement to identify types of psychopathologies, but without a consideration to the contents of the items endorsed. The MMPI-2 standard scales contain heterogeneous contents, and their structures are multidimensional; thus, they would not be suitable to assess unique, affect-related constructs. For our investigation, we used six subscales from the Harris-Lingoes subscales, content scales, and supplementary scales of the MMPI-2 (described below).

The Harris-Lingoes subscales offer dimensionally homogeneous subscales from each of the clinical scales, based on rational contents (Graham 2002). The subscales provide the clinical descriptions and underlying factors of the syndromes assessed by the MMPI standard clinical scales (Ward 1997). These subscales are high in both reliability and validity (Graham 2002). MMPI-2 content scales, a revised version of the content scales based on the MMPI, were developed by Butcher, Graham, Williams, and Ben-Porath (1990) and have a high internal consistency and construct validity (Ben-Porath, McCully, and Almagor 1993; Ben-Porath and Sherwood 1993; Butcher et al. 1990; Graham 2000). The content scales are more effective measures of psychological characteristics than the MMPI-2 standard clinical scales (Levitt and Gotts 1995). MMPI-2 supplementary scales were developed using "item-analytic, factor analytic, and intuitive procedures" (Graham 2000, 146) and tap into constructs and concepts that were not previously addressed by the standard clinical scales. These scales reportedly provide more meaningful psychological constructs previously untapped by the MMPI-2 standard clinical scales (Craig, Ammar, and Olson 1998; Ward 1995). To capture the psychological elements relevant to the SMH, the following MMPI-2 special scales (Butcher and Williams 2000), which empirically assess the conceptual basis of the SMH, were used: (a) Psychomotor Acceleration (MA2), a desire for elation and "restlessness"; (b) Depression (DEP), depressed, apathetic, sad, guilty, and hopeless affects; (c) Cynicism (CYN), anger and negative feelings toward self and others; (d) PTSD (posttraumatic stress disorder; PK), a severity of trauma, including experiences of great emotional turmoil, intrusive thoughts, and feeling misunderstood and mistreated; (e) Repression (R), emotional inhibition and denial; and (f) Overcontrolled Hostility (OH), rigid inhibition of hostility. The current study used the MMPI-2 computer-generated score summary from National Computer Systems (Graham 2002).

PARTICIPANTS

The total database sample consisted of 521 clients who participated in the program between 1997 and 2002. Clients who had taken the MMPI-2 but later dropped out from the program were included in the current analyses. The study protocol was reviewed and approved by the Institutional Review Board of Long Island University, with which Jesse J. Suh was affiliated at the time of the analysis.

We used the following criteria to assess the validity of the MMPI-2 scores and to exclude invalid MMPI-2 scores, as suggested by Butcher and Williams (2000): (a) Lie Scale is less than or equal to T score of 70; (b) Infrequency Scale is less than or equal to T score of 99; and (c) K Defensiveness Scale is less than or equal to T score of 80. These scales assess the client's cooperativeness, openness, and willingness to disclose personal information (Butcher and Williams, 2000). Of the 521 MMPI-2 available case protocols, 402 cases were valid and 119 cases were invalid.

A client's drug of choice was established on the basis of drug use histories from referring sources, drug treatment histories, and clinical interviews. Of the 402 participants, 84 clients (20.9 percent) did not have substance abuse or treatment histories (no-drug- of-choice group). Alcohol, cocaine, heroin, and "other" drug users consisted of 64 (15.9 percent), 123 (30.6 percent), 94 (23.4 percent), and 37 (9.2 percent) cases, respectively. "Other" drugs consisted of marijuana, amphetamine, and "diet pills." The majority of the 402 clients were single/never married (65.7 percent), female (64 percent), and African American (66.7 percent; Hispanic, 18.3 percent; Caucasian, 7.0 percent), and their ages ranged between 17 and 71 years ($M = 36.7$, $SD = 9.9$).

Procedure

All clients underwent randomly administered urine drug screening to ensure that they were substance free for the duration of the program. At the time of the admission, a master's-level clinician interviewed each participant to review drug use histories. Jesse J. Suh then reviewed referral documents, past drug treatment histories, and clinical interviews to determine the participant's drug of choice.

Within the two-week period after the admission, doctoral-level graduate students administered a set of assessment measures, including the MMPI-2, the Rorschach (Exert 2003), the Thematic Apperception Test (Murray 1974), and the Human Figure Drawing test (Harris 1968; Moppets 1968). These tools were administered to assist the participants in the course of individual and group therapy treatments. The MMPI-2 was administered in a group setting. The MMPI-2 instructions from Butcher, Dahlstrom, Graham, Tellegen, and Kaemmer (1989) were used. The clinicians reviewed the completed MMPI-2 response sheets to ensure that all clients completed the forms properly. The completed answer sheets were then scanned twice to verify their accuracy, and a score summary was generated.

DATA ANALYSIS

All 402 clients were included in the data analysis. Student's t tests were used to compare the means for the drug groups on continuous variables (e.g., age), and chi-square analyses were conducted for categorical variables (e.g., ethnicity and level of education). Three separate logistic regression analyses were conducted to predict each drug group (i.e., alcohol, cocaine, and heroin) using six MMPI-2 scales (R, OH, Ma2, DEP, PK, and CYN) in the regression equation. Because the dependent measures are dichotomous variables, we used logistic regression, a test to statistically examine a relationship between a dichotomous variable and continuous variables, to estimate the relationship between each drug group and the selected MMPI-2 special scales. For each predictor, a specified drug of choice was the comparison category (coded 1), and no-drug-of-choice (i.e., no history of drug abuse) and drug-of-choice groups other than the specified group were the reference category (coded 0). A backward stepwise selection based on Wald statistics, a method to add or drop a variable from a model, was used to fit the model, using both an alpha entry criterion and an alpha deletion criterion of .05. Because of the number of covariate variables, we used the stepwise technique to reduce the number of models under consideration (Shatland, Cain, and Barton 2001). Estimated odds ratios (ORs) and 95 percent confidence intervals (CIs) were calculated for all variables. All analyses were conducted using the SPSS 12.0 software package.

Table 8.1. Demographic Information for Each Drug Group

			Drug of choice groups		
Variable	Overall[a] N = 402	No drug history (N = 84; 20.9%)	Alcohol (N = 64; 15.9%)	Cocaine (N = 123; 30.6%)	Heroin (N = 94; 23.4%)
Age (M [SD])	36.7 (9.9)	34.2 (10.2)	39.7 (11.4)*	37.9 (6.9)	37.4 (10.8)
Female (% within group)	254	66 (81.5)*	38 (60.3)	74 (60.7)	54 (57.4)
African American (%)	264 (66.7)	47 (56.6)	40 (62.5)	94 (77.7)**	58 (61.7)
Education level (%)					
Under high school**	201 (50.3)	47 (57.3)	29 (35.3)	57 (46.4)	45 (47.8)
High school grad/GED	133 (33.3)	22 (26.9)	21 (32.9)	43 (35.0)	33 (35.1)
Marital status (%)					
Married/living with partner	49 (12.4)	8 (10.1)	11 (17.2)	17 (14.0)	7 (7.6)
Never married	260 (65.7)	53 (64.6)	39 (60.9)	82 (67.8)	60 (65.2)

Overall[a] includes the mentioned four drug groups and the participants in the "other" drug-of-choice group, consisting of marijuana, amphetamine, and "diet pills."
*p .05. **p .01.

Table 8.2. Mean t Scores (and Standard Deviations) for Each Drug-of-Choice Group

Variable	No drug history (n = 84)	Alcohol (n = 64)	Cocaine (n = 123)	Heroin (n = 94)	Total (n = 402)
Overcontrolled hostility	56.65 (8.3)	59.25 (10.7)*	54.92 (9.9)	56.02 (9.0)	56.61 (9.7)
Repression	52.24 (9.0)	56.59 (10.7)**	49.83 (9.2)	48.17 (9.7)**	51.17 (10.0)
Depression	60.13 (10.6)	53.64 (8.9)**	60.65 (9.5)	60.24 (8.9)	63.46 (8.5)
Psychomotor acceleration	51.72 (8.8)	47.59 (10.8)**	56.60 (9.1)**	54.89 (9.9)	53.25 (10.1)
Posttraumatic stress disorder	61.39 (12.6)	55.45 (12.9)**	62.90 (11.9)	64.61 (11.9)*	62.02 (12.4)
Cynicism	58.69 (8.4)	56.86 (11.0)**	59.90 (10.2)	66.27 (10.9)**	60.67 (10.7)

Note: All *t* tests conducted between each drug-of-choice group versus all other drug-of-choice groups.
*p < .05. **p < .01.

Results

PARTICIPANT CHARACTERISTICS

Table 8.1 presents the demographic information of the sample. An analysis of variance demonstrated that age was significantly different between the drug groups, $F(4, 397) = 6.4$, $p < .05$. Fisher's least significant difference test indicated that the alcohol group was significantly older ($p < .05$) than the no-drug group. A significantly greater proportion of women (26 percent) than men (10.5 percent) reported no problems with substances, $x^2(3, N = 402) = 13.8$, $p < .05$. African American clients (77.7 percent) were more likely to report cocaine as the preferred substance than was any other ethnic group, $x^2(12, N = 402) = 38.4$, $p < .05$. Those in the alcohol group had obtained a higher level of education (i.e., post–high school; 21.9 percent) than those in other drug groups, $x^2(6, N = 402) = 39.2$, $p < .05$. Marital status was not significantly different between the groups.

MMPI-2 SCORES FOR DRUG GROUPS
AND FOR MEN AND WOMEN

Six MMPI-2 variables measuring affect-related constructs were compared between different drug groups and between men and women. An analysis of variance showed that the alcohol group (vs. other groups) obtained significantly higher scores on OH, $F(1, 397) = 5.7$, $p < .05$, and R, $F(1, 400) = 23.6$, $p < .05$, and significantly lower scores on DEP, $F(1, 400) = 30.3$, $p < .05$; Ma2, $F(1, 396) = 25.2$, $p < .05$; PK, $F(1, 397) = 22.4$, $p < .05$; and CYN, $F(1, 400) = 9.9$, $p < .05$. The cocaine group scored significantly higher on Ma2, $F(1, 396) = 13.0$, $p < .05$, when compared with all other groups. The heroin group obtained significantly

Table 8.3. Comparison of Mean (and Standard Deviation) Minnesota Multiphasic Personality Inventory: Two Special Scales between Men and Women

Variable	Men (n = 148)	Women (n = 254)
Overcontrolled hostility	57.30 (9.34)	56.17 (9.92)
Repression	50.80 (10.34)	51.28 (9.85)
Depression*	60.94 (9.26)	58.79 (10.03)
Psychomotor acceleration	52.75 (9.65)	53.49 (10.37)
Posttraumatic stress disorder	62.41 (12.79)	61.77 (12.30)
Cynicism	60.29 (11.56)	60.84 (10.27)

*$p < .05$.

higher scores on PK, $F(1, 400) = 5.4$, p < .05, and CYN, $F(1, 396) = 36.7$, p < .05, and significantly lower scores on R, $F(1, 400) = 11.3$, p < .05. The MMPI-2 scores for the four drug groups are provided in table 8.2.

Men scored significantly higher on DEP than did women, $F(1, 395) = 4.4$, p < .05. On other measures, there was no significant difference in scores between men and women. Table 8.3 presents scores for men and women.

PREDICTING DRUG OF CHOICE

Alcohol as Drug of Choice

According to Khantzian (1999), alcohol softens the users' rigid defenses and allows them to relieve these constricted emotions. In an overall model containing R, OH, Ma2, DEP, PK, and CYN, the probability that alcohol as the drug of choice may be predicted from the observed MMPI-2 variables (overall likelihood ratio) was statistically significant—$x^2(6, N = 402) = 54.4$, $p < .05$—indicating that at least one of the sample coefficients differs from zero. Findings from the logistic regression model for the alcohol group are reported in table 8.4.

Backward elimination began with a full model containing all control variables. The final model consisted of R and DEP, $G(2) = 48.6$, p < .05. The participants with higher R scores (estimated OR = 1.07, 95 percent CI = 1.04 –1.10, p < .05) and DEP scores (estimated OR = 0.92, 95 percent CI = 0.89– 0.96, p < .05) were more likely to belong in the alcohol group. Each additional MMPI-2 T score on R increased the odds of belonging in the alcohol group by approximately 7 percent when controlling for DEP in the model. DEP showed an inverse relationship. Each increase of one point in the DEP score decreased the odds of belonging in the alcohol group. Overall, using the two predicting variables, the final model correctly predicted 85 percent of the cases, indicating adequate sensitivity and specificity of the model.

Cocaine as Drug of Choice

Khantzian et al. (1990) claimed that cocaine abusers' need to regulate inner depressive states or to maintain their restlessness (hypomania) draws them to the powerful, energizing effects of cocaine. The probability that cocaine use may be predicted from the observed MMPI-2 variables (overall likelihood ratio) for a model containing all six variables was 18.6 (df = 6, p < .05), indicating that at least one variable coefficient differed from zero.

Findings from the logistic regression model are reported in table 8.4. In a backward stepwise elimination analysis, the final model contained Ma2, $x^2(1, N = 402) = 13.0$. Higher Ma2 scores predicted one's membership in the cocaine group (estimated $OR = 1.06$, 95 percent CI = 1.02–1.09, $p < .05$). Each ad-

Table 8.4. Summary of Logistic Regression Models Predicting Drug-of-Choice Group

Drug of choice and variable	Wald	Odds ratio	5% confidence interval
Alcohol (6-variable model)			
Overcontrolled hostility (H)	0.20	0.99	0.96–1.03
Repression (R)*	12.58	1.07	1.03–1.11
Depression (DEP)*	10.45	0.91	0.86–0.96
Psychomotor acceleration (Ma2)	3.52	0.97	0.93–1.00
Posttraumatic stress disorder (PK)	0.07	1.01	0.96–1.06
Cynicism (CYN)	2.99	1.03	1.00–1.07
Final model[a]			
R*	17.07	1.07	1.04–1.10
DEP*	22.43	0.92	0.89–0.96
Cocaine (6-variable model)			
OH	0.01	1.00	0.97–1.04
R	0.12	0.99	0.96–1.03
DEP	1.59	1.04	0.98–1.10
Ma2*	12.84	1.08	1.03–1.12
PK	3.61	0.95	0.91–1.00
CYN	0.21	0.99	0.96–1.03
Final model[a]			
Ma2*	12.2	1.06	1.02–1.09
Heroin (6-variable model)			
OH	0.35	1.01	0.98–1.04
R	0.84	0.99	0.96–1.02
DEP	1.56	0.97	0.93–1.02
Ma2	1.24	0.98	0.95–1.01
PK	0.21	1.01	0.97–1.05
CYN*	23.68	1.08	1.05–1.12
Final model[a]			
CYN*	31.80	1.07	1.05–1.10

Note: For each predictor, a specified drug of choice was the comparison category (coded 1), and no-drug-of-choice and drug-of-choice groups other than the specified group were the reference category (coded 0).
[a] A backward stepwise selection based on Wald statistics was used to fit the final model, using an alpha entry criterion of .05 and an alpha deletion criterion of .05.
*$p < .01$.

ditional T-score point in Ma2 increased the odds of belonging to the cocaine group by approximately 6 percent. Overall, the model with Ma2 correctly predicted 86.4 percent of the cases.

Heroin as Drug of Choice

Logistic regression revealed that the full model was statistically significant, $x^2(6, N = 402) = 41.9$, $p < .05$, indicating that at least one of the sample coefficients differed from zero. Findings from the logistic regression model for the heroin group are reported in table 8.4. In a backward stepwise elimination analysis, CYN remained as the only significant predictor for the heroin group, $x^2(1, N = 402) = 36.0$, $p < .05$. The participants with higher scores on CYN were more likely to belong in the heroin group (estimated $OR = 1.07$, 95 percent CI = 1.05–1.10, $p < .05$). Each additional point in CYN increased the odds of belonging to the heroin group by approximately 7 percent. Overall, the model with CYN correctly predicted 77.1 percent of the cases.

Discussion

The results of the present investigation partially confirm Khantzian's (1997) clinical observations and show that specific psychological characteristics are associated with the drug of choice.

ALCOHOL AS DRUG OF CHOICE

Alcohol abusers reportedly use rigid defenses to inhibit emotions (e.g., repression), and their alcohol use disinhibits these defenses (Khantzian 1997). We found that an individual's tendency to repress emotions increased the probability of belonging in the alcohol group. This is consistent with a finding that alcohol abusers present with a high degree of defensiveness (Isenhart and Silversmith 1996) and use repression and denial as their primary psychological defenses (Eshbaugh, Tosi, and Hoyt 1993a; Wells, Tosi, Eshbaugh, and Murphy 1993). Additionally, abstinent alcohol abusers demonstrated more "flattening" emotional experience compared with cocaine users (Aguilar de Arcos, Verdejo-Garcia, Peralta-Ramirez, Sanchez-Barrera, and Perez-Garcia 2005), indicating that the observed emotions were not due to substance-induced or withdrawal-related symptoms. The tendency to excessively inhibit hostility (OH), however, did not play a significant role in predicting alcohol preference. In a series of empirical studies conducted by Eshbaugh et al. (1993a; Eshbaugh, Tosi, and Hoyt 1993b), alcohol abusers of all subtypes presented with the tendency to inhibit or deny uncomfortable affects, although women were more likely to deny their experience of hostility and resentment than men. Our alcohol group had significantly higher OH scale scores than those in other drug groups, but we did not observe a significant difference between men and women in their tendency to inhibit hostility. In our study, a decrease in depressive emotion (DEP) led to a higher likelihood of preferring alcohol. Nichols (2001) suggested that low scores on the DEP scale signify a high degree of defensiveness and "denial of depressiveness" (p. 207). In our sample, the alcohol abusers scored significantly lower on the DEP scale, when compared with other drug groups, suggesting that our alcohol group could be more prone to deny depressive affects. It is possible that their denial of depressive affect may be a significant factor in choosing alcohol as a preferred substance.

COCAINE AS DRUG OF CHOICE

Khantzian (1997) has proposed that cocaine is partly alluring to those individuals with the need for an experience of hypomania. Our results showed that a higher level of desire for elation and restlessness (Ma2) significantly predicted cocaine preference, as proposed in the SMH. Such a state of restlessness has been identified as a subtype of depression (Arieti and Bemporad 1980) or as introjective psychopathology (Blatt 1998) in those individuals who show obsessive tendencies or who are excessively goal oriented. Depressive affect (DEP) was not a significant predictor of cocaine preference, although Denier, Thevos, Latham, and Randall (1991) previously found that cocaine users were more likely to show depression than controls. The DEP scale is reportedly a good indicator of affective and cognitive components of depression (Levitt and Gotts 1995). However, the DEP scale could also be considered a multifactorial variable. For example, Nichols (2001) suggested that DEP component subscales, such as DEP-1 (lack of drive) or DEP-2 (dysphoria), would capture more specific phenomena of depressive affect (Nichols 2001). Given that cocaine is alluring to anergic individuals (Khantzian et al. 1990), the DEP-1 subscale, rather than DEP, might have been more suitable to predict cocaine preference.

HEROIN AS DRUG OF CHOICE

Heroin helps to sooth the experience of anger and trauma (Khantzian 1999). In our logistic regression model, a high level of anger and negative feelings toward others and themselves (CYN) significantly predicted heroin use. This is consistent with a finding that opiate abusers hold a more self-directed critical stance and maintain an "access to considerable anger and aggression" (Blatt, Rounsaville, Eyre, and Wilber 1984, 349). Blatt, McDonald, Sugarman and Wilber (1984) also reviewed the clinical reports and research investigations of opiate addicts and emphasized the purpose of opiates as containing and modulating painful affects and primitive impulses. Additionally, they noted the painful emotions leading to intense feelings of anger and rage and the opiate use as protecting "some addicts from giving direct expression to these destructive impulses" (Blatt, McDonald, Sugarman, and Wilber 1984, 177).

Although Heffernan et al. (2000) reported that the risk for opiate use increases threefold for those with a history of childhood trauma, we found that the severity of trauma symptoms (PK) did not predict heroin preference. The PK scale, which was developed to assess the presence of trauma symptoms

(Keane, Malloy, and Fairbank 1984), is effective in identifying traumatized combat veterans (Butcher and Williams 2000). Because trauma-related symptoms are often indistinguishable from mood or anxiety disorder symptoms, the PK scale may not differentiate the experience of trauma from a mood disorder (Nichols 2001). This raises the possibility that our use of the PK scale did not adequately isolate the severity of trauma in our sample. The PK scale might be sensitive to current trauma symptoms and not the occurrence of childhood trauma, which might not manifest in adult trauma symptoms.

A greater proportion of male compared with female participants were more likely to report past substance problems. The result is not a surprising one, as men are more likely than women to abuse alcohol or other substances (Anthony, Warner, and Kessler 1994). Our finding underscores the importance of the sex difference in addiction. Because sex difference was not a primary focus of our investigation and there was a disparity in male and female sample sizes, we did not examine the predictive effects of the sex difference on drug preference. Future investigations should involve predicting drug preference while controlling for demographic variables, including gender, age, and race.

Our results support the important relationship between the capacity to manage emotional states and addiction. Poor affect regulation has been identified as a risk factor for adult substance abuse (Cooper, Frone, Russell, and Mudar 1995; Cooper, Russell, Skinner, Frone, and Mudar 1992; Thorberg and Lyvers 2005). Additionally, negative mood states, including depression, anxiety, and anger, induce craving and drug-related responses in substance abusers (Childress et al. 1994). Consequences of immature defense mechanisms, such as negative affect (Colder and Chassin 1997), emotional dysregulation (Tarter et al. 1999; Tarter, Blackson, Brigham, Moss, and Caprara 1995), and poor emotional coping techniques (Eftekhari, Turner, and Larimer 2004), have also been identified as risk factors for substance abuse in adolescents. In longitudinal studies, adolescents used substances to cope with their negative emotions, and their negative affect was significantly linked to an increase in substance use (Turner, Larimer, Sarason, and Trupin 2005; Wills, Sandy, Shinar, and Yaeger 1999). It is unlikely that this relationship between poor affect regulation and substance use results from residual drug effects or drug withdrawal effects, because Thorberg and Lyvers (2005) found that even after an extended period of abstinence substance abusers were still deficient in regulating their emotions. This result raises the possibility that inadequate defense mechanisms may predate drug use.

The emphasis of early experiences and the subsequent emotional capacity cannot be minimized. During infancy, with the use of responsive and supportive maternal objects, and the subsequent experience of attachment to consistent figures, one's capacity for self-organization and affect regulation develops

(Fonagy and Target 2003). When the intersubjective attunement between the caregiver and the child becomes incongruent or pathological, such a type of affect mirroring can disrupt the mentalization process, and the defects in affective capacity may manifest in the form of psychopathology. Fonagy and Target (2003) suggested that these affect-regulating modes become the prelude to adult patients presenting narcissistic personality disorder and borderline personality disorder. Kohut (1977) referred to these more serious impairments as "defects in the self" and has hypothesized that substances are often used as a remedy. Drawing from Khantzian's clinical experience in working with substance abusers, Khantzian et al. (1990) also hypothesized that drug abuse represents an attempt to self-correct vulnerabilities associated with affect mismanagement. That is, substance abuse is an expression of vulnerabilities and dysfunction in regulating and maintaining self-esteem, self-care, and interpersonal relations. Experiencing emotions, such as rage, shame, loneliness, or depression, as intolerable and overwhelming, substance abusers regulate their affect life using drugs and maintain the feeling states that they cannot achieve on their own (Khantzian 1997).

In terms of treatment implications, a patient's drug preference might provide vital clues to the specific painful emotions with which the patient predominantly suffers, and it may guide clinicians to implement appropriate psychotherapeutic interventions. Khantzian and colleagues (1990) developed a modified psychodynamic psychotherapeutic approach that incorporates supportive, semi-structured techniques. While engaging patients with empathy and reflective modes, the clinician would allow the unfolding of the patient's inner experience and patterns of psychological defense. In this reflective space, the patient develops an understanding of painful emotions and their maladaptive defenses involved in the substance addiction and makes changes in behavioral patterns. The discovery of specific psychological and emotional qualities within each substance group can enhance the understanding of the dynamics of substance addiction and could assist clinicians in designing treatment interventions according to the patient's unique characteristics. Treatment goals would involve ameliorating or improving these psychological characteristics—relieving emotional suffering or learning to make emotions less restrictive. For example, a recovering alcohol-dependent patient who represses emotions would benefit by learning to acknowledge and manage those emotions. For heroin users, managing aggression would help them maintain abstinence. In a cognitive–behavioral therapy setting, the identification of distressful emotions could guide the therapist–patient dyad to distinguish automatic thoughts and dysfunctional behaviors leading to relapse. Applying these SMH concepts to Dodes's (2003) formulation of substance addiction, the psychoanalytic treatment would deal with managing and tolerating their experience of helplessness.

Our study sample included substance users who had remained drug free for three months or longer, allowing us to control for the possible research confounds of measuring drug- or withdrawal-induced dysphoric affects. However, the sample included clients who had already developed substance use disorders, raising a possibility that their experience of dysphoric affects could have derived from their chronic substance use. Prospectively following a group of at-risk participants and a group of controls from a time before the development of substance use disorders would alleviate this study's limitation (see Chilcoat and Breslau 1999; Chilcoat and Breslau 1998, for examples).

The interpretation of our findings needs to be examined in light of additional methodological limitations. First, one potential measurement problem involves the reliability of the participants' drug-of-choice reports. This measure was based on each participant's report (i.e., drug preference, substance use and treatment history) and past treatment documents rather than a structured diagnostic interview, which is more commonly used in addiction research. It is also possible that some participants may have concealed or minimized their substance use history. Second, although the logistic regression is the most appropriate statistical test in our investigation, there exist several disadvantages to using the stepwise elimination techniques (Derksen and Keselman 1992). Additionally, the backward stepwise elimination procedure requires numerous statistical tests. Thus, additional predictors increased the likelihood of Type I error (i.e., false-positive error). Cross-validation samples should be conducted in future investigations to reduce the risk of Type I error.

The SMH is a psychoanalytically informed theory of substance addiction that considers the emotional and psychological dimensions of the substance use disorders. In previous investigations, the SMH was tested using the MMPI-2 standard clinical scales, which are based on descriptive diagnosis and its related symptoms. Additionally, these scales embody only the surface of numerous underlying heterogeneous contents within each scale (Butcher and Williams 2000). Therefore, the previous studies may have misconstrued the SMH as a function of clinical, descriptive diagnosis or symptoms rather than Khantzian's (1997) focus on the affective experience of the abusers. In this study, Khantzian's SMH was examined using MMPI-2 special scales, which are more valid psychological measurements in assessing affect-related constructs. Our results partially confirmed Khantzian's (1997) clinical observations and demonstrated the relationship between psychological characteristics and drug of choice. Our findings advance the theoretical formulation of the SMH and underscore the importance of psychoanalytic perspectives in understanding drug addiction. One future research possibility would include developing assessment tools that would validly measure the affective experience, as described in the SMH. Such advancement in approximating the constructs, such as underlying affects and subjective states of distress, in future investigations would enhance our understanding of the substance addiction.

References

Aguilar de Arcos, F., Verdejo-Garcia, A., Peralta-Ramirez, M. I., Sanchez-Barrera, M., and Perez- Garcia, M. (2005). Experience of emotions in substance abusers exposed to images containing neutral, positive, and negative affective stimuli. *Drug and Alcohol Dependence, 78,* 159–67.

Aharonovich, E., Nguyen, H. T., and Nunes, E. V. (2001). Anger and depressive states among treatment-seeking drug abusers: Testing the psychopharmacological specificity hypothesis. *American Journal on Addictions, 10,* 327–34.

Anthony, J. C., Warner, L. A., and Kessler, R. C. (1994). Comparative epidemiology of dependence on tobacco, alcohol, controlled substances, and inhalants: Basic findings from the national comorbidity survey. *Experimental and Clinical Psychopharmacology, 2,* 244–68.

Archer, R. P., Griffin, R., and Aiduk, R. (1995). MMPI-2 clinical correlates for ten common codes. *Journal of Personality Assessment, 65,* 391–407.

Arieti, S., and Bemporad, J. R. (1980). The psychological organization of depression. *American Journal of Psychiatry, 137,* 1360–65.

Beck, A. T., Steer, R. A., and Brown, G. K. (1996). *Manual for the Beck Depression Inventory-II.* San Antonio, TX: Psychological Corporation.

Ben-Porath, Y. S., McCully, E., and Almagor, M. (1993). Incremental validity of the MMPI-2 content scales in the assessment of personality and psychopathology by self-report. *Journal of Personality Assessment, 61,* 557–75.

Ben-Porath, Y. S., and Sherwood, N. E. (1993). *The MMPI-2 content component scales: Development, psychometric characteristics, and clinical application* (MMPI-2/MMPI-A Test Reports No. 1). Minneapolis, MN: University of Minnesota Press.

Blatt, S. J. (1998). Contributions of psychoanalysis to the understanding and treatment of depression. *Journal of the American Psychoanalytic Association, 46,* 723–52.

Blatt, S. J., McDonald, C., Sugarman, A., and Wilber, C. (1984). Psychodynamic theories of opiate addiction: New directions for research. *Clinical Psychology Review, 4,* 159–89.

Blatt, S. J., Rounsaville, B., Eyre, S. L., and Wilber, C. (1984). The psychodynamics of opiate addiction. *Journal of Nervous and Mental Disease, 172,* 342–52.

Butcher, J. N., Dahlstrom, W. G., Graham, J. R., Tellegen, A., and Kaemmer, B. (1989). *Minnesota Multiphasic Personality Inventory-2 (MMPI-2): Manual for administration and scoring.* Minneapolis, MN: University of Minnesota Press.

Butcher, J. N., Graham, J. R., Williams, C. L., and Ben-Porath, Y. S. (1990). *Development and use of the MMPI-2 content scales.* Minneapolis, MN: University of Minnesota Press.

Butcher, J. N., and Williams, C. L. (Eds.). (2000). *Essentials of MMPI-2 and MMPI-A Interpretation* (Vol. 2). Minneapolis, MN: University of Minnesota Press.

Castaneda, R., Lifshutz, H., Galanter, M., and Franco, H. (1994). Empirical assessment of the self- medication hypothesis among dually diagnosed inpatients. *Comprehensive Psychiatry, 35,* 180–84.

Chilcoat, H. D., and Breslau, N. (1998). Posttraumatic stress disorder and drug disorders: Testing causal pathways. *Archives of General Psychiatry, 55,* 913–17.

———. (1999). Pathways from ADHD to early drug use. *Journal of American Academy of Child and Adolescent Psychiatry, 38,* 1347–54.

Childress, A. R., Ehrman, R., McLellan, A. T., MacRae, J., Natale, M., and O'Brien, C. P. (1994). Can induced moods trigger drug-related responses in opiate abuse patients? *Journal of Substance Abuse Treatment, 11,* 17–23.

Colder, C. R., and Chassin, L. (1997). Affectivity and impulsivity: Temperament risk for adolescent alcohol involvement. *Psychology of Addictive Behaviors, 11,* 83–97.

Cooper, M. L., Frone, M. R., Russell, M., and Mudar, P. (1995). Drinking to regulate positive and negative emotions: A motivational model of alcohol use. *Journal of Personality and Social Psychology, 69,* 990–1005.

Cooper, M. L., Russell, M., Skinner, J. B., Frone, M. R., and Mudar, P. (1992). Stress and alcohol use: Moderating effects of gender, coping, and alcohol expectancies. *Journal of Abnormal Psychology, 101,* 139–52.

Craig, R. J. (1988). Psychological functioning of cocaine free-basers derived from objective psychological tests. *Journal of Clinical Psychology, 44,* 599–606.

Craig, R. J., Ammar, A., and Olson, R. E. (1998). Psychological assessment (MMPI-2) of male African-American substance-abusing patients with and without histories of childhood physical abuse. *Journal of Substance Abuse, 10,* 43–51.

Denier, C. A., Thevos, A. K., Latham, P. K., and Randall, C. L. (1991). Psychosocial and psycho-pathology differences in hospitalized male and female cocaine abusers: A retrospective chart review. *Addictive Behaviors, 16,* 489–96.

Derksen, S., and Keselman, H. J. (1992). Backward, forward, and stepwise automated subset selection algorithms: Frequency of obtaining authentic and noise variables. *British Journal of Mathematical and Statistical Psychology, 45,* 265–82.

Dodes, L. M. (2003). *The heart of addiction.* New York: HarperCollins.

Dodgen, C. E., and Shea, W. M. (2000). *Substance use disorders: Assessment and treatment.* London: Academic Press.

Eftekhari, A., Turner, A. P., and Larimer, M. E. (2004). Anger expression, coping, and substance use in adolescent offenders. *Addictive Behaviors, 29,* 1001–8.

Eshbaugh, D. M., Tosi, D. J., and Hoyt, C. N. (1993a). Some personality patterns and dimensions of male alcoholics: A multivariate description. In D. J. Tosi, D. M. Eshbaugh, and M. A. Murphy (Eds.), *A clinician's guide to the personality profiles of alcohol and drug abusers: Typological descriptions using the MMPI* (pp. 17–30). Springfield, IL: Charles C. Thomas.

———. (1993b). Women alcoholics: A typological description using the MMPI. In D. J. Tosi, D. M. Eshbaugh, and M. A. Murphy (Eds.), *A clinician's guide to the personality profiles of alcohol and drug abusers: Typological descriptions using the MMPI* (pp. 31–38). Springfield, IL: Charles C. Thomas.

Exner, J. E. (2003). *The Rorschach: A comprehensive system. Volume 1: Basic foundation and principles of interpretation* (4th ed.) Hoboken, NJ: Wiley.

Fonagy, P., and Target, M. (2003). *Psychoanalytic theories: Perspectives from developmental psychopathology*. New York: Brunner-Routledge.

Freud, S. (1961). Civilization and its discontents. In J. Strachey (Ed. and Trans.), *The standard edition of the complete psychological works of Sigmund Freud* (Vol. 21, pp. 59–145). London: Hogarth Press. (Original work published 1923).

Ganellen, R. J. (1996). *Integrating the Rorschach and the MMPI-2 in personality assessment*. Mahwah, NJ: Erlbaum.

Graham, J. R. (2000). *MMPI-2: Assessing personality and psychopathology* (Vol. 3). New York: Oxford University Press.

————. (2002). *MMPI-2: Assessing personality and psychopathology* (Vol. 4). New York: Oxford University Press.

Greene, R. L. (2000). *The MMPI-2: An interpretive manual* (Vol. 2). Boston: Allyn & Bacon.

Greene, R. L., Adyanthaya, A. E., Morse, R. M., and Davis, L. J., Jr. (1993). Personality variables in cocaine- and marijuana-dependent patients. *Journal of Personality Assessment, 61,* 224–30.

Harris, D. B. (1968). *Goodenough-Harris Drawing Test Manual*. New York: Harcourt, Brace, and Jovanovich.

Heffernan, K., Cloitre, M., Tardiff, K., Marzuk, P. M., Portera, L., and Leon, A. C. (2000). Childhood trauma as a correlate of lifetime opiate use in psychiatric patients. *Addictive Behaviors, 25,* 797–803.

Isenhart, C. E., and Silversmith, D. J. (1996). MMPI-2 response styles: Generalization to alcoholism assessment. *Psychology of Addictive Behaviors, 10,* 115–23.

Keane, T. M., Malloy, P. F., and Fairbank, J. A. (1984). Empirical development of an MMPI subscale for the assessment of combat-related posttraumatic stress disorder. *Journal of Consulting and Clinical Psychology, 52,* 888–91.

Khantzian, E. J. (1985). The self-medication hypothesis of addictive disorders: Focus on heroin and cocaine dependence. *American Journal of Psychiatry, 142,* 1259–64.

————. (1997). The self-medication hypothesis of substance use disorders: A reconsideration and recent applications. *Harvard Review of Psychiatry, 4,* 231–44.

————. (1999). *Treating addiction as a human process*. Northvale, NJ: Jason Aronson.

————. (2003). Understanding addictive vulnerability. *Neuro-Psychoanalysis, 5,* 5–21.

Khantzian, E. J., Halliday, K. S., and McAuliffe, W. E. (1990). *Addiction and the vulnerable self: Modified dynamic group therapy for substance abusers*. New York: Guilford Press.

Khantzian, E. J., Mack, J. E., and Schatzberg, A. F. (1974). Heroin use as an attempt to cope: Clinical observations. *American Journal of Psychiatry, 131,* 160–64.

Kohut, H. (1977). Preface. In J. D. Blaine and D. A. Julius (Eds.), *Psychodynamics of drug dependence* (pp. vii–ix). Northvale, NJ: Jason Aronson.

Koppitz, E. M. (1968). *Psychological evaluation of children's human figure drawings*. Needham Heights, MA: Allyn & Bacon.

Levitt, E. E., and Gotts, E. E. (1995). *The clinical application of MMPI special scales* (Vol. 2). Hillsdale, NJ: Erlbaum.

Morgenstern, J., and Leeds, J. (1993). Contemporary psychoanalytic theories of substance abuse: A disorder in search of a paradigm. *Psychotherapy, 30,* 194–206.

Murray, H. A. (1974). *Thematic Apperception Test*. Cambridge, MA: Harvard University.

Nichols, D. S. (2001). *Essentials of MMPI-2 Assessment.* New York: Wiley.

Rado, S. (1933). The psychoanalysis of pharmacothymia (drug addiction). *Psychoanalytic Quarterly, 2,* 1–23.

Schinka, J. A., Curtiss, G., and Mulloy, J. M. (1994). Personality variables and self-medication in substance abuse. *Journal of Personality Assessment, 63,* 413–22.

Shatland, E. S., Cain, E., and Barton, M. B. (2001). The perils of stepwise logistic regression and how to escape them using information criteria and the output delivery system. In *Proceedings of the13th Annual SAS Users Group International (SUGI), USA* (pp. 222–26). Cary, NC: SAS Institute.

Spielberger, C. C. (1996). *Manual for the State-Trait Anger Expression Inventory.* Odessa, FL: Psychological Assessment Resources.

Tarter, R. E., Blackson, T., Brigham, J., Moss, H., and Caprara, G. V. (1995). The association between childhood irritability and liability to substance use in early adolescence: A 2-year follow-up study of boys at risk for substance abuse. *Drug and Alcohol Dependence, 39,* 253–61.

Tarter, R., Vanyukov, M., Giancola, P., Dawes, M., Blackson, T., Mezzich, A., et al. (1999). Etiology of early age onset substance use disorder: A maturational perspective. *Development and Psychopathology, 11,* 657–83.

Thorberg, F. A., and Lyvers, M. (2005). Negative mood regulation (NMR) expectancies, mood, and affect intensity among clients in substance disorder treatment facilities. *Additive Behaviors, 31,* 811–20.

Turner, A. P., Larimer, M. E., Sarason, I. G., and Trupin, E. W. (2005). Identifying a negative mood subtype in incarcerated adolescents: Relationship to substance use. *Addictive Behaviors, 30,* 1442–48.

Ward, L. C. (1995). Correspondence of the MMPI-2 and MCMI-II in male substance abusers. *Journal of Personality Assessment, 64,* 390–93.

———. (1997). Confirmatory factor analyses of the anxiety and depression content scales of the MMPI-2. *Journal of Personality Assessment, 68,* 678–91.

Wells, C., Tosi, D. J., Eshbaugh, D. M., and Murphy, M. A. (1993). Comparison and discrimination of male and female alcoholic and substance abusers. In D. J. Tosi, D. M. Eshbaugh, and M. A. Murphy (Eds.), *A clinician's guide to the personality profiles of alcohol and drug abusers: Typological descriptions using the MMPI* (pp. 63–73). Springfield, IL: Charles C. Thomas.

Wetzler, S., Khadivi, A., and Moser, R. K. (1998). The use of the MMPI-2 for the assessment of depressive and psychotic disorders. *Assessment, 5,* 249–61.

Wills, T. A., Sandy, J. M., Shinar, O., and Yaeger, A. (1999). Contributions of positive and negative affect to adolescent substance use. Test of a bidimensional model in a longitudinal study. *Psychology of Addictive Behaviors, 13,* 327–38.

CHAPTER 9

The Self-Medication Hypothesis and Psychostimulant Treatment of Cocaine Dependence

AN UPDATE

With John J. Mariani and Frances R. Levin

Although effective pharmacologic treatments have been developed and widely employed for opioid, nicotine, and alcohol dependence there are no FDA-approved pharmacotherapies for cocaine dependence. Cocaine dependence (CD) remains one of the most debilitating and lethal addictions and remains widely prevalent in society; there are approximately 1.6 million current users of cocaine in the US (Substance Abuse and Mental Health Services Administration 2011), and the past-year prevalence of CD is estimated to be 1.1 percent (Compton et al. 2007). Standard psychosocial treatments for CD are only moderately effective, with an average abstinence rate of approximately 30 percent (Dutra et al. 2008). The need for effective pharmacotherapy for CD remains. In 1983, one of us (EJK) reported on a case in which there was marked improvement of an extreme case of IV CD treated with methylphenidate (MP) (Khantzian 1983). The patient suffered with comorbid attention-deficit disorder. The patient has been followed now for 30 years and has experience no relapse to cocaine. In a subsequent publication we reported on two additional cases of individuals who suffered with CD who also responded favorably to psychostimulant treatment (Khantzian et al. 1984). For reasons not exactly clear these promising outcomes were essentiality ignored for over a decade as far as follow-up clinical trials or controlled studies testing the efficacy of psychostimulant treatment for cocaine dependency, although recent studies are promising (Mariani et al. 2012). As we will elaborate subsequently, in our experience we believe that such patients can respond favorably to psychostimulant substitution because they are self-medicating painful subjective states and feelings due to the dopaminergic dysregulation associated with cocaine dependence.

The main effects of cocaine are due to the inhibition of catecholamine reuptake, particularly dopamine, by binding to the dopamine transporter (White et al. 1998). Substitution pharmacotherapy is effective for opioid (Amato et al. 2005) and nicotine (Berrettini and Lerman 2005) dependence, and is a plausible strategy for treating cocaine dependence. However, cocaine interactions with neurotransmitter systems are more complex and indirect than nicotine and opioid agonist actions. Psychostimulants, including amphetamine, methamphetamine, methylphenidate, bupropion, and modafinil, have been studied as substitution treatments for cocaine dependence, both in patients with (Schubiner et al. 2002; Levin et al. 2006) and without (Mariani et al. 2012; Grabowski et al. 1997, 2001; Shearer et al. 2003; Dackis et al. 2005; Poling et al. 2006; Anderson et al. 2009; Mooney et al. 2009; Grabowski et al. 2004; Schmitz et al. 2012) co-occurring attention deficit/hyperactivity disorder (ADHD). The results of these studies have been mixed with regard to effects on cocaine use, with the most consistent therapeutic effects reported for dextroamphetamine (Castells et al. 2010; Mariani and Levin 2012) and methamphetamine (Mooney et al. 2009). Amphetamine and cocaine have similar pharmacological and clinical characteristics; they differ mainly in onset of action and half-life. The mechanism of action of amphetamine is to both block dopamine reuptake and promote dopamine release.

Animal studies evaluating the potential of psychostimulants as treatments for CD have been promising. Rats have been shown to have dose-dependent decreases in cocaine-reinforced responding with dextroamphetamine administration (Negus and Mello 2003). Dextroamphetamine has also been shown to reduce cocaine self-administration in rhesus monkeys (Czoty, Martelle, and Nader 2010) and that this effect diminishes after discontinuation of dextroamphetamine, suggesting that prolonged treatment may be necessary to produce a sustained reduction in the reinforcing effects of cocaine (Martinez et al. 2011). Generally, these preclinical data support the hypothesis that psychostimulants are potentially efficacious treatments for CD deserving of further study, although animal models of addiction can only be suggestive of potential clinical utility.

The results of brain imaging studies have provided additional support for the potential utility of psychostimulant treatment of cocaine dependence. Findings with the positron emission tomography (PET) raclopride displacement procedure have shown that deficient dopamine transmission is associated with failure to respond to behavioral treatment (Volkow et al. 2010). Stimulant medication may correct this deficit, and by enhancing dopamine release, may improve the salience of competing reinforcers to cocaine. Using PET and 2-deoxy-2-fluoro-D-glucose (FDG) to measure brain glucose metabolism as a marker of brain function, MP administration was associated with blunting of regional brain responses to cocaine cues (Rush, Stoops, and Hays 2009). These brain imaging findings can be interpreted as supporting the hypothesis that psychostimulant administration has the potential to "normalize" brain function for individuals with cocaine dependence.

Human laboratory experiments have also yielded results supporting the potential value of psychostimulant treatment of cocaine dependence. Cocaine use during dextroamphetamine maintenance has been reported to be safe and tolerable at moderate doses (Rush et al. 2010). Dextroamphetamine administration has been found to reduce cocaine self-administration, most likely by altering the reinforcing effects of cocaine (Katusic et al. 2005). These carefully controlled experiments point to the feasibility of using psychostimulants to treat individuals actively using cocaine. Controlled trial experience with using psychostimulants to treat CD has been mixed. A recently conducted metanalysis (Castells et al. 2010) pooled the results of 16 clinical trials that investigated bupropion, dextroamphetamine, methylphenidate, modafinil, mazindol, methamphetamine, and selegiline. Psychostimulants were not associated with improvements in cocaine use, retention in treatment, or sustained abstinence, although sustained abstinence did differ by type of drug used, and was higher with bupropion and dextroamphetamine. We believe the approach of looking at all dopamine agonists as having equal potential is flawed. In our view, the existing evidence, as well as our clinical experience, suggests that more potent classical stimulants (e.g., amphetamines and methylphenidate) have the highest potential to be effective. Cocaine is a powerful stimulant medication; a pharmacotherapy that substantially modifies the reinforcing effects of cocaine needs to compete with its pharmacodynamic actions.

In a significant number of these cases dating back to the first published cases in the early 1980s and up to the present, the responses to MP treatment have been dramatic and sustained. In this report we report on an additional recent case example of marked improvement with sustained released MP, the rationale for such treatment, preliminary studies of stimulant treatment of non-ADHD cocaine dependent patients, and explore the basis for further study of this potentially promising treatment.

The Case of Bobby and the "Miracle Cure"

The patient reported here was treated in the summer of 2011 for the first time with sustained release MP and in his own words described his response as a "miracle." Bobby is a 49-year-old married handyman who is currently separated from his wife, mainly as a result of Bobby's many relapses to his drug of choice, cocaine—in its crack form. He has also been subject to heavy periodic alcohol use and dependence. Bobby has been followed by one of us (EJK) for six years. He has a moderately severe learning disability that has rendered him borderline illiterate. Furthermore he describes attentional problems, restlessness, and hyperactivity growing up as a child.

He has responded to mood stabilizer, antidepressants, and disulfiram which have provided some degree of relief from persistent feelings of depression, anxiety, agitation, and impulses to resort to alcohol. The periodic use of cocaine has been the most unrelenting clinical problem. MP treatment was recently reconsidered because of marked deterioration in his condition from the drug use including suicidal depressive feelings. After consulting with a colleague (JM) doing research with stimulant drug substitution for stimulant dependent patients, sustained release MP was prescribed 36 milligrams (Concerta®), a long-acting form of MP, subsequently adjusted to 27 milligrams per day. Within 24 hours of commencing the MP the patient left a voice message describing the effects of the treatment as a "miracle" exuding gratitude for the relief the medication had afforded him. Bobby maintained contact by phone almost daily until his scheduled appointment a week later continuing to be elated about his improved mood and expressing appreciation for his new-found sense of well-being. When seen in person he again excitedly proclaimed that it was a miracle how much better he felt and emphasized that he now had a choice about using cocaine, much like the patient first treated with MP indicated in the early 1980s. He bragged that he was eight days abstinent. Not insignificantly, two mornings before his visit he described how he was not sure if he had taken his medication (when it turned out he had) and mistakenly took a second dose. Loudly and animatedly he said, "I didn't like it at all. It was too much."

Four weeks after commencing the MP in a context of developing severe back pain he reverted to using some illicitly obtained oxycodone which in turn led to a "limited" amount of cocaine. He quickly reassured his psychiatrist that he felt he did not have to continue the cocaine, uncharacteristic for him prior to being treated with the MP. Despite his back pain he indicated he has become much better organized, has been catching up with chores and tasks at home that he had been ignoring. Despite his back pain he has remained buoyant and more optimistic in his outlook. At the time of writing this chapter Bobby has been abstinent from cocaine use for eight months.

Mixed-Amphetamine Salts Treatment of Cocaine Dependence

A 32-year-old man with CD presented for treatment with one of the authors (JJM). He had a history of opioid dependence successfully treated with buprenorphine, but over the past year, developed a pattern of nightly cocaine use. The patient would stay up late every night using cocaine and compulsively tinkering with old computers. This pattern caused problems with work attendance and financial difficulties due to the cost of the cocaine. The patient would experience progressively more intense cocaine cravings while at work and then buy cocaine immediately arriving home each evening. Motivational and cognitive-based interventions were ineffective in changing the pattern of cocaine use. Extended-release mixed-amphetamine salts were started at a dose of 20 milligrams per day and gradually titrated to a dose of 30 milligrams every morning and 20 milligrams at 1 p.m. Very soon after initiation of amphetamine treatment the patient's cocaine use ceased. The patient also reported elimination of cocaine craving and a cessation of the compulsive computer tinkering each evening. The patient has achieved six months of abstinence from cocaine. The plan is to continue amphetamine treatment for a total of one year and then gradually taper off.

Interestingly, these positive findings have been difficult to replicate in clinical trials with cocaine-dependent trials. Our group has carried out several trials assessing MP with cocaine abusing adults. Unfortunately, the primary outcomes did not demonstrate a significant difference between those receiving MP and those receiving placebo. However, in these studies older sustained-release MP preparations were used, resulting in less consistent absorption and perhaps diminished efficacy of the medication. Importantly, our studies, as well as additional ones conducted by other experienced groups, have found little evidence of medication misuse/abuse. This should not be interpreted to mean that abuse of prescribed stimulants is not possible. The risks and benefits of prescribing stimulants should be thoughtfully considered with the patient and an appropriate decision should be made.

Methylphenidate Treatment of Cocaine Dependence: A Self-Medication Perspective

There is six time greater risk for developing substance use disorders (SUDs) among patients with ADHD compared to people who do not have the disorder (Wilens 2004) and such patients experience earlier onset and more severe SUDs (Wender 1979). There is an older clinical literature describing the enormous distress and dysfunction associated with ADHD, previously designated as minimal brain dysfunction (MBD), characterized by lack of emotional control, attentional and learning disabilities, depressive affect, marked irritability, low self-esteem, anergia, and restlessness (Huessy, Cohen, and Blair 1979; Yang, Shang, and Gau 2011). The recent literature on ADHD documents a disproportionately high co-occurrence of bipolar, depression, and anxiety disorders (Cumyn, French, and Hechtman 2009; McIntyre et al. 2010; Khantzian 1997). In objectively cataloging and classifying the symptoms associated with each diagnostic category what is often lost is the enormous subjective psychological suffering experienced with psychiatric disorders, including ADHD. The emphasis on painful feeling and emotional states is central to the self-medication hypothesis (SMH). Namely, it is not so much a psychiatric diagnosis or conditions that an individual self-medicates, rather the hypothesis underscores the psychological suffering associated with SUDs.

The observations about the SMH were derived from the clinical work of psychodynamic investigators dating to the early 1970s. Terms such as "drug of choice," "preferential use of drugs," and "self-selection" were coined to describe how individuals found certain drugs appealing, contributing to the articulation of the SMH (Khantzian 1985). The two main aspects of the SMH are (a) that individuals use addictive drugs to relieve their suffering and distress, and (b) that there is a considerable degree of psychopharmacologic specificity in an individual's drug preference (Khantzian 1985, 2003). Although the SMH derives from a psychodynamic perspective emphasizing deficits in affect defense and psychological pain associated with regulating self-esteem, relationships, and self-care, it is also consistent with the fact that individuals self-medicate the pain and suffering associated with psychiatric disorders (Khantzian 2003). The concept of self-medication has been applied to a variety of substance-symptom pairings such as cannabis use and aggression (Arendt et al. 2007), nicotine use and schizophrenia (Segarra et al. 2011), and alcohol consumption and mood (Swendsen 2000). However, the empiric evidence base is inconsistent, and some reports have not supported self-medication mechanisms of substance use disorders (Hall and Queener 2007; Carrigan and Randall 2003; Chambers 2009).

From a self-medication perspective, it is important to consider what affects or painful co-occurring psychiatric symptoms might be targeted to alleviate the distress that individuals wittingly and unwittingly attempt to relieve with their drug of choice. We have reviewed elsewhere in more detail the action of the classes of abused drugs (Khantzian 1985). For the purposes here, we described how stimulants act as augmentors for hypomanic, high-energy individuals as well as persons with atypical bipolar disorder. They also appeal to people who are de-energized and bored, and to those who suffer from depression, often of a subclinical variety. In addition, stimulants, including cocaine, can act paradoxically to calm and counteract hyperactivity, emotional lability, and inattention in persons with ADHD.

For the purposes of this report, we focus on the actions of illicit psychostimulants in considering treatment with prescribed psychostimulants. When considering treatment of CD with or without co-occurring with ADHD, it is important to explore and identify the painful feeling states or affects that patients are trying to relieve with their drug of choice. Such distress might or might not be associated with diagnosable psychiatric disorders. In the case of successful treatment of ADHD, it is arguable whether improvement is the result of "curing" the disorder, or whether improvement is the result of alleviating the painful affects and dysphoria that patients experience with the disorder. It is our clinical experience that the sense of well-being patients express with treatment is likely the result of relieving the gnawing depressive affect, anhedonia, and dysphoria associated with the pain and dysfunction of dopaminergic dysregulation. The SMH suggests that it is not so much euphoria but the relief of dysphoria that individuals experience when they respond to addictive drugs. As we indicated in a previous publication (Khantzian et al. 1984), it is likely that craving or desire for drugs is rooted in the corrections and relief from suffering patients experience with their drug use. In the first case reported here, and in the reported case in 1983 (Khantzian 1983) the substitution of the more long acting stabilizing form of MP (compared to the short acting destabilizing action of snorted, IV, and free base cocaine) corrects the predisposing and resultant chemical and emotional instability associated with CD. In doing so, it is our experience that the desire or craving for cocaine is reduced or eliminated. In the case of non-ADHD patients with CD, explorations of what painful affects and psychiatric conditions such individuals are self-medicating are useful and can guide treatment choices and be therapeutically beneficial. The SMH is rooted in a seemingly simple question—namely, asking patients, "What did the drug do for you when you first used it?" (Khantzian 1985). As we have indicated some patients describe how stimulants heighten expansive, hypomanic, high-energy states, or modes of relating. In other instances individuals discover that stimulants counteract states of anergia and related depressive symptoms if not frank coexisting depression. In other cases depressive reactions are accompanied by agitation or irritability. Psychostimulants might be used as augmenting agents when antidepressants alone produce only partial remission. When irritability, anger, or agitation complicates depression or sub-clinical bipolar or mixed states, mood regulators may be combined with stimulants or antidepressants. In our experience it is likely that mood regulators are useful because they act effectively as affect modulators and make painful/intense feeling more manageable and tolerable. In effect, the SMH suggests that a patient's self-medication provides an important clue in predicting which psychopharmacological approach might best relieve the patient's psychiatric symptoms.

Barriers to Acceptance of Psychostimulant Treatment

The use of psychostimulants to treat CD is controversial for several reasons. First, psychostimulants are controlled substances with well-recognized risks for misuse, diversion, and compulsive use. Second, cardiovascular risks are associated with the therapeutic use of psychostimulants, and there is concern that these risks would be additive. Finally, the tradition of substance use disorder treatment in the United States is heavily influenced by 12-step approaches, which tend to deemphasize medication treatments, particularly substitution pharmacotherapy. Clinicians would be well advised to prepare and instruct patients to be discreet when in 12-step meetings in discussing their treatment with psychostimulants. If and when it does come up they might explain it as treatment for an underlying psychiatric condition(s).

However, the field must follow where the evidence leads us, regardless of our preconceived preferences for therapies for substance use disorders to be benign, non-abusable medications. A similar dynamic has existed in the treatment for opioid dependence, where the evidence supporting the use of agonist replacement treatment (e.g., methadone and buprenorphine) is as strong as for any therapies in any field of medicine, yet many clinicians and institutions have strong reservations about their use. This is not to gloss over the safety limitations of psychostimulant treatment of cocaine dependence, and these risks will need to be managed as treatment models have emerged, perhaps using methadone and buprenorphine treatment as a model.

The main risks of psychostimulant treatment of CD are cardiovascular. In some cases, where cardiac disease risk factors are present, obtaining a baseline electrocardiogram would be indicated. As with all psychostimulant treatment, baseline and intermittent monitoring of pulse and blood pressure should be performed. However, normal readings do not preclude the risk of elevated pulse and blood pressure if prescription stimulants and cocaine are used simultaneously. Some medical conditions, such as a history of myocardial infarction, stroke, and poorly controlled hypertension, would be contraindications for psychostimulant treatment of cocaine dependence.

References

Amato, L., Davoli, M., Perucci, C. A., et al. (2005). An overview of systematic reviews of the effectiveness of opiate maintenance therapies: Available evidence to inform clinical practice and research. *Journal of Substance Abuse Treatment* 28:321–29.

Anderson, A. L., Reid, M. S., Li, S. H., et al. (2009). Modafinil for the treatment of cocaine dependence. *Drug Alcohol Dependence* 104:133–39.

Arendt, M., Rosenberg, R., Fjordback, L., et al. (2007). Testing the self-medication hypothesis of depression and aggression in cannabis-dependent subjects. *Psychological Medicine* 37:935–45.

Berrettini, W. H., and Lerman, C. E. (2005). Pharmacotherapy and pharmacogenetics of nicotine dependence. *American Journal of Psychiatry* 162:1441–51.

Carrigan, M. H., and Randall, C. L. (2003). Self-medication in social phobia: A review of the alcohol literature. *Addictive Behavior* 28:269–84.

Castells, X., Casas, M., Perez-Mana, C., et al. (2010). Efficacy of psychostimulant drugs for cocaine dependence. *Cochrane Database Systematic Reviews*, CD007380.

Chambers, R. A. (2009). A nicotine challenge to the self-medication hypothesis in a neurodevelopmental animal model of schizophrenia. *Journal of Dual Diagnosis* 5:139–48.

Chiodo, K. A., Lack, C. M., and Roberts, D. C. (2008). Cocaine self-administration reinforced on a progressive ratio schedule decreases with continuous D-amphetamine treatment in rats. *Psychopharmacology (Berl)* 200:465–73.

Compton, W. M., Thomas, Y. F., Stinson, F. S., et al. (2007). Prevalence, correlates, disability, and comorbidity of DSM-IV drug abuse and dependence in the United States: Results from the national epidemiologic survey on alcohol and related conditions. *Archives of General Psychiatry* 64:566–76.

Cumyn, L., French, L., and Hechtman, L. 2009. Comorbidity in adults with attention-deficit hyperactivity disorder. *Canadian Journal of Psychiatry* 54:673–83.

Czoty, P. W., Martelle, J. L., and Nader, M. A. (2010). Effects of chronic D-amphetamine administration on the reinforcing strength of cocaine in rhesus monkeys. *Psychopharmacology (Berl)* 209:375–82.

Dackis, C. A., Kampman, K. M., Lynch, K. G., et al. (2005). A double-blind, placebo-controlled trial of modafinil for cocaine dependence. *Neuropsychopharmacology* 30:205–11.

Dutra, L., Stathopoulou, G., Basden, S. L, et al. (2008). A meta-analytic review of psychosocial interventions for substance use disorders. *American Journal of Psychiatry* 165:179–87.

Grabowski, J., Rhoades, H., Schmitz, J., et al. (2001). Dextroamphetamine for cocaine-dependence treatment: A double-blind randomized clinical trial. *Journal of Clinical Psychopharmacology* 21:522–26.

Grabowski, J., Rhoades, H., Stotts, A., et al. (2004). Agonist-like or antagonist-like treatment for cocaine dependence with methadone for heroin dependence: Two double-blind randomized clinical trials. *Neuropsychopharmacology* 29:969–81.

Grabowski, J., Roache, J. D., Schmitz, J. M., et al. (1997). Replacement medication for cocaine dependence: Methylphenidate. *Journal of Clinical Psychopharmacology* 17:485–88.

Hall, D. H., and Queener, J. E. (2007). Self-medication hypothesis of substance use: Testing Khantzian's updated theory. *Journal of Psychoactive Drugs* 39:151–58.

Huessy, R., Cohen, S., and Blair, C. (1979). Clinical explorations in adult minimal dysfunction. In *Psychiatric Aspects of Minimal Brain Dysfunction in Adults*, edited by L. Bellak. New York: Grune & Stratton.

Katusic, S. K., Barbaresi, W. J., Colligan, R. C., et al. (2005). Psychostimulant treatment and risk for substance abuse among young adults with a history of attention-deficit/hyperactivity disorder: A population-based, birth cohort study. *Journal of Child Adolescent Psychopharmacology* 15:764–76.

Khantzian, E. J. (1983). An extreme case of cocaine dependence and marked improvement with methylphenidate treatment. *American Journal of Psychiatry* 140:784–85.

―――――. (1985). The self-medication hypothesis of addictive disorders: Focus on heroin and cocaine dependence. *American Journal of Psychiatry* 142:1259–64.

―――――. (1997). The self-medication hypothesis of substance use disorders: A reconsideration and recent applications. *Harvard Review of Psychiatry* 4:231–44.

―――――. (2003). The self-medication hypothesis revisited: The dually diagnosed patient. *Primary Psychiatry* 10:47–54.

Khantzian, E. J., Gawin, F., Kleber, H. D., et al. (1984). Methylphenidate (Ritalin) treatment of cocaine dependence—a preliminary report. *Journal of Substance Abuse Treatment* 1:107–12.

Levin, F. R., Evans, S. M., Brooks, D. J., et al. (2006). Treatment of methadone-maintained patients with adult ADHD: Double-blind comparison of methylphenidate, bupropion and placebo. *Drug and Alcohol Dependence* 81:137–48.

Mariani, J. J., and Levin, F. R. (2012). Psychostimulant treatment of cocaine dependence. *Psychiatric Clinics of North America* 35 (2): 425–39.

Mariani, J. J., Pavlicova, M., Bisaga, A., et al. (2012). Extended-release mixed amphetamine salts and topiramate for cocaine dependence: A randomized controlled trial. *Biological Psychiatry* 72:950–56.

Martinez, D., Carpenter, K. M., Liu, F., et al. (2011). Imaging dopamine transmission in cocaine dependence: Link between neurochemistry and response to treatment. *American Journal of Psychiatry* 168:634–41.

McIntyre, R. S., Kennedy, S. H., Soczynska, J. K., et al. (2010). Attention-deficit/hyperactivity disorder in adults with bipolar disorder or major depressive disorder: Results from the international mood disorders collaborative project. *Primary Care Companion to the Journal of Clinical Psychiatry* 12:1–6.

Mooney, M. E., Herin, D. V., Schmitz, J. M., et al. (2009). Effects of oral methamphetamine on cocaine use: A randomized, double-blind, placebo-controlled trial. *Drug and Alcohol Dependence* 101:34–41.

Negus, S. S., and Mello, N. K. (2003). Effects of chronic D-amphetamine treatment on cocaine- and food-maintained responding under a progressive-ratio schedule in rhesus monkeys. *Psychopharmacology (Berl)* 167:324–32.

Poling, J., Oliveto, A., Petry, N., et al. (2006). Six-month trial of bupropion with contingency management for cocaine dependence in a methadone-maintained population. *Archives of General Psychiatry* 63:219–28.

Rush, C. R., Stoops, W. W., and Hays, L. R. (2009). Cocaine effects during D-amphetamine maintenance: A human laboratory analysis of safety, tolerability and efficacy. *Drug and Alcohol Dependence* 99:261–71.

Rush, C. R., Stoops, W. W., Sevak, R. J., et al. (2010). Cocaine choice in humans during D-amphetamine maintenance. *Journal of Clinical Psychopharmacology* 30:152–59.

Schmitz, J. M., Rathnayaka, N., Green, C. E., et al. (2012). Combination of modafinil and D-amphetamine for the treatment of cocaine dependence: A preliminary investigation. *Front Psychiatry* 3:1–6.

Schubiner, H., Saules, K. K., Arfken, C. L., et al. (2002). Double-blind placebo-controlled trial of methylphenidate in the treatment of adult ADHD patients with comorbid cocaine dependence. *Experimental and Clinical Psychopharmacology* 10:286–94.

Segarra, R., Zabala, A., Eguiluz, J. I., et al. (2011). Cognitive performance and smoking in first-episode psychosis: The self-medication hypothesis. *European Archives of Psychiatry and Clinical Neurosciences* 261:241–50.

Shearer, J., Wodak, A., van Beek, I., et al. (2003). Pilot randomized double blind placebo-controlled study of dexamphetamine for cocaine dependence. *Addiction* (Abingdon, England) 98:1137–41.

Substance Abuse and Mental Health Services Administration. (2011). *Results from the 2010 National Survey on Drug Use and Health: Summary of National Findings.* Publication No. SMA 11-4658. Rockville, MD: Office of Applied Studies.

Swendsen, J. D., Tennen, H., Carney, M. A., et al. (2000). Mood and alcohol consumption: An experience sampling test of the self-medication hypothesis. *Journal of Abnormal Psychology* 109:198–204.

Volkow, N. D., Wang, G. J., Tomasi, D., et al. (2010). Methylphenidate attenuates limbic brain inhibition after cocaine-cues exposure in cocaine abusers. *PLOS ONE* 5:1–9.

Wender, P. 1979. *Psychiatric Aspects of Minimal Brain Dysfunction in Adults.* New York: Grune & Stratton.

White, F. J., and Kalivas, P. W. 1998. Neuroadaptations involved in amphetamine and cocaine addiction. *Drug and Alcohol Dependence* 51:141–53.

Wilens, T. E. (2004). Impact of ADHD and its treatment on substance abuse in adults. *Journal of Clinical Psychiatry* 65:38–45.

Yang, L. K., Shang, C. Y., and Gau, S. S. (2011). Psychiatric comorbidities in adolescents with attention-deficit hyperactivity disorder and their siblings. *Canadian Journal of Psychiatry* 56:281–92.

CHAPTER 10

The Psychodynamics of Addiction and Its Treatment

AN INTERVIEW WITH *NEW THERAPIST*

***New Therapist* (*NT*):** What are some of the essential elements of good inpatient addiction treatment?

Edward J. Khantzian (EJK): I have recently put "kindness" at the top of the list in several articles. This might seem so self-evident as to be superfluous, but in practice too often it is not readily honored. In addition I include elements of comfort, empathy, avoidance of confrontation, patience, and instruction. Kindness is important because addicted individuals suffer with a sense of unworthiness that predisposes to and results from addiction. It is not apt to be present when unwittingly we operate with modes of impassivity or more strictly interpretive modes of interaction, traditions that linger and carry over from now passé styles of therapeutic detachment and neutrality. Furthermore, given the problems of disbelief and distrust that problems of addictions can evoke in us, attitudes of kindness are often hard to adopt and maintain. Given the problems of disordered emotions, discomfort, low self-esteem and troubled relationships so often associated with addictive disorders, approaches that incorporate attitudes of comfort and empathy become crucial. Addictive behavior can cause therapists to feel crazy and angry and thus evoke confrontations that can be injurious, but they must be done with restraint, when necessary, and done in a way that preserves self-esteem. Patience and instruction remain important therapeutic ingredients, since addicted individuals so often are confused, out-of-touch, and not knowing about their emotions. All these elements are important in assuring a strong therapeutic relationship and alliance.

***NT*:** How can therapists be assisted in understanding, addressing and modifying addicts' vulnerabilities that contribute to their using drugs?

EJK: I have advocated that clinicians need to adopt and flexibly maintain a focus to deal with the complexities and challenges associated with addictions. A basic reminder is that what goes on in the contexts of individual and group treatments in most respects reflects what goes on outside of the treatment relationship for the individual and is a powerful telltale of what their addictive vulnerabilities are about. Modern relational therapies instruct therapists to monitor the subjective reactions and emotions that patients evoke as a means to guide them about their patients' suffering and distresses and what needs therapeutic focus. I have discovered that maintaining a focus on four areas of vulnerability in self-regulation is fruitful and principally involved in addictions—namely, difficulties in regulating affect life, self-esteem, relationships and self-care.

NT: Working with addicts provokes powerful and intense feelings. How can therapists in these situations be aware of caring for themselves?

EJK: In addition to Freud's dictum for mental health—"to love and to work" (*lieben und arbeiten*)—I would add "spielen" (to play). This applies to ourselves as clinicians as much as it applies to our patients. Letting go and finding enjoyment elsewhere beyond the work can be re-invigorating and revitalizing for us. As the recovery traditions also instruct, a sense of humor helps. Employing periodic gut checks as to what we are feeling, self-scrutiny, and reflection also help. But when the going gets rough, as well it can in this work, not bearing and suffering our reactions alone, but sharing them with colleagues and friends, can make a significant difference.

NT: About 40 years ago you began to conceptualize your view of addiction as an attempt by the user to self-medicate painful and uncomfortable inner states. What were some of the responses of your colleagues?

EJK: Because one of the predominant paradigms at the time of publishing my self-medication hypothesis (SMH) was a psychodynamic one, and my ideas were grounded in that tradition, it was met with considerable interest and acceptance. Beyond that, in lay articles and in non-psychiatric journals it was positively reviewed and endorsed. Five years after the publication of the SMH in the *American Journal of Psychiatry* (1985), the associate editor of the *Journal of the American Medical Association*, in an editorial article on nicotine dependence, said, "The notion of 'self-medication' is one of the most intuitively appealing theories about drug abuse" (Glass 1990, 1583). As anticipated in your next question, many in the recovering traditions were skeptical, including physicians of that persuasion, and would respond saying, "Keep it simple." One highly regarded colleague and academic was inclined to say, "Alcohol causes depression,

depression doesn't cause alcoholism." As an aside, I never said depression causes alcoholism; rather, the SMH emphasizes that painful feelings and psychological suffering, which may or may not be associated with psychiatric conditions, predispose to addiction.

NT: How do you think the idea of addiction as self-medication sits alongside the view held by some, especially AA, that addiction is a disease?

EJK: It depends upon whom you ask. As many as there are who debunk it, I find many, including those who endorse a disease concept, who feel the SMH is complementary with the disease concept of addiction. A nurse one day quipped, "Addiction is a disease of disordered emotions." More often, I find that clinicians are most comfortable with the paradigm. That is, in the clinical context, therapists and counselors find that it is an alliance building approach to inquire and pursue what an individual's drug of choice does for them. This is in contrast to the prevailing tendency to judge and shame individuals for what the drugs do to them and loved ones, this in addition to the shame and guilt addicted individuals shower on themselves. Needless to say, some are sharply critical and dismissive of the SMH—including some neuroscientists, who consider it a "primary disease." As two authors recently put it, the SMH is "dangerously false and misleading" (DuPont and Gold 2007).

NT: Many theorists believe that, for treatment to be effective, it requires an awareness of the underlying psychological processes and mechanisms. Psychodynamic theory does this. What elements and techniques do you think non-psychodynamic theories, such as cognitive behavioral therapy, dialectical behavioral therapy and motivational interviewing, might share with psychodynamic therapy?

EJK: Both as predisposing and resultant factors, addictions are disorders of emotion, cognition, and attitude. Therapies that work do so because they address these factors. Some individuals are more in need of addressing the pain residing in confused or overwhelming emotions or troubled self-other relationships. For others, the problems are rooted in cognitive distortions or beliefs. For yet others, the need to examine issues of impulsivity and faulty decision making are the order of the day; and finally, who would argue against treatments that target motivational factors and disavowal of problems. In my opinion and experience, effective clinicians draw upon and integrate elements of all these paradigms to address the factors that emerge and become apparent in the course of treatment. If we can consider the various paradigms as different channels needing variable attention and attunement, the challenge then becomes one of picking the channel that best suits a given patient or client at any given time. Effective therapists flexibly switch and adopt approaches best suited for patients' needs and issues.

NT: Some theorists view addiction as the pursuit of pleasure. How compatible is this view with the belief that drug use is an attempt at self-medication?

EJK: Pleasure is not unimportant, but it is not lasting or sustaining. Nor in my opinion is it a prime motivating factor in addictions. In my experience and that of relational therapists, we are more contact and comfort seekers than we are pleasure seekers. Furthermore, in my estimation, there is an undue and misleading emphasis on pleasurable reward as a major motivating factor in drug/alcohol dependency. Some of this resides in a misunderstanding of what substance-dependent people experience and achieve with their substance use and dependency. I have concluded that addictively prone individuals suffer with distressing states of anhedonia and dysphoria and substances provide temporary relief from these painfully vague and confusing states. Little wonder that, when these distressful and elusive feelings are changed or relieved, it is experienced or erroneously interpreted as euphoria or a "high." This is principally what is "rewarding" about addictive drugs.

NT: You identify difficulties in self-regulation of feelings, self-esteem, self-care and relationships as contributing to an individual's pain and distress that leads them to self-medicate with drugs. What leaves individuals more or less equipped to self-regulate emotions?

EJK: In life we need our emotions to guide us in being in touch with our inner psychological terrain and to negotiate our relationships with the human and nonhuman environment. We need to love and care about ourselves and we need connection to caring others in order to take care of ourselves. Adequate protection, nurturing, bonding, and affirmation in the growing-up years determines whether we are equipped to be aware of and know our emotions, like ourselves and trust others enough to ensure we avoid danger and harm, especially behaviors and relationships associated with the dangers associated with addictions. Addictively prone individuals more often have been subjected to traumatic abuse and neglect such that these capacities for self-regulation have been severely compromised or lacking. They self-medicate the pain associated with their difficulties in regulating their emotions, self-esteem, and relationships. Their deficits in being unable to use their emotions as guides for their behaviors causes major dysfunctions and deficits in self-care and leaves them in harm's way, especially those involved with substance use and dependency.

NT: Jeffrey Roth, an addictions psychiatrist and group psychotherapist, has referred to addiction as a disease of isolation. How does this view tie in with your understanding of addict's struggles to manage their interpersonal relationships?

EJK: I totally agree. One of my patients in group therapy described his dilemmas with relationships as being a "born-again isolationist". Recovering individuals reveal their difficulties and ambivalence about their connections to others in their aphorisms such as "we don't have relationships, we take hostages"; or "we are relief-seeking missiles." Too often, patients and clinicians are misguided by an outdated and erroneous conception of maturity as the capacity to be "autonomous and independent" when, more correctly, an essential aspect of maturity resides in the capacity for interdependence. Life problems are not best solved alone and least of all are the problems of addiction solved alone. Rather, problems are best solved in a context of mutual concern and care.

NT: Attachment theory has gained prominence over the past two decades in addiction treatment. When individuals struggle to behave in a caring way towards self, indulging instead in dangerous and harmful drug usage, might this arise from an early attachment failure between themselves and their primary caregivers?

EJK: I believe that the SMH and attachment theory are mutually enriching paradigms. I was recently honored by the Bowlby Center to deliver the 20th John Bowlby Memorial Lecture. In their invitation to deliver the lecture, the conveners of the conference, including Sir Richard Bowlby, the son of John Bowlby, indicated that the SMH and my ideas of addiction as a self-regulation disorder clearly linked up with Dr. Bowlby's ideas of the disrupting and damaging nature of trauma, neglect, and broken bonds in early stages of development. That is, they leave such individuals prone to life struggles with regulating emotions, self-esteem, relationships, and self-care, thus making addictively prone individuals more likely to self-medicate their suffering with addictive substances. What is significant here, with relatively little specific reference to attachment theory on my part over the years in my publications, and independent of my work, the originators and adherents of attachment theory affirmed that the concepts of self-medication and self-regulation disturbances associated with addictions were entirely consistent with the addiction as an attachment disorder.

NT: Mentalization-based therapy has gained prominence in many areas of mental health. Do you think it might be a useful way to assist patients to begin to identify and think about their overwhelming thoughts and feelings?

EJK: The principles and practice of mentalizing therapies are preeminently applicable to and efficacious for the dilemmas with which addictively prone individuals suffer. Helping drug dependent persons to identify, put into words and express their thoughts, feelings, and behaviors is to help such individuals use these processes to deal therapeutically with the issues of disturbed self-regulation problems that otherwise have been short-circuited into self-harmful addictive behavior. Psychoanalytic concepts of alexithymia, hypo-symbolization and disaffected states were identified by Krystal, Wurmser, and McDougall, respectively, as important factors in the development of addictions in the last half of the 20th century. These investigators appreciated the importance of helping individuals to understand how these factors contributed to their addictive problems. Mentalizing provides tools and approaches that specifically attunes to and addresses the affective deficits with which addicted individuals suffer.

References

DuPont, R. L., and Gold, M. S. (2007). Comorbidity and "self-medication." *Journal of Addictive Disorders* 26 (1):13–23.

Glass, R. (1990). Blue mood, blackened lungs: Depression and smoking. *Journal of the American Medical Association* 264:1583–84.

Part III

TREATMENT OF ADDICTIVE DISORDERS

In a recent publication, I suggested that treating addictive disorders, as with other medical and psychiatric conditions, should rest on the principle that effective treatment best occurs when the underlying processes and mechanisms involved in the disorder are understood and targeted. We now have more than half a century of empirical and clinical studies, with the benefit of illuminating diagnostic tools and better contemporary psychodynamic appreciation, to identify the nature of coexisting psychopathology. Such appreciation is crucial in guiding our treatment interventions.

The existence of psychiatric disorders and psychodynamic dysfunction that has been identified to co-occur with substance use disorders is too great to be by chance. The development of addictive disorders is much more probable with dually diagnosed individuals because they are likely to experience the short-term ameliorating and pain-relieving effects of addictive drugs. Whether the acquisition of addictive drugs occurs in a doctor's office or in the process of experimentation in nonmedical situations, the prevalence of addictive substances is pervasive in modern society, and in the process of exposure to them, wherever that may occur, vulnerable individuals are at risk to *discover* their pain-relieving psychoactive properties.

For the purposes of this section of the book, I draw primarily on the contemporary psychodynamics findings previously reviewed as the basis for guiding the modes of intervention that are necessary to effectively engage and therapeutically treat addicted individuals. Whether psychotherapy occurs in individual or in group settings, old psychoanalytic approaches of passivity, detachment, and strictly interpretive responses should be avoided. In my lectures, I caution clinicians and counselors that if they subscribe to the "wooden Indian school of therapy" (i.e., unexpressive and minimally interactive modes) such an approach would be ineffective, if not harmful, in responding to the needs of substance-dependent individuals—namely, addressing the deficits in and problems with affects, self-esteem, relationships, and behavior with which they suffer.

Affect deficits are best responded to with an active process of drawing out, identifying, labeling, and helping addicted individuals better know and find words for their feelings—that is, the elusive feelings that get short-circuited with the use of addictive substances. The recent paradigm of "mentalization" introduced by Jon G. Allen, Peter Fonagy, and Anthony Bateman, wherein therapists develop and maintain a focus with patients to access feelings, thoughts, and behavior and put them into words, is preeminently applicable for helping addicted patients. Patients benefit from the understanding that their incapacity to deal with their feelings is intimately involved with drug use and dependence.

In contrast, for those who are overwhelmed by intense feelings of rage, agitation, angry depression, and the like, efforts by therapists to help such patients contain and moderate their reactions are critically important. It is important to keep in mind that a positive treatment relationship and the therapist's concern for the patient's well-being is in and of itself an important containing influence. Exploring, identifying, and acknowledging the sources of their intense emotions, and validating them, lends to a sense of understanding and feeling understood that helps patients detoxify such intense states. Furthermore, linking their intense emotions with their drug of choice also becomes a basis of understanding and containing their intense emotions. It is also the case that judicious use of medications that modulate intense and unmanageable affect can often help make psychotherapeutic exploration and resolution more achievable.

The impaired sense of self, low self-esteem, and related interpersonal difficulties are best responded to with active support and empathic engagement. We extensively review in this section how and why this is so. These elements are crucial to counter the sense of shame, shattered self-esteem, and lack of self-love so common a predisposing and resulting part of addictive process.

In chapter 11, I review an evolution in my thinking on the nature of the psychopathology associated with addiction. As previously indicated, my work in addiction studies started with the implementation of a methadone maintenance program. Thus, it should not be surprising that in my early papers I stressed "pervasive, primitive, narcissistic dynamics" driving the impulse to use addictive drugs. This was an admittedly more troubled population; however, as I began to see in my private practice—in groups and individually—patients who were using alcohol, cocaine, and other drugs, many of them coming from 12-step programs, I witnessed in them more resiliency and characterologic strength. I began to feel more comfortable working as much with their strengths and defenses and, at the same time, developing a focus to work on their self-regulation vulnerabilities that predisposed them to addiction—that is, to focus on sectors of vulnerability in personality organization. As I have indicated, this shift had implications for establishing a stronger therapeutic alliance, especially for group psychotherapy in my private practice. I elaborate on group therapy as a special corrective for these vulnerabilities. I stress that groups are therapeutic because they are powerfully containing and transformative.

Chapter 11 was a paper published in one of the early issues of the then new journal, the *Journal of Groups in Addiction & Recovery*. As pursued in chapter 12, the interview with Martin Weegmann, a distinguished clinician and widely published scholar in Great Britain, allowed me to further detail the corrective benefits of group therapy. Beyond a stimulating interview drawing me out on many aspects of group work with addicted patients, he probed for personal and professional factors and experiences in my background to explore the origins of and the development of my interest in this work. I say it was stimulating in that his questions evoked in me some of my personal beliefs and passions that are not ordinarily and usually expressed or evident in my publications.

Chapter 13 is another collaborative effort with Martin Weegmann. We explore the utility and effectiveness of three modern psychodynamic approaches (Kleinian, Kohutian, and Bowlbian perspectives) in treating the vulnerabilities addictively prone individuals live with that made their addiction likely. In-depth analysis of several cases offer insights into how fine-tuning the applications of these perspectives provided access to and resolution of core conflicts and deficits that were at the heart of their suffering and their addictive attempts to cope with their suffering.

In chapters 14 and 15, I believe I have described, as best as I ever have, how an appreciation and understanding of the psychodynamic deficits and vulnerabilities associated with addiction can guide effective individual psychotherapy (chapter 14), and how and why it can explain the effectiveness of 12-step programs. In chapter 14, I list and explain how the important elements of kindness, empathy, patience, balance of listening and speaking, and the like are crucial in responding to the affect deficits, shattered sense of self, disturbed relationships, and self-care that are so pervasive with addictive disorders; in the case of 12-step programs, in chapter 15, I explore how the traditions of nonjudgmental acceptance, storytelling, natural bonding, and sharing experiences become natural, extraordinary antidotes and correctives for these same vulnerabilities.

CHAPTER 11

Reflections on Group Treatments as a Corrective for Addictive Vulnerability

When Dr. David Brook approached me to make a contribution to this series of papers on group treatments for substance use disorders (SUDs), I originally had planned to write an overview article on psychodynamic group therapy, reviewing our own work and that of others, and to focus on my particular interest on modified dynamic group therapy (MDGT) (Khantzian et al. 1990). As the deadline approached, my plan began to feel increasingly daunting. I shared my reaction with David indicating that the prospect of "rehashing" my work and that of my collaborators (Golden, Halliday, Khantzian, and McAuliffe 1993; Khantzian et al. 1990; Khantzian, Golden, and McAuliffe 1995; Khantzian, Halliday, Golden, and McAuliffe 1992), as well as the work of respected colleagues (Brown and Yalom 1977; Matono and Yalom 1991; Vanicelli 1982; Yalom 1974), felt redundant and not as challenging as this subject matter usually seems to me. I asked him for some latitude in offering some musings and reflections, rather than a more academic or pedagogical approach, on what has been a keen interest of mine—namely, how and why groups help people, particularly individuals with addictive disorders, to feel better and to change.

Based on my clinical experiences working with patients with SUDs in both individual and group psychotherapies, I am convinced that problems in self-regulation and the psychological suffering that ensues are at the root of addictive disorders. I have found group treatments to be preeminently suited to address these problems. Group work is especially effective to unearth the nature of these problems and offers a means to relieve the distress and address the co-occurring characterologic problems that interact with their suffering. In the following paragraphs, I describe how these ideas developed in the contexts of my clinical experience, and how they in turn generated a model for group therapy for patients with SUDs.

An Evolving Perspective (1970–1980)

When I first began teaching about patients with SUDs I emphasized "severe and pervasive co-existent psychopathology," a focus that shifted as I worked with more patients. I stressed primitive and narcissistic dynamics as being at the root of the impulse to use and become dependent on substances of abuse. In part, this formulation was a function of my initial experience starting in the early 1970s working with patients coming to a methadone maintenance treatment program, patients who admittedly were more characterologically disturbed. These patients had high rates of comorbid depression, as well as a disproportionately high incidence of personality disorder (Khantzian and Treece 1985). During this time, I continued to see increasing numbers of alcohol-dependent patients in my private practice and with the advent of the "cocaine epidemic" in the 1980s, I was seeing more cocaine-dependent patients as well. I became increasingly impressed with the degrees of resiliency and characterologic strength in the patients I was treating, especially those in recovery (e.g., 12-step programs). Both in individual and group psychotherapy, I found it increasingly more comfortable (for me and my patients) to work with their strengths and to consider the special ways my patients suffered and the ways they attempted to disguise their suffering from themselves and from others. This shift in my thinking increased the therapeutic alliance and, further, had special implications for group psychotherapy in my practice.

My emphasis shifted from a focus on psychopathology to more of a focus on sectors of vulnerability in personality organization. Increasingly, I stressed the interrelationships between patients' distress, their characterologic defensive patterns, problems with control, and their compulsion to use addictive substances.

A close and related companion to the issues of pain and suffering in SUDs is the problem with control. Patients with SUDs have repeatedly demonstrated that a core feature of their addictive illness is their inability to control their lives in an adaptive manner. As much as SUDs can be seen as a loss of control over substance use, they may also be seen as an attempt to control their lives using an external, if not self-destructive, source of support. As our patients in recovery so often remind us, "alcohol" is only mentioned once in the 12 steps of Alcoholics Anonymous (AA); otherwise the steps are a metaphor for life and a means to help individuals who have difficulty regulating themselves to better do so.

In my own work, spanning three decades working with patients who suffer with SUDS, I have evolved an understanding of addictive vulnerability as a disorder in self-regulation. The core features of substance abusers' inability to regulate their lives involves their emotions (or affects), self-esteem, relationships, and behaviors (e.g., self-care) (Khantzian 1990, 1995, 1999). Originally when I first began to work with substance abusers I was in the middle of my psychoanalytic training, which then (and now) influenced me to believe that I could engage my patients and understand them best if I used an analytic and adaptive perspective. I assumed that the patients coming to the methadone program were using opiates to cope with life problems. Because opiates are physical pain killers, I presumed they might also be a means to ameliorate psychological pain. As I continued to evaluate in greater depth the nature of their suffering, and treated increasing numbers of patients in individual and group psychotherapy in our methadone program, I became aware of a more specific reason for the appeal of these analgesic agents. Namely, opiates increasingly seemed to me to be compelling for my patients because they had discovered the powerful anti-range and anti-aggression action of these drugs. The predominance of these affects in the methadone patients was not surprising given that so many of them had been both victims and perpetrators of traumatic violence and abuse.

This clinical observation was the beginning of the second stage of my thinking, and an important part of the groundwork of what I and others would increasingly refer to as the "self-medication hypothesis." The increasing numbers of addicted patients that I saw in my private practice presented compelling clinical evidence that there were unique affect states with which they struggled that made the specific action of each class of drugs appealing (Khantzian 1975, 1985, 1997). The self-medication perspective, however, raised questions and inconsistencies that needed explanation. Two important ones were (1) many individuals suffer with painful affects, but they do not self-medicate them or become addicted; and (2) the use of addictive substances caused as much, if not more, pain than they relieve. In this context, my thinking evolved to consider addictive involvement as a self-regulation disorder (Khantzian 1990, 1995, 1997) and, subsequently, on a related basis, to also consider the nature of the disordered person or disordered personality that makes it more likely that individuals will experiment, become dependent on, and relapse to addictive substances (Khantzian 1999).

Group Therapy as a Corrective (1980–2000)

Group psychotherapy provides a special forum for these vulnerabilities in self-regulation and related defenses to unfold and to provide corrective experiences for our patients to find relief for their pain and opportunities to change and grow. Bill, an articulate professional man working with me in a group in which we repeatedly came around to exploring such vulnerabilities, provided the following vivid vignette to explain the sources of his self-regulation difficulties and how alcohol became a magical elixir to counter his inner distress and constricting defenses.

My childhood was a period of isolation and loneliness—there was restriction suppression, repression, oppression and depression. I distinctly recall my first drink, at 17 years old, and how it changed all of that. I recall the frosted highball class, the two ice cubes, unscrewing the red top of the Beefeaters gin bottle, the cracking of the ice cubes when the liquor splashed over them, the strong odor of the juniper berries. I recall the tightening of my throat when the foreign solution burned going down—and then I recall the unfettering from my emotional chains that followed. I began to feel free—free to feel. I felt happy, even giddy—unashamed, unpretentious and uninhibited. I felt that I finally was a member of the human race, "one of the guys," an equal.

I often like to quote Fenichel's quote (1945) [source unknown], to demonstrate an essential truth about alcoholism. The quote is "The superego is that part of an individual that is soluble in alcohol." Obviously, as we know from everyday experience, and as Fenichel was suggesting, alcohol is a good superego solvent.

Actually, modern psychodynamic theory (Krystal and Raskin 1970; Khantzian 1990) would suggest alcohol is at least as good an ego solvent and helps individuals who are constricted around dependency and nurturance needs to overcome restricting ego defenses, as Bill's dramatic vignette demonstrates. Alcohol lessens our defensive inhibitions and our anxiety levels, enabling a "repressed" individual to become more expressive, as Bill described. His vignette also reveals that beyond the major painful affects with which he struggled, he also experienced anguishing problems with his self-esteem and an inability to connect to others without the benefit of alcohol. In addition to the suffering entailed in the self-regulation problems with emotions, self-esteem, and relationships, Bill and so many other patients like him also succumb to addictive disorders because they cannot regulate their self-care—namely, they repeatedly fail to consider, anticipate, or fear the consequences and dangers of the behaviors that lead up to and are involved in SUDs. At the same time our patients suffer with their self-regulation vulnerabilities, they also defend against them. Their often seemingly impregnable defenses disguise at the same time they reveal the substance abuser's significant vulnerabilities in self-regulation.

Therapies that are effective successfully target both the pain and the defenses. In my experience group psychotherapy, with or without individual psychotherapy, has been an extraordinary vehicle for achieving this end. By the early 1980s, group therapy was a regular if not essential part of my armamentarium in trying to help my patients understand their vulnerability to becoming dependent on substances of abuse. In the context of a semi-structured, supportive, friendly and safe group experience I was impressed how much my patients could reveal and teach me and each other about what the core dynamics were around addictive vulnerability. These "friendly and supportive" elements became increasingly important operatives, and my patients had to help me and each other to loosen up and relax enough to be ourselves and to learn the value of healthy play in groups. This included the ability to laugh, as much as the ability to cry, about ourselves and our problems. I believe as practitioners we have not emphasized enough how groups are fun, uplifting, and extraordinary sources of support in engaging self with others in pursuing "mutual concerns" (Balint 1972) and addressing what needs to be addressed in order to get better and to change.

How Do Groups Work?

Group therapy works because it acts as a containing influence, and over time, the therapeutic group process increasingly serves as a transformative experience. In the group, members help each other to focus on what is needed to survive, given the major problems that members have with behavioral and emotional dysregulation. In my experience the natural anxiety, fear, and apprehension that is evoked in members and the leader when a group member is engaged in life threatening activities, and the range of reactions that are expressed, are often crucial in motivating the patient to do something about his or her behavior. Further, the understanding and nonjudgmental responses from others who are experiencing similar problems positively influence the troubled member. Where friends and family have reacted with impatience, anger or rejection, the members' commitment to each others' safety and well-being generate empathic concerns and expressions of appropriate fear and apprehension that the patient cannot feel for him/herself to guide their behavior. Often, the suggestion that it is time for detoxification and confinement is spontaneously initiated by group members who have similarly had to accept this realization, and it is often offered with hopeful and positive descriptions of their own experiences.

At other times the group leader enlists the patient to face the needed intervention, and catalyzes a process that encourages other patients to express their experiences and convictions about the benefits of a needed intervention—expressions that come from multiple perspectives that might not otherwise be available, when they are needed so much. The group members and leader can also play a crucial role in examining distress and/or the dangerous and mindless reactions that are part of the underpinnings of addictive behavior. In other instances when the same reactions herald potential relapse after varying lengths of sobriety or abstinence, the group members and leader may act to forestall relapse. More specifically, the members and group leader are alerted to spot the dysregulation of affects, self-esteem, relationships and self-care that are a constant threat to susceptible individuals when they are confronted with inevitable life stresses and distress.

Beyond containing addictive behavior, groups play an equally important, if not more important, role in transforming behavior, particularly the characterologic styles and patterns of behavior that predispose to addictive behaviors. In psychoanalytic/psychodynamic practice, the measure of improvement is not based primarily on symptom reduction. Rather, improvement is measured in terms of structural change, that is, how a person has been in their characteristic ways of relating, feeling, and behaving, and how they have changed as a consequence of treatment, indicates improvement. Do their character flaws or "defects" that cause them to repeat the same maladaptive patterns of being and behaving that predisposes them to their symptoms (in this case, the addictive use of drugs) change over time, and is there an emergence of more flexible, alternative ways of dealing with life problems and vicissitudes? In this respect, effective group leaders stimulate a process to assure that the group goes beyond the important matters of safety and support, but also foster a climate for self-examination and an understanding of how we are all more or less programmed (or not well enough programmed) to repeat and perpetuate self-defeat, or worse still, self-destruction.

As one patient who suffered so much with his sadness, bitterness, and loneliness put it, "I'm a born-again isolationist." In group, the constant challenge for him, myself, and the others was to monitor how he was constantly lapsing into taking leave of us in group even as he sat there, and was doing so in most of his other social circles.

In psychiatric and psychodynamic practice, we have few, if any, well-grounded traditions to proscribe behaviors other than confrontation. Most experienced clinicians, including myself, however, agree that as a therapeutic intervention confrontation is overrated, overused (especially in addicted populations), and more often ineffectual and/or damaging. Yet the need for containment and transformation for individuals suffering with SUDs begs for proscription of behaviors in the short term (e.g., abstinence) and long term (e.g., characterologic self-defeating behaviors) to get better. In the foregoing pages, I have described how in group psychotherapy a kind of confrontation can evolve that preserves self-esteem and is not damaging but still succeeds in addressing the essential need for containment and transformation. During these years, I have formulated principles about how and why group treatments work (some of which I repeat here from previous publications).

1. Groups are excellent forums to foster self-examination, especially in the domain of feelings, and the characterologic defenses and behaviors that mask patients' feelings.
2. Groups provide powerful antidotes for problems with self-esteem.

3. Groups foster effective connection with others and facilitate a process to examine how and why individuals operate to make connection unlikely or impossible.
4. Groups are extremely beneficial in helping individuals to face their behavioral dysregulation and their problems with self-care.
5. Groups are contexts where people seeking help can be remarkably sensitive and sensible in meeting each other's needs.
6. Groups are contexts in which it is very difficult to practice "pretend and pretense." That is, you might not know what you are feeling (even if you are acting as if you did), or you can posture and deny your vulnerability and act as if you are okay (when you are not), but in effective groups others will gently and supportively confront your denial and defenses.

In writing this chapter, I realize that much of what I have said about group psychotherapy as a corrective for addictive vulnerability is equally true about 12-step programs such as AA (Khantzian 1995; Khantzian and Mack 1989, 1994). Nevertheless, the two perspectives do not or need not compete. For reasons which are explainable, or not so explainable, patients have varying degrees of acceptance of different approaches. Self-help and psychotherapeutic groups have many similar and overlapping features upon which I will not elaborate here. I would only emphasize that under a trained group leader, group psychotherapy has certain advantages to 12-step programs. I offer a partial list as follows.

1. Group psychotherapy is more interactive.
2. A group leader can actively maintain a needed focus.
3. A group leader can more efficiently maintain the correct timing of needed interventions.
4. A group leader can function to stimulate needed responses and contain and forestall disruptive or counterproductive interactions.
5. A group leader can set limits on destructive or unacceptable group interactions.
6. A group leader can both analyze and catalyze processes that help group members appreciate the reciprocal relationship between the distress they suffer and their characterological defenses, and how this interaction is intimately interwoven into their penchant to adopt the use of addictive substances and behaviors.
7. A group leader can speak instructively, authoritatively, and if necessary, even charismatically, to draw attention to what a member or members need to hear to ensure their safety, sanity, and sobriety.

Conclusion

Group psychotherapy is a corrective for addictive vulnerability because a human context is created for patients with SUDs to play out and reenact their self-regulation problems with affects, self-esteem, relationships, and self-care, as well as the characterologic defenses that disguise and betray them. Group leaders instill confidence and hope that our patients do not need to passively endure their vulnerabilities. As I have already mentioned, suffering is at the core of addictive vulnerability. The worst fate, however, is not to suffer, but to suffer alone. Group members learn they can help each other actively identify and modify in self and others their tendency to be unaware, deny, or remain oblivious to their pain, suffering, and defenses, and the costly nature of their addictive solutions.

References

Balint, E. (1972). Fair shares and mutual concerns. *International Journal of Psychoanalysis* 53:61–65.

Brown, S., and Yalom, I. D. (1977). Interactional group therapy with alcoholics. *Journal of Studies of on Alcohol* 38:426–56.

Fenichel, O. (1945). *The Psychoanalytic Theory of Neurosis.* New York: Norton.

Golden, S., Halliday, K., Khantzian, E. J., and McAuliffe, W. E. (1993). Dynamic group therapy for substance abusers: A reconceptualization. In *Group Psychoanalytic in Clinical Practice,* edited by A. Alonso and H. Swiller, 271–87. Washington, DC: American Psychiatric Press.

Khantzian, E. J. (1975). Self selection and progression in drug dependence. *Psychiatry Digest* 10:19–22.

———. (1985). The self-medication hypothesis of addictive disorders. *American Journal of Psychiatry* 142:1259–64.

———. (1990) Self-regulation and self-medication factors in alcoholism and the addictions: Similarities and differences. In *Recent Developments in Alcoholism,* Vol. 8, edited by M. Galanter, 225–71. New York: Plenum.

———. (1994). How AA works and why it's important for clinicians to understand. *Journal of Substance Abuse Treatment* 11:77–92.

———. (1995). Self-regulation vulnerabilities in substance abusers: Treatment implications. In *The Psychology and Treatment of Addictive Behavior,* edited by S. Dowling, 17–41. Madison, CT: International Universities Press.

———. (1997). The self-medication hypothesis of substance use disorders: A reconsideration and recent applications. *Harvard Review of Psychiatry* 4:231–44.

———. (1999). *Treating Addiction as a Human Process.* Northvale, NJ: Jason Aronson.

Khantzian, E. J., Golden S. J., McAuliffe, W. E. (1995). Group therapy for psychoactive substance use disorders. In *Treatments of Psychiatric Disorders: The DSM IV Edition,* edited by G. O. Gabbard, 832–39. Washington, DC: American Psychiatric Press.

Khantzian, E. J., Halliday, K. S., Golden, S., and McAuliffe, W. E. (1992). Modified group therapy for substance abusers: A psychodynamic approach to relapse prevention. *American Journal on Addictions* 1:67–76.

Khantzian, E. J., Halliday, K. S., and McAuliffe, W. E. (1990). *Addiction and the Vulnerable Self: Modified Dynamic Group Therapy for Substance Abusers.* New York: Guilford.

Khantzian, E. J., and Treece, C. (1985). DSM-III psychiatric diagnosis of narcotic addicts: Recent findings. *Archives of General Psychiatry* 42:1067–71.

Krystal, H., and Raskin, H. A. (1970). *Drug Dependence: Aspects of Ego Functions.* Detroit: Wayne State University Press.

Matano, R. A., and Yalom, I. D. (1991). Approaches to chemical dependency: Chemical dependency and interactive group therapy—a synthesis. *International Journal of Group Psychotherapy* 41:269–93.

Vannicelli, M. (1982). Group psychotherapy with alcoholics. *Journal of Studies on Alcohol* 43:17–37.

Yalom, I. D. (1974). Group psychotherapy and alcoholism. *Annals of the New York Academy of Science* 233:85–103.

CHAPTER 12

More Reflections on Group Therapy

INTERVIEW BY MARTIN WEEGMANN

MW: Dr. Khantzian, you have been a student in his field for around 30 years and have an international reputation for having developed a modern, clinically—and research—relevant psychodynamic understanding of addiction. Could you say something about how you first found yourself drawn to this field?

EK: In good part what drew me to the addiction field was a matter of circumstance and chance. Probably more importantly, what sustained my interests had to do with my personal background, my training and mentoring. The circumstance and chance part had to do with the fact that I was chief of psychiatric liaison at The Cambridge Hospital during the late 1960s and early 1970s when the "heroin epidemic" was overtaking the United States. Because I was positioned in the medical-psychiatric interface, I was the logical designee to pursue a treatment program for heroin addiction which was rampant in Cambridge Mass. On the personal side, my mother as a young person was a survivor of the massacres that occurred in Turkey in the second decade of the 20th century. My father, also of Armenian descent, was a political and social activist when he arrived in this country, hoping for a better life and a better society. I believe my mother's appreciation of human suffering which she endured and witnessed during the massacres, and my father's convictions about a more just social order, combined to stir in me an early sensitivity about what is disordered in our human nature and in society.

I trained in psychiatry at the Massachusetts Mental Health Center (MMHC), a program that was still steeped in psychoanalytic traditions of probing for the psychodynamic underpinnings of psychopathology. A most central influence for many of us in training at MMHC was the influence of a great teacher/clinician, Elvin Semrad, who had the capacity to demonstrate with patients that unbearable affect had precipitated their major mental illness. Inspiring teachers following in Semrad's footsteps were superb mentors such as Les Havens and John Mack who upheld and further instilled the notion that human psychological distress was more often the focus that should be appreciated by the student as well as the patient. I was also fortunate that my training analyst was at least as concerned about my discomforts as he was about the content of my unconscious.

Upon completion of my psychiatric training in 1967, and after a year of staff work at MMHC I shifted my main academic and training activities to our then fledgling department of psychiatry at the Cambridge Hospital. As I have indicated, within two short years we were barraged by the heroin problem, thus being the stimulus for initiating the methadone maintenance program in 1970. Needless to say, despite being in the middle of my psychoanalytic training, I had to overcome my own stereotype (i.e., counter-transference) of heroin addicts as menacing, unfeeling individuals. Adopting an adaptational perspective, my initial prejudices were quickly overcome by my discovering the preeminently human vulnerabilities of the heroin dependent patients I was evaluating and treating. Above all beyond their behavioral difficulties, more than anything, I quickly became aware how discomforted by and intolerant of feelings these patients were. Of course what I was realizing was that my personal background and mentoring was serving me well—namely, that at its roots, most human problems had suffering and distress at their roots. I believe this understanding has been a principal factor in engaging and sustaining my interests in understanding and treating individuals with addictive vulnerability.

MW: What interests me about what you say is that you heard about or witnessed two large-scale disasters—that of the Armenian holocaust, somewhat occluded in the West, but no doubt much alive in the memories of your parents, and that of the heroin epidemic, not just a few individuals but a veritable social and group phenomena. Can you say anything more about the basis of your identification with people at the margins of society?

EK: Interesting that you chose the term "margins." In the epilogue of my book, *Treating Addiction as a Human Process* published in 1999,[1] I make a plea for "marginality." However, I use the term "marginality" not in its contemporary usage of being peripheralized (and as your question suggests). Rather I use it more in the sense that Harvard sociologist Everett Stonequist popularized in 1937 in his book *The Marginal Man*.[2] To quote from my book:

1. Khantzian, E. J. (1999). *Treating Addiction as a Human Process.* Northvale, NJ: Jason Aronson.
2. Stonequist, E. V. (1937). *The Marginal Man: A Study in Personality and Culture Conflict.* New York: Charles Scribner's Sons.

For Stonequist, marginality referred more to residing between different worlds, or more precisely, being in the margins between different cultures, different ethnic/religious groups, and between different ways of thinking and/or viewing the world. He described how it was the lot of certain individuals to never feel entirely comfortable in one world or another but rather to be destined to reside between them, never totally free to join one or the other, and ultimately positioned to see both the folly and wisdom in different domains. In this respect, I consider myself a "marginal man." Both my parents came from a different world and thus I am a first generation ethnic that by Stonequist's description makes me a marginal person. (Khantzian 1999, 666)

As you can see marginality has a different connotation for me, but I believe it helps to get to your question of what might make it likely that I could identify with individuals who are "at the margins."

As Stonequist suggests, having identifications in more than one world makes it easier (and perhaps even compels) to tune into a world or domain other than one's own. When we started the Methadone Maintenance Program (MMP) in the early 1970s I quickly became aware of the degrading and glorifying terms the opiate dependent patient used to describe themselves their practices, and the drugs they used. One term, "junky," stood out as a way they refereed to themselves and each other. This might have contributed to my counter-transference that they were "menacing, unfeeling individuals," thus they were of another world, certainly not mine. I believe, however, that being of another mind, that is to dwell between the two worlds, facilitated and perhaps compelled a need in me to explore parallels and similarities in each other's worlds. Clearly in the non-addicted world we also refer to ourselves, and each other, in degrading and glorifying ways.

A very imposing, large African American male who was one of our first MMP patients embodied this theme for him and me. He was principled, admirable and attractive at the same time that he was unprincipled, deplorable and off putting. Given the extreme parallel emotions he evoked in me, and as we got to know each other better, I once quipped with him that we could write a history of the MMP together. I suggested that the title would be "The Memoirs of a Junky and a Puritan." Left unsettled was who would write which part.

MW: Yes, marginality and being caught "between worlds" can have advantages in terms of seeing and understanding. Coming to the figure of the "addict," we know that all societies have intoxicants, favoured or otherwise, and that all substances or activities have the potential for being used excessively; what is it about the modern "drug addict" that attracts so much stigma and social opprobrium? Why are they feared and what are the sources of shame/hostility attached to what they do? Can they, paradoxically, say something useful about who *we* are?

EK: Your question is in three parts which are interrelated and, as you suggest, are linked to the penchant to get stuck too much in one's own world. Briefly, with regard to stigma and the opprobrium that addicts evoke, the opposite of "marginality" probably is "insularity"; it is that unrelenting human tendency to wall-in or wall-out ourselves from others around beliefs, prejudices, and stereotypes—the proverbial "us versus them" reaction. The process, in my opinion, is more often fueled by another basic aspect of life—namely, the inevitability of pain and suffering. Our suffering can stimulate growth and change, or it can cause immature and mean-spirited reactions, including insensitivity, entitlement, and externalizing one's hatred for his/her lot in life. Unfortunately, active addicts, in regressive states of their own, behave badly and provocatively and thus become easy targets for nonaddicts' discontents and intemperate reactions.

Clearly, those who are nonaddicts also struggle, more or less, with their discontents, powerlessness, and fears. The feelings of shame and hostility this engenders resonate with the feelings and shame of the addict. The vulnerabilities of addicted individuals frighten us because they remind us too much of our own vulnerabilities involving loss of control (i.e., emotions and behavior) and powerlessness.

Perhaps what the lot of addicted individuals might best teach us, if they could make their case clear, and often they do in recovery, is that we all struggle with issues of suffering, discontrol, and powerlessness. The addicted person is not alone in craving for alternatives which relieve them and/or empower them.

MW: If I could take you back to the early days, as a psychiatrist and psychoanalyst in a methadone prescribing service, I am interested in knowing about how you found your way in conceptual terms. Did you identify with a particular psychoanalytic approach at the time? And did you use other, non-psychoanalytic models of intervention as well?

EK: My psychoanalytic training was through the Boston Psychoanalytic Society and Institute (BPSI). I was trained to consider and interpret mental life "from the ego side," the emphasis being to stay with what was observable. This was to avoid wild speculations about the unconscious and running the risk of being a "couch diver" (i.e., someone who unjustifiably speculated about deep unconscious processes). The emphasis thus was more on a structural psychology rather than a conflict psychology. This better suited my temperament to stay with the here-and-now aspects of the therapeutic relationship, an approach I believe to be particularly well suited for personality disordered patients. My early and ongoing interactions with our methadone patients repeatedly left me pondering how these patients were unique. What was it in their backgrounds and personality makeup that made them so intolerant of painful feeling and so prone to action and activity? I became particularly interested in trying to understand the special ways the patients experienced their emotions and how they expressed, or failed to express, their feelings. At the same time I wondered about their repeated mishaps and unregulated behaviors that caused such patients so much self-harm. They seemed to be less governed by self-destructive drives (a not uncommon psychoanalytic theory), but that their self-harm was more the result of developmental deficits in which self-care functions were diminished or absent.

I believe my perspective and treatment approaches were also guided by the then burgeoning developments in psychopharmacology. Within the two decades surrounding my psychiatric training we had gone from an era of referring to "major" and "minor" tranquilizers (my first year of training) to designating our psychotropic medications by their specific actions (by the second year of training), that is, anti-anxiety, anti-depressant, and anti-psychotic agents. Based on these developments, not insignificantly, I found myself wondering what particular affects or kinds of distress our methadone patients might be self-medicating, and how might this dictate their treatment needs with respect to both psychopharmacologic and psychosocial approaches.

MW: In the early days, did you take any patients into intensive psychotherapy, even into analysis? (If so) what were some of your overall recollections?

EK: It was virtually impossible to administer the methadone program and at the same time treat patients in the program. This was because we had to often make unpopular administrative decisions which made it difficult to maintain a consistent positive treatment relationship with the patients. Being in the middle of my psychoanalytic training I was therefore anxious to take "all comers" in my private practice to learn as much as I could about these challenging patients. The patients I saw were almost exclusively in individual psychotherapy on a once- or twice-a-week basis. They were dependent either on alcohol, opiates, or amphetamines (the stimulants of the 1970s), or some combination of these agents. By the early 1980s I was combining individual psychotherapy with group psychotherapy. I also realized that I had one patient in psychoanalysis that unknown to me, prior to commencing analysis, was alcoholic. Despite differences in their socioeconomic backgrounds, I was surprised that there were more similarities than differences in the dynamics and vulnerabilities displayed by the methadone patients, the private therapy cases, and the one psychoanalytic patient. Of course what I was observing was much of what I have lectured and written about over the subsequent three and a half decades. Some of the most bewildering and bedeviling aspects of therapeutic work were the patients' not knowing or expressing their feelings (processes I came to understand later as "alexithymia" and disaffection), the intolerability of painful affects, and the apparent obliviousness to the potential and actual danger and self-harm inherent in the practices and behaviors associated with their addictions.

One striking parallel comes to mind between the methadone patients and the one psychoanalytic patient who was alcoholic. It involved a counter-transference reaction on my part, which to some extent still persists—namely, the visceral reaction of recoil and/or alarm that I experience witnessing the dangerous and self-injurious behavior and activities that patients enact and report. In the case of the methadone patients, I recall the same monotonous tone and indifference when I probed for feelings when the patient first broke the "needle barrier" (i.e., the transition from snorting, smoking, or swallowing drugs to shoot them intravenously). The tone and indifference of the patients were elicited in response to my reaction of repugnance (but put more tactfully) which I shared with them. They would say such things as "no, doc, I didn't feel scared . . . or uncomfortable; no, I didn't give it much thought." Meanwhile, I am feeling and thinking, "My God, how scary, how dangerous . . . to put a drug in your veins . . . and not know who your pharmacist is." On a less dramatic count, as I listened to the gifted and promising psychologist in his analysis I was similarly alarmed as he described the embarrassment and other risks he chanced with his excessive drinking. The parallel that I am referring to here is the absence or underdevelopment of "self-care" functions in addictions prone individuals, wherein they repeatedly fail to attend to or be fearful of warnings of danger in the face of the risks associated with their behavior.

MW: Those difficulties around self-care, anticipation of needs, a devil-may-care stance of many substance misusers, which you have written about so persuasively, seemed to have been thought about in two different ways historically. There are those who, like yourself, tend to identify developmental deficits, gaps in maturity and self-integration, subtle or pervasive early trauma and those, I am thinking of some Kleinian analysts (e.g., Rosenfeld, Joseph), whose talk a different language—of malignant narcissism, attacks on linking, destructive or perverse states of mind and the like. Are these differences of emphasis or differences of kind?

EK: Funny you should ask. A quote, source unknown, but I believe by a Kleinian, once said, "It is better to be wicked and bad than helpless and lost." The implication of the quote in this context raises the issue of what is primary and what is secondary—namely, does being lost and helpless breed narcissism or does narcissism cause people to act heedless and as if self-care is beyond or beneath them. I believe so many of the traits of personality disordered individuals people such as bravado, postures of self-importance, contemptuous attitudes toward others, imperiousness, narcissistic rage (the list could go on) are indeed "empowering" defenses in the face of an inner sense of enfeeblement, vulnerability, and helplessness. I am not sure if it is a difference of emphasis or of kind. I suspect it is a matter of temperament and training that causes some of us to prefer the more observable and what is experienced in the treatment relationship versus the preference to draw on complex formulation of the inner terrain of object relations theory which is more inferential and possibly more speculative. (You see, I reveal my bias.) In my experience, the lessons learned from the developmentalists line up more readily with what I and the patient can observe and experience in the treatment relationship. In the case of self-destructive behavior, for example, a Kleinian might speculate that the patient is trying to kill themselves as a "bad object," whereas a developmentalist would invite the patient and the therapist to use the latter's alarm, when it is absent in the patient, to try and understand where they were developmentally cheated or deprived of adequate warning signals in the face of danger. I believe the latter is more empathic and alliance building. When all is said and done, it is likely that one paradigm does not fit all. As Richard Chessick suggested in his book, *The Technique and Practice of Listening in Intensive Psychotherapy* (1989), we need to adopt different "channels" to appropriately tune in on our patients' needs and dilemmas, and if, for example, we feel a "here and now" interactional model is not accessing or tuning in empathically to the patient one might best adopt the object relational model of Klein.

MW: Returning to practice, could you tell me about your initial efforts to see patients in groups? What prompted this and how did you approach it practically?

EK: Group experiences dating back to my late teen have been an important part of my personal and professional development. I have been the beneficiary of some very wise and savvy (and even charismatic—in the best sense of the word) teachers and mentors in this respect. It therefore was not surprising, I believe, to navigate toward and consider using groups for therapeutic ends early in my career as a clinician. When we first started "the methadone program at Cambridge in 1970 we decided to use an intake "rap group" to serve as an introduction to the program and also as a holding process until the patients satisfied federal eligibility requirements for methadone treatment. They were frequently large groups numbering from 12 to 18 participants. The groups were powerful and intense, instructive and revealing. They could also be unsettling and disruptive, albeit often beneficial. We soon decided to harness the beneficial aspect and curtail the disruptive aspects by replacing the rap groups with smaller therapy groups as the central therapeutic feature of the methadone program. Despite the fact that a significant portion of the patients were personality and behaviorally disordered, and thus very challenging, those of us who led such groups quickly came to appreciate the supportive, relational, and transformative influences of group therapy.

I did not begin to regularly use group therapy in my private practice until 10 years later. By then I felt sufficiently experienced and established as an addiction specialist to put some of my individual therapy patients in my groups, and to exercise the opportunity of referrals from other clinicians. A particular realization which influenced me was the growing appreciation that most of my patients needed more support and contact than individual therapy, once or twice a-week, provided. From that vantage point I proceeded to start one and then a second group. Practical and therapeutic considerations that guided me were matching patients (mostly along a subjective, intuitive sense of who might or might not get along with whom), establishing a "critical mass" (i.e., number of patients in the group—six to eight seem to work best for me), techniques which elicited and maximized group cohesive interactions and ones which minimized disruptive or fragmenting interactions. In individual preparatory sessions I shared my "philosophy" of groups—namely, that groups were a place for helpful contact with others, a place to reflect about self and others, a place of safety and confidentiality, and a place which could enhance self-understanding, growth, and change. I expressed the expectation that nobody deliberately hurt another person, and when I was concerned about balance in one direction or the other, that group members should strive for a balance between listening and speaking. I also expressed the usual expectations about payments, punctuality, announcing or calling in about absences, etc. I tried to do most of this in a supportive easy manner, avoiding the pitfall of turning my philosophy and expectations into rigid guides or slavish rules.

MW: Who—and what traditions—influenced your "group philosophy" in particular?

EK: In my personal development and in my career as a clinician I was fortunate to have the influence and guidance of some special and distinguished individual who employed groups as a means to help people find the best in themselves and each other. In my late teens I was invited to join a "study group" led by a Universalist-Unitarian minister, Emerson Schwenk. He was a frustrated therapist with a Rogerian orientation. His kindness, charisma and deep curiosity about human nature and how people got along in groups ignited in me a beginning belief that I too could eventually exercise some of my own potentials in these respects. Through that same group, one of the members recommended me to be a participant in a month-long summer workshop in human relations conducted by the Boston University Human Relations Center. This was in the mid-1950s at a time when the National Training Laboratory (NTL) had come into a place of prominence in studying group processes. Some of their most distinguished faculty—Warren Bennis, Miriam Ritvo, Robert Chin, and Kenneth Benne—comprised the faculty of the Summer Workshop. Dr. Benne seemed to take a special interest in me and encouraged me to appreciate an aptitude in myself for connecting with others and the multiple ways in which the roles and reactions of group participants could enhance or inhibit the helpful influences of groups. I had to wait almost 10 years to begin to test out and clinically apply the early strivings in me about understanding human nature and the special ways it played out in groups. Namely, by my second year of psychiatric training we were obliged to start a therapeutic group and to participate in a didactic training group; I was also asked to run a support group for the staff of a research unit for the severely mentally ill. Two special teachers stand out—Elvin Semrad and Max Day. The former, Dr. Semrad, I have already characterized and his concern about appreciating and acknowledging the central role of painful affect as a driving influence in psychopathology. In addition he had a deep abiding interest in group therapy as a therapeutic instrument. Dr. Day was of the same mold and, in our didactic training, group as our leader, he had a special knack for helping us to appreciate the subtleties of distress and emotional pain that groups can both provoke and resolve.

My least satisfactory experiences with groups, from which I also learned and benefited, were with the therapy groups we were required to lead with patients from the outpatient department, and with the staff support group. In the former case, my supervisor was a tightly wrapped man who seemed more invested in sounding enigmatic and super wise rather optimizing the comforting and connecting aspects of groups. In the case of the support group, either because of my own inexperience, reserve, and anxiety, or the passivity of my supervisor, a daunting element of restraint and prolonged silences persisted and made it a deadly experience for me and the staff, a group in which the staff needed much more from me and from each other.

Early in my career I also was fortunate enough to have met and befriended Norm Neiberg, Scott Rutan, and Ann Alonzo, all highly respected, established clinicians who were ardent advocates for group therapy. I believe all three of them eventually became Presidents of the American Group Psychotherapy Association. Lester Luborsky and associates on supportive-expressive psychotherapy and "core conflictual relationship themes (CCRT), Irving Yalom and Stephanie Brown on interpersonal group psychotherapy with substance abusers, and along similar lines, Marsha Vanicelli and more recently Philip Flores on the centrality of relational needs, were also influential.

MW: Can you tell us more about the origin of the group experiences that you reflect on in *The Vulnerable Self*, with the Harvard Cocaine Recovery Project?

EK: The group experiences reflected upon was a direct outgrowth of the Harvard Cocaine Recovery Project (HCRP). Dr. William McAuliffe, the principal investigator of the project, thought it would be valuable to compare a cognitive-behavioral/relapse prevention experience with a conventional group therapy approach, in turn compared to a control group in which the patients were assigned to attend Cocaine Anonymous meetings—participants in all three groups were also assigned to a counselor who monitored their group participation. An implied condition of my involvement in the project was that I would spearhead writing a manual for the psychodynamic group therapy model which I had recommended. Dr. McAuliffe was a taskmaster—his influence being both burdensome and motivating. I had not thought of writing a book about group therapy, and when he got me to do so I also thought it would not be easy to readily "manualize" the essential and beneficial aspects of a psychodynamic group. The good news was I had available to me two excellent and enthusiastic students, Drs. Sarah Golden and Kurt Halliday, both eager to learn how to run psychodynamic groups for substance abusers. Dr. Golden eventually collaborated on several chapters in the book, and Dr. Halliday ultimately obtained his doctorate based on studying the impact of Modified Dynamic Group Therapy (MDGT) on ego functions in the participants.

I met with Sarah and Kurt on a weekly basis in supervision, initially imparting my philosophy of groups, how they can be helpful, the parameters of group structure and function, and some basic aspects of technique and technical considerations. After that it was reviewing on a week-to-week basis what was going on in their groups. Because it was a federally funded project, we had the luxury of recorded transcripts which allowed us to follow group process in detail. In addition, both Sarah and Kurt had a gift for the work and were open and receptive to guidance and suggestions. In addition, they provided me with many astute insights of their own as to what was special about the population of cocaine dependent patients we were treating (remembering that what I had learned was in private practice under very different circumstances). So the origins were the result of an interaction between some of my special experiences and interests, the gifts and experiences of my collaborators Sarah and Kurt, and the unique needs and experiences with which the cocaine patients were struggling in their attempts at recovery. I would also speculate that it was a very positive experience in my development in that I was being forced to think about and share with my collaborators what I had thought about over the years that were corrective and transformative about group experiences. That is, until then, my patients were the main individuals with whom I had shared my thoughts about groups.

MW: What are the most important qualities for group psychotherapists working with substance misusers?

EK: For starters, a singularly important quality for a group therapist is to consistently maintain a concern about how comfortable and connected the group members are with each other, including the group leader. Namely, the ongoing question the group leader might be asking, "Would I be comfortable with what is going on here?" An empathic group leader might consider this the "Golden Rule" of group psychotherapy. From this basic vantage position the group leader can entertain what he or she can do about it, in concert with the members, to assure comfort and connection. If a group therapist can continue to ask him- or herself, "How would I feel with what transpires in the group therapy?" they are best positioned to facilitate analytic and facilitating responses which assure, balance (e.g., speaking/listening; asking for vs. offering help, etc.), cohesion, comfort and interdependence. Working with the assumption that substance misusers are individuals who have trouble (self-regulation difficulties) with knowing/ tolerating/expressing feelings, self-esteem, relationships, and self-care, a group therapist must be constantly attuned to these vulnerabilities. He or she must be ready to facilitate interactions that positively influence such vulnerabilities and discourage or curtail negative interactions which heighten the vulnerabilities. To achieve such ends, it is important for group therapist to know when to be passive (a good group therapist knows he or she does not have a corner on the market of what is helpful or beneficial), and when to be more active. One best not be a "know-it-all" at one extreme, or an impassive "wooden Indian" at the other extreme. Capacities for listening empathically, speaking knowledgeably and evocatively, a lively and involved sense of humor, can all serve a group therapist well in meeting the needs of substance dependent patients. An effective group therapist must be constantly mindful of how his or her responses and that of the group members can enhance or undermine self-esteem for group members. An effective group leader addresses problematic group interactions by modeling and expecting responses from group members that will preserve self-esteem at the same time concerns for problematic behaviors which occur inside and outside the group are tactfully expressed and processed. The corollary here is that aggressive confrontations by group therapists or members are rarely helpful and, more often, are counterproductive or damaging.

MW: Your emphasis on comfort and reducing resistance reminds me of the spirit of motivational interviewing. Do you agree? And if so, how do you differ?

EK: In most respects I agree. Motivational interviewing (MI) derives from Carl Roger's non-directive counseling method. William Miller has adopted this approach with modifications which include stages and the recommendation that the therapist be more directive (the latter in contrast to Roger's non-directive method). His method again places a premium on techniques which promote a nonjudgmental interviewing approach. MI respects that psychological change is a process and not an event. This suggests to me that MI appreciates the importance of comfort and assuring satisfactory connection. Miller's approach has been manualized and provides a detailed description of how to proceed with stages of initiating and maintaining the treatment relationship. There is little here with which I could take issue, as long as the imperative is empathic listening and speaking. My caveat, which could be offered for any method of treatment, is that such an approach can become too stylized and regimented. I think this is a risk of a staged or manualized approach. In the absence of such a structure or program, the clinician runs the risk of losing the focus and, perhaps, getting lost, especially the inexperienced. The advantage of less structure, as is the case with the psychodynamic method, is that the clinician can cultivate a better sense of attunement, spontaneity, and authenticity in reaction the patient's needs, rather that maintaining concerns about adhering to a more programmed method.

MW: How, in a group, might you deal with persistent boundary breaking or, say, a glamorizing of drug use?

EK: Most likely, I would begin to consider in my own musings first, and then out loud with the group, what it might mean as far as current and ongoing group dynamics, what it might mean in terms of characteristic behaviors for the individuals involved, and what it might have to do with issues of distress which might be driving such behavior. If the behavior is imminently threatening or dangerous to the individuals or the group, I would ask who in the group is alarmed about the behavior, and if such reactions are not apparent or forthcoming from the members, I would sound the note of alarm. In other instances, I sometimes can see alarm on one of the member's face, yet the person might not be aware of their own reaction. In such a case, I might call on that person to check out the reaction which I tell them I see on their face. Obviously if the behavior is destructive and persistent and the members are ineffectual in stopping themselves or each other, it is the responsibility of the leader to take action. This might include an interruption of group participation for the individual(s) involved, or in extreme cases, termination from the group of the problematic individual(s). Frankly, except for my early experience with the methadone rap groups, the latter extreme injunction has not been necessary. Coming back to the behavior that might be in question, I would point out it is probably symptomatic of what the members' vulnerabilities are about (for example, how individuals behave when they are unthinking or not using feelings to guide them—i.e., the self-care vulnerability), and at the same time try to devise or orchestrate reactions (hopefully, elicited from the members, and if not, use my own concerns) to curtail the behavior. As the troublesome behavior subsides, I would then work with the members to try to explore how the particular problem adversely affects the individual and/or the group. Speaking of boundaries, if problem behaviors or reactions can be kept within some reasonable boundaries, the problem can become an opportunity. As I suggested in my prefacing remark, it can become an opportunity to help group members understand how behaviors affect group process and how group interactions can evoke certain behaviors. As I also suggest, the group is a forum which actually fosters a climate in which people can be themselves and identify in each other characterological vulnerabilities and flaws which cause certain behaviors that can be problematic in their lives. When boundary problems occur in the group they are invariably related to the characterologic issues that get them in trouble outside the group. And certainly in my experience, and I suspect for others who are attuned to the affect recognition/tolerance problems that are so much a part of addictive vulnerability, one rather quickly begins to appreciate how much troubling behavior is linked to troubled and troubling feelings. The group becomes a very effective place for members to grow in their appreciation of this link, and how the supportive and empathic interactions which effective groups foster can serve as an extraordinary corrective for such vulnerabilities. As for the specific of patients "glamorizing" drug use, or, as the patients call it, "war stories," such interactions can serve multiple purposes for the individuals and the group, but, in my experience, it more often seems to be avoidance of problematic feelings that the group and or certain individuals are unwilling or unable to face. The group leader encourages the patients to be aware of this trend and to bring it to each other's attention or, if it is not being identified by the members, the leader can point it out.

MW: The word "recovery," from substance misuse, often feels too simple for me. The journey through from one world to another, or the rite of passage, particularly for those committed to abstinence, seems immense: rebuilding of self, relationships, social circumstances, moral direction, and so on. How do you see it?

EK: I periodically have joked that many of my patients coming from the recovery traditions of AA and NA have seemed more mature than some of my so-called well-analyzed colleagues. What my "joke" is about is that successful psychological treatments of any kind, at their best, stimulate emotional growth and personality change. To paraphrase Enid Balint, a psychoanalysis might overcome neurosis but not necessarily make an individual more mature, but with group experiences an individual might not be less neurotic but they are inevitably more mature. Working with patients in groups, keeps forcing on us and our patients the realization that we keep wanting to have the world comply with our preferences for how we manage our lives and how we conduct ourselves. Group experiences help us to carry on the cost-benefit analysis of our ways of doing business. In some instances the group affirms the merit if not the magnificence of our strengths, and when they are less than meritorious, we are gently and persistently reminded that the case is otherwise, as we jar ourselves and others with the disadvantages of holding out for our own ways. The edgy smooth out, the timid become bolder, the boorish become more considerate, and the pompous become more humble. Best of all, as your question suggests, we are freer, or less enslaved by our previous insistent ways of being. We are freer to explore possibilities of what we can better discover in ourselves and others, in the myriad of possibilities in relationships, in the caring about ideas, in appreciating new-found values, and in realizing the needs of other human beings. The gift of recovery goes far beyond relieving the symptoms of addictive behavior. The processes that an individual goes through to achieve sobriety albeit arduous and painful, stimulates growing capacities for a more flexible life; we better cope with experiences and relationships that otherwise were impossible, at the same time unforeseen possibilities are perceived as opportunities rather than impediments which cannot be overcome.

MW: I'd like to finish with a question about values. Perhaps the central tragedy of addiction is a loss of meaning, as more and more salience attaches to the drug. Rebuilding requires a reconstruction of meaning, which lends purpose to the change a person tries to bring about. But what of the values that sustain the therapist? Am I right in sensing the influence of humanist values in your own outlook?

EK: I sat down to write my response to your question on a day when I interviewed in a case conference a very difficult, refractory-to-treatment substance dependent patient. He was in a general medical treatment unit, recovering from amputation of the toes, fingers of his right foot being necessitated by frost-bite which had occurred secondary to a debilitating drug-alcohol run which had reduced him to living on the street. He had been dismissive of treatment alternatives which were being proposed on his unit, and during my interview with him he alternated a seeming compliance with a dismissive and disdainful attitude. Of significance was a horrendous childhood history of sexual and physical abuse. At a number of points during the interview I alternated between feeling therapeutic despair and my own disdain in response to his confusion which was intermixed with his testy attitude of contempt.

Your question made me think what kind of values help a clinician to hang in with such a difficult patient. It reminded me again of where we started with this interview—namely, in our lot as humans we share with our patients the inescapability of suffering, and our patients are not the only ones who can react to that suffering in unredeeming ways. Indeed, humanistic values of compassion and care help us to appreciate how the challenges of life can be difficult enough, but how much more difficult it must be to have suffered the trauma of a holocaust, whether it be a people or an individual. I remain convinced that suffering is at the heart of addictive disorders, whatever else might be going in the brain with such conditions. Our humanistic values keeps us attuned to what is essentially important with our patients—namely, how they experience their suffering and the ways they express or fail to express their pain and discomfort. I believe our values help us to sustain the distress and the less than redeeming feelings that our patients' reactions can engender, as suggested by the mutual reactions I and the patient experienced in the above interview.

MW: Dr. Khantzian, thank you for your time and the pleasure of this interview.

CHAPTER 13

"Dangerous Desires and Inanimate Attachments"

MODERN PSYCHODYNAMIC APPROACHES TO SUBSTANCE MISUSE

With Martin Weegmann

Although psychodynamic approaches to addiction have not been prominent in the field, compared with a range of other psychosocial models, it is our contention that such approaches offer a unique and subtle complement to our understanding of the nature of addition and addictive suffering, an understanding in depth. We regard this approach as complementary rather than competing with others, such as motivational enhancement, relapse prevention, 12-step facilitation and so on. A psychodynamic perspective is of great value to clinicians in their efforts to reach an emotionally hard-to-reach population of clients and formal psychoanalytic therapy (and, more commonly, psychodynamically informed therapy) can be of considerable help to many clients as they forge the psychic journey that underpins recovery. Not only this, but psychodynamic understanding is a solid resource to the clinician, regardless of the approach they use, as a way of better containing the complicated and uncomfortable emotions and reactions they can feel in response to their clients.

Laying out our general convictions, we think that it is difficult to comprehend the nature of additive suffering, as well as the successful overcoming of such suffering, without:

- Postulating some notion of the "internal world," with an intricate layering of affect, cognition, memory and learning. Addiction represents a life lived *in extremis,* requiring a corresponding concept of "extreme internal worlds."
- An understanding of "irrationality," by which we mean that thinking, action and judgment becomes disconnected, short-term and self-defeating (see Sutherland's [1993] interesting exploration of concept of the dimension of irrationality in all human affairs).

- An appreciation of powerful psychological forces, if one wills, including unconscious, in which individuals are caught between quite different positions and motivations. Indeed, the very term "psycho-dynamic" has from its inception been concerned with such forces and their configurations, which are hard to describe except perhaps by metaphors. Thus individuals with addiction often present as torn individuals, struggling with "different selves" and contradictory "self states," as captured by such popular expressions as "like Jekyll and Hyde," "it wasn't me" or "I'm out of character when using."
- An understanding of the serious dysregulations of life, emotion and relationships associated with substance misuse. This requires thinking about predisposing addictive vulnerabilities and the devastating, traumatizing consequences of immersion in a world of using. Chronic substance misuse has an enveloping effect on individuals, subsuming more and more aspects of their lives, from which people protect themselves by complicated rationales and defenses. Unfortunately, blunted empathy, for self and others, and denial of one's wider needs is a concomitant of this envelopment (Weegmann and Khantzian 2011).
- Acknowledging the complicated emotions, reactions and strains that are aroused in workers who help those with substance misuse, traditionally called "counter-transferences" and which are seldom explicitly addressed by other approaches.
- An in-depth understanding of the process by which individuals can and do exit addictive careers, re-building damaged selves. A concept of "internal recovery" is proposed to describe this process of psychic change.

Early psychoanalytic and psychodynamic treatments rested principally on a passive model of interaction by the therapist in which she/he was detached, remote, and depended mainly on interpretive interventions. We do not shrink from criticism of such approaches, which have suffered from old-fashioned, Freudian formulations, obscure language and speculative concepts, usually focused on the entirely regressive and self-destructive aspects of the disorder. By contrast, contemporary psychodynamic theory and practice places greater emphasis on the centrality of emotions, self-regulation, interpersonal relations, self-care, the treatment alliance, and here-and now observations. Emphasis is placed on active support, empathy, a focus on recurrent themes that occur in and out of therapy, and an emphasis on developmental factors to understand current emotional and relational difficulties clients experience in treatment that parallel experiences outside of treatment (Weegmann and Khantzian 2011). Collaborative, active and phase-appropriate therapy is important in assessment and treatment of addictive disorders. In their contribution to the American textbook *Psychotherapy for the Treatment of Substance Misuse*, Lighdale, Mack, and Frances

(2011, 243) state, "Application of psychodynamic understanding—including attention to the unconscious, child development, ego function, affect regulation and efforts to enhance self-esteem and deal with shame and other narcissistic vulnerability—widens the range of patients who can be treated." Similarly, colleagues in the United Kingdom have explored the rich variety of ways in which such understanding can help (Weegmann and Cohen 2002).

We begin by highlighting three different psychodynamic traditions, followed by our integrative view of addiction as a disorder of self-regulation.

Primitive Emotional States; Kleinian Views

Just as Freud saw the child within the adult, Melanie Klein saw the infant within the child (Segal 1973). What happens from the earlier stages of development onward constitute developmental templates through which the growing infant makes sense of the world and manages rudimentary emotional life. Klein was centrally concerned with the earliest forces, as it were, of mental life and what it is that enables small steps to integration and growth to proceed. Her, albeit cumbersome, terms to characterize struggles around growth were the "paranoid-schizoid position," marked by threats, persecutory anxieties and all-good/all-bad polarities and the "depressive position," in which the infant is able to experience a more mixed world and to experience early forms of guilt and initiate reparative efforts. She posited "positions" rather than stages, because of the to-and-fro movement between them, continuing to a degree throughout life and in response to stress, when we are all capable of "reverting" in our response and coping.

Space does not permit a full review of the Kleinian tradition, in relation to substance misuse, but we venture the following hypotheses:

(a) Addiction increasingly creates, or re-creates, early emotional states. It reinforces a primitivization of emotions, returning people, as it were, to more paranoid-schizoid functioning; a battle ensues between omnipotent ways of dealing with the world, assisted by drugging, versus the desire to change (English 2009).

(b) Drug use is anti-growth, with addiction seen as a form of psychic evasion and evacuation of pain. Developmental "shortcuts" in the form of "fixes," "rushes," and "highs" impair or halt maturation (Hyatt-Williams 1978).

(c) There is often a wavering of positions, in which addicted individuals at one point see the damage they are doing, struggling to resist its intense pull, whilst at another point succumb to it, rejecting the need for change or any consideration of reality. This reflects a deep, powerful form of ambivalence, more malignant than the "motivational dilemmas" postulated by motivational interviewing approaches. It is an added reason why presumed "change for the better" (e.g., stopping use) can lead to a paradoxical counterreaction (e.g., returning to use), as change is felt to be dangerous. This wavering of psychic positions is often seen between and within sessions, with moment-to-moment shifts in motivation and the expression of contradictory aims.

(d) Dependence on drugs is a striking enactment of what one distinguished Kleinian analyst calls "psychic retreats" (Steiner 1993). Psychic retreats are defined as pathological organizations based around powerful avoidances, whose functioning and maintenance feels like a matter of survival to the person concerned. Related terms come to mind: sanctuaries, bastions, refuges; interestingly, however, some of the terms that refer to avoidances can also refer in our field to places of healing, constituting a different kind of retreat. While not referring to specifically to addiction, Steiner writes of such retreats, "Whether idealised or persecutory, it is clung to as preferable to even worse states which the patient is convinced are the only alternatives" (1993, 2). One of the tragedies of drug addiction is how the seeking of retreats can become a way of extreme and habituated life.

(e) The process of recovery from addiction involves a process of repair—to self, body, spirit and relationships. Reparation is central to the depressive position and psychic integration. Reparation is fragile and personalities can easily revert to simpler, more primitive postures. In the analysis of a violent man, Anderson (1997) refers to an "internal tyranny" that would periodically assert itself, with rapid shifts in which his client could make progress, only to "put the boot in" at a subsequent stage. Thus, guilt is difficult to experience and old ways are difficult to relinquish.

VIGNETTE

Peter sought help for his problems from a psychologist, acknowledging that his life was "mortgaged" to self-destruction and self-neglect. He was ashamed of this and was worried that he had left it "too late to change." Peter easily undermined his own progress, throwing caution to the wind. In one session, he observed, "I can put it this way, the nearest thing I can find to being at ease, really at ease, is by using. And OK, I hate where it leads me, the day after, but I keep going back, by which time it's a classic 'fuck it.'" He was puzzled by the seeming commitment by his therapist, offering the (serious?) joke, "You've either got to be mad or very brave to deal with me." There was an appreciative side to his also, in his comment that "I almost gave up on trying to understand myself over the years—you know, just became an unquestioning addict."

COMMENT

The psychologist was aware that Peter's state of motivation and goals were forever oscillating and that this was evident in the consulting room, where Peter turned to his psychologist both as a symbolic ally against drugs, while undoing and even mocking the help offered at one and the same time. Drug misuse had indeed constituted a form of psychic retreat for Peter, from the wider demands, responsibilities and potential of the world and self, hence the "unquestioning addict." His therapy illustrated just how precarious was his struggle to get beyond the "addict" which dominated his life, internal and external.

Comforting Self-Objects: Kohutian Views

Kohut (1971, 1977) appreciated how troubled early parenting interactions around admiring, being admired, comfort, and soothing left individuals so affected to suffer with troubled self-states and poor self-esteem. Although he did not systemically consider how these formulations related to the development of substance use disorders, he offered important observations about how self-disturbances could predispose to and result in dependence on substances. Kohut and subsequent recent investigators have emphasized how the addictively prone suffer from a lack of inner cohesion, fragmentation, feelings of powerlessness, and helplessness. Originally Kohut (1971) stressed that substances were not sought out as substitutes for loved or loving objects but were adopted as a "replacement for a defect in psychological structure" (46). Subsequently he emphasized disturbances in the organization of self-structures characterized by states of disempowerment, helplessness, and low self-regard resulting in defenses of grandiosity, disavowal of need, and self-sufficiency, alternating with exaggerated needs for comfort and validation from others. Based on this latter conceptualization he proposed that substance users resort to their drugs to lift these defenses and allow self-soothing and revitalization of a better sense of well-being that they are otherwise so devoid of. Balint (1968) anticipated this view when he described alcoholics' dependency as a "basic fault." He proposed it is "something wrong in the mind, a kind of deficiency which must be put right" . . . [to establish a sense of] . . . "harmony—a feeling that everything is now well between them and their environment-and . . . the yearning for this feeling of harmony is the most important cause of alcoholism or, for that matter, any form of addiction" (56).

Dodes (1996, 2002) and Director (2005) have extended these ideas to explain recurrent relapse and the compulsive nature of addiction, and Khantzian (2003) to clarify the repetitious nature of addictive behavior as a means to control addictive suffering. Dodes explained how feelings of helplessness and related narcissistic rage were key in relapse and use of drugs, and Director described emotional states of powerlessness and unimportance and reactive attitudes of omnipotence leading to repeated relapse.

Little wonder that low to moderate doses of alcohol release restricted, self-sufficient individuals from their constricting defenses, or stimulants activate and enliven those suffering with their states of emptiness, feeling vacuous, or impotent; and similarly boost or augment defensive postures of grandiosity and invincibility. Opiates, and heavy doses of alcohol on a different basis, cause individuals struggling with threatening and disorganizing aggression and rage to discover how these agents can feel like a magical elixir to produce a state of comfort and containment when otherwise it is elusive. Whether is an incomplete and impoverished sense of self, intense disorganizing affect, or restricting and immobilizing defenses, it is not surprising that the powerful feeling altering properties of addictive drugs can become so alluring and compelling for those whose sense of self and self-regard is insufficient or underdeveloped.

VIGNETTE

Mary was asked to write an imaginative "Letter to Alcohol" as part of her therapy. Amongst the things expressed included, "When I drink you . . . the buzz you give me feels like protection . . . I can control and use you to help me, like a liquid talisman. It makes me feel so calm and peaceful . . . without you I feel so alone, bereft." Mary went on, in the letter, to describe chronic shyness as teenager and how discovery of alcohol lifted confidence, enabling social interaction and assertion.

COMMENT

The letter suggests that self-soothing is part of the compelling attraction of alcohol for Mary. Developmentally it seemed that her resources of self were felt to be wanting and that alcohol did at the time—and subsequently—lift those resources and was increasingly incorporated into her coping with life. We underestimate the "comforting" effects of substances at our peril, even as it co-exists with familiar negative consequences. The letter read somewhat as a "love letter," a tribute, and notwithstanding the physiological dimensions of tolerance and drink dependence, provides a useful insight into how she relates to her substance, at an experiential level. Incorporated into her narcissistic economy as it were, the threat of change and managing without alcohol is considerable.

Inanimate Attachments: Bowlbian Views

Attachment theory is celebrated for its productivity and influence, reaching far beyond the confines of psychoanalysis; it offers not only a theory of attachments but also one of motivation, cognitive appraisal, psychobiology and information processing; a complex disorder, addiction affects all of these domains. Here we enumerate four substantive contributions of attachment theory to addictions and are informed in this respect by the seminal contributions of Phil Flores (2004) in the United States and Bill Reading (2002) in the United Kingdom.

(a) Misattachment to drugs. In their relationships to drugs, people with substance misuse can truly be said to develop "alternative attachments," which are strong, passionate and consuming. In this sense there is a psychic "take over," which distorts thinking, feeling and acting, not to mention the "commandeering" of aspects of brain functions, including learning, reward and memory. The interpersonal consequences of addiction are devastating, summed up in its extremes in the Narcotics Anonymous saying, "We don't make relationships; we take hostages." Features associated with ordinary attachment needs have similarities and parallels with attachment to inanimate substances, such as proximity maintenance, homeostasis, and separation distress and so on. In an evocative turn of phrase, Reading (2002) refers to the transfer by which "affectional bonds" are replaced by "addictional bonds."

(b) Internal working models. As mediators of attachment experiences, Bowlby (1973, 203) explains, "Each individual builds working models of the world and of himself in it, with the aid of which he perceives events, forecasts the future, and constructs his plans." Again, in parallel to ordinary processes of attachment, the user develops an alternative internal working model of the drug, as to what can be expected, what is sought and so on. Drug experiences and memories gain in salience, and just as Bowlby suggested a hierarchy of internal working models, so Reading (2012) argues that the "drug insinuates itself ever higher in the individual's hierarchy of internal working models with a corresponding relegation of person-to-person models to lower status within the hierarchy."

(c) Attachment disorders. The issue of predisposition and early vulnerability to addictive disorders is enormously complex, with attachment theory offering an excellent basis for research. As this is explored elsewhere in the book, we simply comment that there is seldom an easy "either/or" explanation with respect to addictive vulnerability and that developmental pathways into addiction are highly varied (Khantzian 1974). Over time, there is, however, invariably an inverse relation between substance abuse and healthy interpersonal attachments.

(d) Recovery and discovery. Attachment-oriented therapy uses the paradigm of attachment theory as framework for helping those with substance misuse to rebuild their lives, referring to the graded ways in which attachment to drugs and drug mechanisms can be replaced by, hopefully, healthier, human attachments of various sorts.

VIGNETTE

Carl is a 49-year-old orthopedic surgeon whose license was suspended after colleagues discovered and reported that beyond his heavy drinking he had resorted to periodic use of an anesthetic inhalant. He explained that he had resorted to the agent because it was easier to disguise, versus the alcohol, his need to escape persistent feelings of dysphoria. He also added that he thought his use of alcohol in early adolescence was motivated by similar feelings which he discovered was temporarily relieved by alcohol.

As a child he describes a sense of persistent feelings of being disconnected and lonely. Although he feels his mother was well intentioned, he always sensed an emotional vacuum. Carl attributed his mother's emotional shallowness to the fact that she was a middle child among nine siblings. He concluded that mother's remoteness was compounded when she gave birth to twin daughters when he was three years old. He and his therapist adopted the term that his mother did not have enough to go around and that he was "back-burnered" after their birth. His keen intelligence helped in that he retreated to his room as an avid and curious reader and achieved considerable academic recognition and success in school. While his father was kind, he worked long hours in a foundry and was not actively involved with him in his growing up years.

The following is a near verbatim account of his emotional reactions in a therapy session following a weekend visit home to his elderly parents that seemed to repeat and amplify a lifelong sense of anhedonia, despair, and near suicidal depressive feelings.

> His opening statement was "Man! I feel bad when I go home; it sucks the life out of me . . . I regress; it takes the life out of me. I feel irritable, strange. Observing myself I feel bad about my reactions—there's no reason." (In a subsequent group therapy meeting he summed up that weekend with his parents by saying he felt "shitty.") With a little prompting by his therapist, he conceded that this was much like feelings from his childhood wherein he would get quiet. Agreeing, he recalled how it was always very difficult to engage his parents, especially his mother. He used to wonder if they even noticed their disconnection. His therapist asked him to elaborate. Carl gave the example how on this most recent visit

mom kept irrelevantly referring to a Principal's Award in high school that he had received for which he felt there was no great significance. He said he had tried to speak to her about the death of her two sisters who had passed away over the past six months; he also learned for the first time that her father, his grandfather, had been hospitalized for a "nervous breakdown." In both instance he described how she could hardly sustain the conversation and did not express any emotion. He said, "Little or nothing was said or shared." In this context, he shifted and recalled how when he was 12 or 13 years old experiencing a lot of frustration, like there was something missing . . . "I felt hopeless, a weight, like there was no point going on." He wondered out loud that already at that age it explained the pull of alcohol on him. He elaborated a bit about his exchanges that weekend with his father. Carl said he felt again the old despair about the disconnect with his father, and how he had to deal then and now with the gaps in the conversation with him. Touchingly he shifted back to his mother and said, "My mother has a story to tell but she won't tell it." He agreed when his therapist corrected him and said, "She can't."

COMMENT

When Reading speaks of substituting inanimate connections for human ones, Carl's story typifies and gives meaning to how this occurs. His poignant recount and characterization of the weekend was painfully repeating and evoking in the present the long standing distress and discomforting and insecure attachment that haunted him throughout his growing up years into the present. The case illustrates how useful and sensitizing it is bear a clients' attachment styles and proclivities in mind and their subtle re-enactment during the course of therapy. The therapist also has to maintain reflective examination of the nature of their own responses to clients and how these can be optimized.

Bringing It Together: Addiction as Disorder of Self-Regulation

Clinical work with substance users reveals that the complex developmental, troubled self-states, and attachment issues involved in addictions pre-eminently lend themselves to the depth explorative and interactional aspects of psychodynamic psychotherapy. Addicted individuals suffer, the suffering compels them to use, and they know not why. Drug-dependent behavior is driven and notorious for the absence of self-reflection. The problem is that much of the behavior derives from infancy and early development for which there are no memories, words, or mental representations (Gedo 1986; Khantzian 1995; Krystal 1988; Lichtenberg 1983). Dodes (1996) for this reason characterizes addictions as a compulsive disorder. Psychodynamic psychotherapy can be fundamentally useful and beneficial in accessing, identifying, and therapeutically addressing these early predisposing and subsequent developmental factors, as well as the consequences, involved in addictive attachments and behaviors.

In our work we have found it useful to conceptualize addiction as a self-regulation disorder. Guided by object-relation, self-psychology, and attachment theory, a formulation of addiction as a self-regulation disorder allows for an understanding of how deficits and dysfunctions in regulating emotions, self-esteem, relationships, and self-care are important, if not essential, to the development and maintenance of addictive disorders. As we have described, investigators adopting a developmental perspective remind psychotherapist how early life experiences are fundamentally important in subsequently influencing all these aspects of self-regulation in adult life and, when derailed, can contribute to and result in the self-regulation disturbances that govern so much of addictive behavior.

As we have indicated the addictively prone become powerfully and passionately attached to their drugs of choice—dangerous desires. This is so because the drugs work—short term. The psychoactive properties of addictive drugs interact with the suffering and deficits in the regulation of affect, self-states, object relations, and self-care in helping individuals to cope with these deficits. In the case of affects, addictively vulnerable individuals experience their emotions in the extreme, wherein they are intense and overwhelming or elusive or absent; thus feelings are unavailable to guide reactions and behavior (Krystal 1988; McDougall 1984; Krystal and Raskin 1970). Depending on the drug, it relieves or changes the confusion and distress of such extremes in feeling. Similarly, the pain accompanying self-other relationships of emptiness, dissociation, and helplessness, or compensatory disavowal of needs, interpersonal cutoff, and counterdependence powerfully interact with drug effects to create for the while the sense that all is well. It is for these reasons that such reactions are incorrectly characterized as euphoria or pleasure. As Reading (2002) has indicated, the power of addiction resides in the fact that the addictive experience creates the illusion that substances can replace affectional bonds with addictive ones. It is worth noting in this respect, despite deficits in cognitive functions and memory associated with addiction, that drug dependent individuals vividly remember how powerfully "corrective" the ingestion of addictive drugs are, and why Reading observes that the drug experience becomes superordinate to all other interpersonal considerations and priorities.

It is for the above reason that therapist best not be impassive, remote, and insufficiently interactive. Therapists' energy, fine tuning, and readiness to evoke and create words and emotions with patients can support, comfort and reassure, as the interactive and empathic aspects of psychotherapy create an anlage for patients to grow and develop in these underdeveloped aspects of personality organization. The climate of comfort and mutual respect afforded by this more contemporary psychotherapeutic approach also allows for a gentle challenge to interpersonal and psychic isolation and the characterologic defenses that maintain it. Such an approach also allows the emergence, examination, and resolution of disavowed, competing, and ambivalent parts of self that produces so much internal and interpersonal distress, conflict, and addictive responses. The comfort found in drugs is gradually replaced by the comfort initially stimulated in the therapeutic relationship, and subsequently, the comfort that can be experienced in one's relationship with self and others as internal intrapsychic and interpersonal barriers are therapeutically lifted and resolved.

Reflective Practice

As noted, chronic substance misuse undermines reflective self-functions; as habits strengthen, alternatives recede and users immunize themselves, there is a corresponding loss of emotional range, cognitive flexibility and empathy for self and others. Here, however, we briefly touch upon the importance for the therapist in maintaining good reflective functions in the face of the difficult and discomforting feelings that the work can arouse. The traditional term in analytic tradition for this is the "counter-transference," although we believe that this is a somewhat unwieldy term (indeed, we do not always know what the "counter" aspect is; Weegmann 2003). Suffice to note, that in a disorder characterized by dysregulations of life and emotion, extreme internal worlds and irrationality, the worker can find it hard to contain and make sense of the responses which are aroused. After all, we witness chaotic worlds, crisis and drama, escalating situations and reversals (slips, relapses, demotivations) all the time. Misalignments occur easily, as we are baffled by the power of addictions to subvert progress, resulting in challenges to empathy, as illustrated in the following case.

VIGNETTE

Millie is a single woman in her late 40s whom I (EJK) have been following for about 18 months. She has been through no less than six detoxes and four rehab stints during that time. She has experienced severe medical and psychiatric complications as a consequence of the relapses. She is a remarkably bright individual and has succeeded in two professional careers but has languished professionally and vocationally for about the past decade. After several months working with her in individual and group psychotherapy, on a particular morning she was complaining about how her mother just doesn't get that her priorities are different from that of her mother. She gave the example of her 86-year-old mother's inclination to go to bed early (e.g., around 9 p.m.). Millie described how mother might get up subsequently while Millie was still up watching TV and her mother somewhat commandingly would refer to the time, implying, "Isn't this the time to be in bed?" What was striking about this was to witness Millie uncharacteristically bristle in describing this, bitterly complaining how still at the age of 49 years old her mom was still trying to run her life.

Mother is an impressive, regal lady. In the ninth decade of her life she still has a manner and a precise way of talking that makes her convictions about how life should be imposing and difficult to take issue with, an aspect of Millie's relationship with her mom that has always been difficult. This whether it be how she times matters of when it's okay to go to bed, trying to get her mother to understand the compelling disease nature of her alcoholism, or in sharing difficult personal developments and experiences that have caused her shame and guilt.

The example of the timing of when one should be in bed, albeit seemingly trivial, likely reflected a lifelong theme of how Millie could feel misaligned and not understood by her mother. Kohut (1971) referred to "telescoping of analogous experiences" where contemporary relationship issues and interactions reflect parallel examples from childhood for which there are not necessarily lasting memories but which nevertheless mirror lifelong misalignments that are painfully recurrent and nagging and more often beyond conscious awareness.

This dynamic was juxtaposed to how cruelly the addiction was treating Millie, her mother, and certain members of her family as they experienced the repeated cruel nightmarish emergency calls, admissions of ERs, and all the other multiple complications of the disease. What Millie shared in common with several other chronically relapsing patients with whom I was working was the cruelty of the relapses paralleling deep resentment going back to childhood of feeling chronically misaligned with their parent(s)—sometimes in violent, angry confrontations, at other times suffering in silence and feeling not heard or understood. Recently, after an exasperating episode of attempting to get her to a rehab facility, which ultimately was successful, but trying and exhausting, I had a rare reaction, for me, of wanting to give up on Millie. Based on my response and considering Millie's impatience with her mom and cousins in these efforts and the impatience of the family, I came to the conclusions that whatever part empathic failures play in early development there certainly is mutual empathic failure that develops as a consequence of the cruel and daunting consequences of addictive disorders. Perhaps the intersubjective experience of giving-up by me had in it an aspect of repetition in the treatment relationship involving painful perpetuation at the same time an attempt to resolve old relational/attachment issues. After her return from rehab, lasting five months, I shared how my sense of wanting to give up reflected some of her own feelings, and that of her family. She reacted receptively, considering thoughtfully out loud the consequences of the recurrent relapses for her, me, and her mother. It is perhaps significant that interacting with her on the issue of empathic faltering for all of us, for the first time in 18 months there followed a period of no further relapses extending up to the present time (eight weeks).

Internal Recovery

There is a paucity of convincing theories of how people actually get better. This is also true of psychodynamic approaches, where there is a corresponding lack of theory concerning the "psychodynamics of recovery." As experienced practitioners and theorists in the field, while acknowledging the enormous damage caused by addiction and the considerable deficits which make addiction more likely, as individuals seek to alleviate painful states of mind or restricted capacities, we are keenly interested in understanding more about those unpredictable powers of restoration which enable people to exit addictive careers and reconstruct broken lives. Indeed, we each have extensive experience in working with those in medium and long-term recovery. But how is addictive vulnerability reversed, or at least lessened? How is psychological growth and integration promoted? How do individuals move forward, from attachment to inanimate containers to constructive human resources? How are more resilient "self-structures" built? How does internal recovery come about? At this stage in the "science" of recovery, it is perhaps too early to be sure of the answers, although, with the benefit of clinical hindsight, much can be gleaned.

VIGNETTE

Faith's out-of-control drinking and a devastating depression were precipitated when she was terminated from a highly placed executive position in a major health care corporation. A hypercritical, intimidating senior officer was instrumental in her removal from her position. Much of her success and ambition was driven and compensatory. She was raised by an immigrant mother who was insufficiently supportive and, like her boss, hypercritical of Faith, but this was further compounded by her mother taking to her bedroom for years at a time by her own immobilizing depression. For most of her growing up years she says home was an unhappy place given her mother's depression, her father's drinking, and her parents' constant fighting.

She was referred by her psychopharmacologist for individual and group psychotherapy to deal with her heavy drinking. Although she did not adopt abstinence, almost immediately she was successful in significantly cutting back the frequency and amount of her drinking. In her own words, she said she was "self-medicating" her anxiety (in low to moderate doses) and when the anxiety and depression mounted to unbearable levels she would drink to obliterating levels (e.g., the entire bottle of wine) and go to bed.

From the start of treatment Faith quickly formed a positive attachment to her therapist and was openly expressive of her appreciation for the comfort and reassurance she was experiencing from the work with the therapist in her individual and group therapy. In a recent individual visit, even as she was wondering out loud why she was continuing to use alcohol, adding that she was no longer self-medicating, she spontaneously indicated that the antidepressant was relieving her sadness and despair. But she quickly added that her energy levels remained low and the alcohol energized her. She volunteered that she definitely felt better and that she was okay with the controlled drinking but was aware that it was a "slippery slope" and realized she could get back to "numbing" herself with alcohol. The therapist wondered out loud if she might think about what she might be numbing. She thought about how she used to get her "adrenaline lift" from the kudos and recognition she obtained from her position, but then offered that she derived little comfort or satisfaction currently from her reading group, arts and crafts, or prettying up her home. She ended the session wondering about what else might give her a "lift or pleasure."

COMMENT

The progression from Faith's unthinking compulsive drinking to ameliorate her immense suffering to a relatively rapid development of a capacity to think and worry about her troubled state of being and her use of alcohol, was impressive. Her demeanor, especially early in treatment, was a melancholic and anxious one. It was notable to witness the comfort, support, and clarification she drew from her individual and group therapy, as well as the opportunity to share her distress and gratitude in her treatment, interactions that were not likely or available in her family of origins. As much as her therapist was active in appreciating, validating, and supporting her gifts and decency, it was also evident that she was drawing on her individual and group contacts to begin to feel better about and within herself. With the help of her therapist, she was fruitfully considering alternative ways to find comfort and self-acceptance beyond the external praise and admiration she derived from her work performance and career. Literally a therapeutic process was being activated where she could begin to shift from deriving satisfaction from external accomplishments and admiration to one where she was more and more appreciating that her comfort and better sense of self had to come from within. As they say in recovery, "it's an inside job." Put in terms of attachment theory, she was reversing the attachment to the inanimate (i.e., the alcohol) to the human ones afforded by her individual and group therapy. And of course, as she got better, she was also reconnecting to her loving husband and three daughters from whom she had withdrawn as her alcohol use was progressively denying her these vital attachments.

Conclusion

Modern psychodynamic concepts for addressing the range of psychopathologies are equally and preeminently well suited for understanding and treating individuals suffering with addictive disorders. This is especially the case for dealing with difficult and complicated cases that do not respond to traditional treatments. These contemporary approaches also assist clinicians to understand and manage the troubling reactions and feeling they stir in treating providers.

Substance dependent individuals alternate in extreme and opposite states involving their emotions, sense of self and relational problems. These alternating and extreme states are further complicated by difficulties with managing their self-care concerning harm, threat, and danger, especially those associated with addictions. In this chapter we identify and explain how such patterns become enmeshed in and absorb the lives of addicted individuals, and how these modern psychodynamics paradigms allow the identification, exploration, and resolution of these self-destructive and consuming processes. Such models and conceptualizations are critically necessary to counter misleading notions that addictions are driven by pleasure seeking and human self-destructiveness. Such motives are tragically attributed to addicted individuals by society, and addicted individuals themselves, and too often stand in the way of an empathic understanding, more humane attitudes (clinically and at large), and effective treatments.

Clinicians need to remain attuned to the enormous suffering that is at the root of addictive disorders. Contemporary perspectives provided by object relationship, self-psychology, and attachment theory provide complementary pathways to attune to the origins and nature of the suffering. They provide new and more enabling windows on addicted patients' experience and to appreciate and empathically attune to their needs and to free them of the compulsions and repetitions that drive their addictions. Such approaches also encourage therapists to depart from early impassive, strictly interpretive psychodynamic modes.

They allow for and encourage more active and interactive ways to provide patients with instruction, clarification, support, and empathic attunement to better appreciate how substances of misuse have interacted with their suffering to make them powerfully compelling, and to develop alternative paths to deal with their pain and confusion.

References

Anderson, R. (1997). Booting the boot in: Violent defences against the depressive position. In *Reason and Passion: A Celebration of the Work of Hannah Segal*, edited by David Bell, chapter 3. London: Karnac Books.

Balint, M. (1968). *The Basic Fault*. London: Tavistock.

Bowlby, J. (1973). *Attachment and Loss*. Vol. 2, *Separation, Anxiety, Anger*. New York: Basic Books.

Director, L. (2005). Encounters with omnipotence in the psychoanalysis of substance users. *Psychoanalytic Dialogues* 15:567–86.

Dodes, L. M. (1996). Compulsion and addiction. *Journal of the American Psychoanalytic Association* 44:815–35.

———. (2002). *The Heart of Addiction*. New York: HarperCollins.

English, C. (2009). The regulatory function of addiction: Maintaining internal cohesion by the drugging of parts of the personality. *Psychodynamic Practice* 15 (4): 341–49.

Flores, P. (2003). *Addiction as an Attachment Disorder*. Northvale, NJ: Jason Aronson.

Gedo, J. (1986). *Conceptual Issues in Psychoanalysis: Essays in History and Method*. Hillsdale, NJ: Analytic Press.

Hyatt-Williams, A. (1978). Depression, deviation and acting out in adolescence. *Journal of Adolescence* 1:309–17.

Khantzian, E. J. (1987). A clinical perspective of the cause-consequence controversy in alcoholism and addictive suffering. *Journal of the American Academy of Psychoanalysis* 15:521–37.

———. (2003). Understanding addictive vulnerability: An evolving psychodynamic perspective. *Neuro-Psychoanalysis* 5:5–21.

Khantzian, E. J., Mack, J. E., and Schatzberg, A. F. (1974). Heroin use as an attempt to cope: Clinical observations. *American Journal of Psychiatry* 131:160–64.

Kohut, H. (1971). *The Analysis of the Self*. New York: International Universities Press.

———. *The Restoration of the Self*. New York: International Universities Press.

Krystal, H. (1988). *Integration and Self-Healing: Affect, Trauma, Alexithymia*. Hillsdale, NJ: Analytic Press.

Krystal, H., and Raskin, H. A. (1970). *Drug Dependence: Aspects of Ego Functions*. Detroit: Wayne State University Press.

Lichtenberg, J. D. (1983). *Psychoanalysis and Infant Research*. Hillsdale, NJ: Analytic Press.

Lighdale, H., Mack, A., and Frances, R. (2011). Psychodynamics. In *Psychotherapy for the Treatment of Substance Misuse*, edited by M. Galanter and H. Kleber, chapter 23. Washington, DC: American Psychiatric Association.

McDougall, J. (1984). The "disaffected" patient: Reflections on affect pathology. *Psychoanalytic Quarterly* 53:386–409.

Reading, B. (2002). The application of Bowlby's attachment theory to the psychotherapy of addiction. In *Psychodynamics of Addiction*, edited by M. Weegmann and R. Cohen, chapter 2. Chichester: Wiley.

———. (2012). *Addiction and attachment*. Unpublished.

Segal, H. (1973). *Introduction to the Work of Melanie Klein*. London: Hogarth Press.

Steiner, J. (1993). *Psychic Retreats: Pathological Organisations in Psychotic, Neurotic and Borderline Patients*. London: Routledge.

Sutherland, S. (1992/2007). *Irrationality*. London: Pinter and Martin.

Weegmann, M. (2002). The vulnerable self. In *Psychodynamics of Addiction*, edited by M. Weegmann and R. Cohen, chapter 3. Chichester: Wiley.

Weegmann, M., and Khantzian, E. J. (2009). A question of substance: Psychodynamic reflections on addictive vulnerability and treatment. *Psychodynamic Practice* 15:365–80.

———. (2011). Envelopments: Immersion in and emergence from drug misuse. *American Journal of Psychotherapy* 65 (2): 1–15.

CHAPTER 14

Reflections on Treating Addictive Disorders

A PSYCHODYNAMIC PERSPECTIVE

In this chapter, I would like to reflect and draw upon a psychodynamic perspective and four decades of work with drug-dependent patients, to look at the struggles and suffering that make addictions so powerful and compelling. Drawing on that perspective and experience, I would then like to offer some thoughts about essential elements of good treatment and how clinicians can develop a focus to address, understand, and modify in psychotherapy the vulnerabilities that have caused drug-dependent individuals to suffer and behave in the ways that they do. The chapter will sound familiar to many practitioners of my generation, and in this respect, it is intended as a recap and summation of my work, but it is also my aim to introduce these ideas to a new generation of clinicians who are taking up the challenge to provide a humanistic psychological approach to understanding and treating addictive disorders.

Treating addictive disorders, as with other medical and psychiatric conditions, rests on the principle that effective treatment best occurs when the underlying processes and mechanisms involved in the disorder are understood and targeted. Over the past several decades considerable evidence has emerged, as recently reviewed by Shedler (2010) on the efficacy of psychodynamic psychotherapy as an effective model for understanding and treating a wide range of psychiatric disorders. Dating back to the 1980s, there is evidence as well that psychotherapeutic approaches derived from a psychodynamic paradigm are effective in treating addictive disorders (Woody et al. 1986; Carroll et al. 1994; O'Malley et al. 1996). Although there have been few, if any, such studies since the 1990s, Shedler suggests that nonpsychodynamic therapies such as cognitive behavioral therapy (CBT), dialectic behavioral therapy (DBT), and motivational interviewing (MI) incorporate techniques central to psychodynamic theory and practice. Especially in the case of MI, the reader will recognize the empathic and humanistic attitudes explicitly embodied in the evidence-based work of Miller and Rollnick (1991), drawing on the work of Carl Rogers.

From my perspective a psychodynamic approach, more simply put, gets at the human psychological underpinning of addictive behavior. Such a perspective is needed given the stigma, negative stereotyping, and the horrible judgment placed on individuals with addictive disorders, not the least of which addicted individuals place on themselves. More than anything, I would like to stress that suffering is at the heart of addictive disorders and that this consideration should remain central in considering the treatment needs of individuals with addictive disorders. To understand and to be understood is a powerful antidote to the confusion, chaos, and suffering associated with addictions. The treatment relationship offers a humane, comforting, and containing remedy to the dehumanizing, discomforting, and disorganizing causes and consequences of addictive disorders.

What Does a Psychodynamic Perspective Instruct about Addiction?

At the outset I would like to emphasize what addiction *is not*. In my experience, addiction is not about pleasure seeking; nor is it about human self-destructiveness or oral dependency—as some well-accepted formulations suggest. Take, for example, the language of modern day neuroscientists who speak of and seek the "reward" and "pleasure" pathways in the brain to explain the reinforcing properties of addictive substances; or the cynical view that addiction is suicide on the installment plan. In the case of neuroscience, such a paradigm is more suitable to explain the drug effects with short-term or intermittent use, but seems insufficient to explain the complexities of what makes addictive behavior and relapse so powerful and driven. It bears repeating that many individuals experiment with these so-called powerfully addicting drugs but few become addicted. The power in addiction resides in the interaction of the drug with the internal terrain of the person who uses it and discovers its pain-relieving effects if they are susceptible. As for invoking suicidal motives about addictive behavior, it is probably the case that suicidal behavior associated with addiction is more likely the result of the long-term crippling and demoralizing consequences of chronic drug use. Over the course of nearly a half-century of clinical work with addicted individuals I have yet to meet a person who became or remained addicted to drugs because of the pleasurable aspect of their use, or whose motives in initiating and using drugs was suicidal in nature.

Addiction as a Self-Regulation Disorder

A psychodynamic perspective suggests that addiction is fundamentally a disorder of self-regulation. More precisely, individuals with addictions suffer because they cannot or do not regulate their emotions, self-esteem, relationships, and their behavior. As humans we are governed less by instincts and more by coping skills and capacities acquired from the caretaking environment. Requirements for human survival and adaptation place a lifelong challenge on humans for self-regulation. Regulating emotions, self-esteem, relationships, and self-care are among the main functions upon which our survival depends (Khantzian 1999). In my experience, individuals self-medicate the distress and pain associated with their self-regulation difficulties.

Notwithstanding factors of temperament, it is both the good news and the bad news about our human nature that we are not hardwired to adjust to our inner and external environment. That is, we are challenged to learn how to figure out who we are, what goes on inside us, how we feel about ourselves, and how to get along with the human and nonhuman environment that surrounds us. This makes for possibilities of satisfaction and joy or the alternatives of dissatisfaction and misery. The former is the result of adequately comforting, caring, and loving relationships over a person's life span that can insulate against injuries and insults, both relationally and materially. The latter grows out of a range of misalignments, neglect, and trauma over the course of a lifetime. Needless to say, genetic loading and related biological processes are clearly important in the etiology of addictions; alone, however, they are insufficient to account for the development of addictive disorders. Adequate nurturing and protective environments likely can protect and help to overcome harsh external environments as well as factors of biological loading.

Based on work with more than a thousand patients over 40 years of practice ("practice-based evidence"), the self-regulation problems that are central to addictive vulnerability involve the following:

- an inability to recognize and regulate feelings;
- an inability to establish and maintain a coherent, comfortable sense of self and self-esteem;
- an inability to establish and maintain adequate, comforting, and comfortable relationships;
- an inability to establish and maintain adequate control/regulation of behavior, especially self-care.

Although addictions are a multifaceted disorder, in my experience these four areas have proven to be extremely fruitful in exploring some of its key components.

To varying degrees, addiction involves problems with regulating emotions, relationships, self-esteem, and behavior interacting with each other, environmental influences, and genetic factors to make addictive disorders more likely.

Adopting a structure and focus serves both the clinician as well as the patient. This is especially important given that the discomforting and disorganizing aspects of addiction can derail both the person who experiences addiction as well as those who witness it, including the clinician who is challenged to understand and treat it. A focus on self-regulation factors in addictive disorders has proven to be useful to me in identifying the core issues in need of understanding and therapeutic modification. So one might ask if addiction is a self-regulation problem, how do addictive drugs "help" with self-regulation?

- Drugs enhance or contain feelings.
- Drugs affect one's sense of self, well-being, and self-esteem.
- Drugs affect our ability or inability to care about or to connect to others.
- Experimentation with and dependence on drugs are influenced by one's capacity for self-care.

Notice that the word "help" is in quotes. Based on my experience, addiction is an attempt at self-correction that fails. It is the real and illusory nature of addictive drugs and behaviors. Short-term addictive drugs might work; they can provide a temporary fix for what the person suffers with. That is what is "reinforcing" about addictions. Long-term, addictive drugs fail. They do so because they become an end in themselves. They erode any existing human capacities to cope, and preclude possibilities to develop solutions to the challenges of regulating emotions, self-esteem, relationships, and self-care.

WHAT ARE THE PROBLEMS WITH FEELINGS?

The capacity to identify, differentiate, verbalize, and tolerate feelings is on a continuum. As with other aspects of life, there is a normal developmental trajectory for the development of feelings. Henry Krystal, a distinguished psychoanalyst, has been seminal in appreciating this aspect of feeling life (Krystal 1999). At the outset feelings are undifferentiated (i.e., the infant does not distinguish between anxiety and depression), feelings are experienced bodily, and they are without words. Optimally, with normal progression (major trauma can reverse this progression) we come to distinguish feelings (and, for example, know the difference between feeling "nervous" or being "blue"), experience them emotionally, and are able to give words to them. Individuals with characterologic, behavioral, and addictive disorders tend to be more singularly troubled with respect to how they process and express their feelings. I continue to be impressed by how invariably my patients with addictive disorders have trouble being aware of, identifying, and verbalizing their feelings. At one extreme, feelings can be inaccessible, confusing, or vague; at the other extreme patients seem unable to think about, cope with, or tolerate their feelings of anger, rage, anxiety, or sadness. For some the activating properties of stimulants or the releasing effects of sedatives and alcohol give vitality to the emotional lifelessness of not knowing, being confused about, or devoid of feelings; for others heavier doses of alcohol, and related depressants, or opiates calm or relieve the intolerable and threatening emotions of intense anger, rage, and associated agitation.

WHAT ARE THE PROBLEMS WITH SELF-ESTEEM?

Working with individuals with addictions, I have been impressed that problems with self-esteem go beyond the pale of simply not feeling good about self. As the self-psychologists put it, inner states of well-being and cohesion are elusive or lacking (i.e., anxiety about self amplifies into fragmenting disarray); feelings of inadequacy, impoverishment, helplessness, and compensatory rage loom large. Narcissistic defenses of omnipotence and bravado (I call it strutting) detract self and others from appreciating the underlying feelings of inadequacy and emptiness. I tell my students, "Don't assume the person sitting in front of you can handle what they profess they can." Is it any wonder that expansive individuals find the sense of omnipotence induced by amphetamines exhilarating, or that relief of feelings of enfeeblement in the more impoverished is experienced as a magical compensation when such individuals use stimulants? I often wonder if the undue emphasis on pleasure and euphoria ascribed to addictive drugs is a reflection of an inherent problem of anhedonia in addictively prone people. Namely, the activating or pain-relieving action of the drugs powerfully corrects and ameliorates dysphoria or enhances a sense of well-being, and that is what is experienced as "pleasure [and] reward."

WHAT ARE THE PROBLEMS WITH RELATIONSHIPS?

Although early psychodynamic formulations and contemporary stereotypic depictions characterize addicted individuals, especially alcoholic individuals, as "oral . . . clinging . . . dependent," in my experience, and as often described by patients themselves, addicted individuals are more often counter-dependent. That is not to say such individuals do not yearn for or need contact or comfort; the problem more often is they cannot or dare not admit or exercise such needs.

They act as if they do not need others and suffer as "born isolationist(s)" as one patient put it. Feeling cut-off, cold, and alienated are a few of the terms that come to mind to capture the affect states that such isolation engenders. Some of this is grounded in defensive postures of self-sufficiency and disdain for the need of others. In others it seems to be the result of depressive inertia that may make connection to others unlikely or impossible. In part, it is on this basis that some investigators have characterized addiction as an attachment disorder (Flores 2004; Walant 2002). It turns out we are more likely comfort and contact seeking than we are pleasure seeking. Pleasure is momentary and not unimportant, but human connection and the comfort we derive from each other is more sustaining and lasting. Opiates can quiet and contain the rage that threatens relationships; sedatives, especially alcohol, can dissolve defenses against otherwise threatening connection to others (it turns out alcohol is at least as good an ego solvent as it is a super-ego solvent); and stimulants can break through the inertia and inhibitions that do not allow contact with other human beings.

WHAT ARE THE PROBLEMS WITH SELF-CARE?

Self-care functions ensure safety, well-being, and survivability. Early in my career working with intravenous heroin users in a methadone program I found myself having a powerful subjective reaction to the idea of injecting oneself with illicit drugs. I realized my reaction of repugnance to that idea was one of counter-transference (modern theorists would call it an "intersubjective" response—namely, our patients getting us to feel something they need us to feel that they are unaware or incapable of). I decided to tactfully share my recoil and discomfort with the many patients I was evaluating at that time. My inquiry consistently and monotonously elicited reactions of little or no emotions or concerns of alarm about crossing the so-called needle barrier. Subsequently, working with abstinent drug- or alcohol-dependent patients in psychotherapy I was struck by how such lack of worry or thought persisted when no longer addicted. I observed these deficiencies to be involved in interpersonal and physical mishaps, slip-ups around management of important matters of unpaid premiums, lapsed licenses, and preventable medical and dental problems. It is in this context that I began to conclude that a major contributing factor to the development of addictions involved deficits in a capacity for self-care. What I was observing was that addictively prone individuals think and feel differently about potential and real situations of harm and danger. Anxiety, fear, worry, or apprehension are deficient or absent and fail to guide such individuals in risky or self-harmful situations. And there is a failure to draw cause/consequence relationship in the face of risk. Where anticipatory shame and guilt might guide when self-care capacities are better developed, in addictively prone people shame and guilt come after the fact (e.g., "I felt stupid and bad when I did that" [rather than] "I will feel stupid and bad if I do that"). It is the combination of self-care deficits interacting with the pain and suffering involved in self-regulation difficulties that make vulnerable individuals more likely to develop addictive disorders.

Treating the Self-Regulation Problems of Addicted Individuals

Because addicted individuals are overwhelmed or confused by their feelings, because their self-esteem is shaky, because relationships are elusive or absent, and because their self-care is undeveloped or inadequate, I have concluded practitioners should be guided by the following essential elements for their work with patients:

- Kindness
- Comfort
- Empathy
- Avoid confrontation
- Patience
- Instruction
- Self-awareness
- Climate of mutual respect
- Balance—talking/listening

Although many of the listed elements seem self-evident and basic, it is worth commenting upon how and why they are important. I begin with kindness because it is so important, yet, because of certain traditions and tendencies, it often wanes or is absent in the treatment relationship. First of all, most of us are influenced more than we like to think by the early psychodynamic paradigm that fostered reserve and impassivity, thus making kindness in treating clinicians less likely apparent. Second, whether we like to admit it or not, addicted patients foster disbelief or distrust in clinicians (and, worse still, if we are unaware of the mistrust), thus making it less likely to be kindly disposed to our patients.

Appreciating the pain and suffering that is at the root of addictive disorders, we need to remember all the things our addicted patients are uncomfortable about and how not understood they feel. In this respect the role of empathy is critical in countering such distress. I say, "avoid confrontation . . . but if the devil makes you," because addictive disorders are maddening to self and others, including treating clinicians. Our patients make us madly angry and crazy given how insane and irrational addictive behavior can seem or be. I believe this in part is what fosters counterproductive and harmful confrontations, more likely angry than not, in clinicians if they are not careful. But "if the devil makes you," because on certain occasions firm proscribing interventions are necessary to insure safety, confrontations have to be done in such a way that preserve self-esteem and are supportive. We need to keep in mind how out of touch our patients can be with regard to their thoughts and feelings. Thoughtfulness and emotions fail to serve addictively prone patients in assuring self-preservation, and instructive approaches are necessary and consistent with psychodynamic approaches. And finally, regarding the final three bullets, in my estimation self-awareness in the patient and clinician, and the balance between talking and listening, are central for a climate of mutual respect, all key to establishing and maintaining a positive therapeutic alliance.

THE PROBLEM OF COMORBIDITY

Given the high rates of psychiatric comorbidity, including presumed sociopathy, associated with substance use disorders (SUDs), one might ask do the principles of kindness, empathy, and so on that I have outlined here apply in working with patients so affected? I would emphatically respond in the affirmative. Although in many previous publications I have addressed the importance of psychiatric comorbidity, including sociopathy, as predisposing to addiction, I do not focus on these factors here. The essential elements that I have listed apply in what follows considering the enormous suffering and dysregulation associated with the range of psychiatric diagnoses that co-occur with addictive disorders. In the case of sociopathy presumably associated with addiction, I have not met a pure type in my years of clinical practice. Perhaps my impressions would be different if I worked in offender or prison populations. But discussing my findings with clinicians who do work with drug-dependent offenders, they tell me that the disruptive and antisocial behaviors witnessed with such individuals detract from underlying suffering and self-regulation difficulties with which offenders struggle. So whether it be the great pain that patients with co-occurring bipolar disorders or posttraumatic stress disorder (PTSD) endure, or the emotional and behavioral instability associated with personality-disordered individuals, kindness, empathy, and patience should remain the order of the day.

ADDRESSING DISORDERED AFFECTS

Because individuals with addictive disorders tend to experience their emotions in extremes of intense or absent affect, our therapeutic responses must be tailored accordingly. For those who seem cut-off or without words for their feelings ("alexithymia"), clinicians should be prepared to actively elicit, label, and put into words for their patient the feelings that seem elusive or confusing. When patients say they do not know what they are feeling one should be less inclined to consider such reactions as denial or defensive. More likely it is an indication that our patients are often truly out of touch with and confused by their emotions. The recent work of Allen and associates (2008) on "mentalizing" helps us to consider the fundamental importance of labeling, clarifying, and processing thoughts, emotions, and behaviors, a basic aspect of individual psychotherapeutic work. The storytelling traditions in group therapy as well as 12-step programs are extremely helpful in cultivating a growing capacity to recognize and process emotions as members listen and share their experiences and stories.

In instances where affects are more intense, overwhelming, and intolerable, therapeutic efforts should be geared to helping patients modulate and contain feelings that are threatening for self and others. In this respect the therapeutic alliance is in and of itself an important containing influence. Yet, for those whose grievances and rage are lodged in major trauma and neglect, the therapist should be undisguised in acknowledging and validating the legitimacy of such intense feelings. The time-honored tradition of exploring and clarifying the origins and displacements of intense affect and how they became connected to drug use can be invaluable ("the truth will set you free"). Helping patients mentalize about and reframe their experiences can assist them in working out alternative ways to ameliorate the distress associated with intense affect and reversion to drug use. Given the natural pressure in groups for balance, the modulating and interpersonal benefits of therapeutic and self-help groups can be extremely beneficial in containing intense affect. Finally a brief word is in order about the judicial use of psychotropic medications in helping to modulate intense or overwhelming affect. In my experience the modulating action of medications reduces the intensity of feelings to tolerable levels and thus permits therapeutic examination and modification of otherwise intolerable emotions.

ADDRESSING DISORDERED SELF-ESTEEM

Honoring the supportive and empathic traditions of psychotherapy is crucial in offsetting the enormous problems with self-esteem that predispose to, and are the consequence of, addictive disorders. This is because an inner sense of well-being and cohesion that ordinarily helps us to feel together is elusive or lacking. Feelings of helplessness, states of alienation and vacuousness, and for some compensatory rage, accompany the low self-regard that such patients experience. This is where kindness and patience is especially important. The rage is both reactive and defensive. I have to constantly remind myself that such reactions and defenses should be approached gingerly and respectfully, albeit such defenses can be off-putting. More often, behind such responses are feelings of emptiness and impoverishment. For those who are more visibly enfeebled and seem vacuous I try to use my own energy to strengthen and activate in my patients a better sense of self and vitality. Beyond the importance of mirroring and validating patients in individual psychotherapy, I have found the accepting and celebratory aspects of group experiences to be a major corrective for the self-esteem problems associated with addictive disorders.

ADDRESSING DISORDERED RELATIONSHIPS

Predisposing and resulting self-esteem problems associated with addictions leave affected individuals feeling unworthy, especially for the support, care, and affection of others. Little wonder such people are avoidant and isolative, if not defensively off-putting. Kindness and empathy remain the order of the day. From my perspective, impassive and strict interpretive approaches recapitulate and perpetuate relationship problems. Individual psychotherapy can address and focus on contradictory attitudes of relational manipulations and disavowal of needs and problems with counter-dependence can and should be addressed and clarified. Keeping in mind the attachment difficulties with which addicted patients struggle, individual and group psychotherapy are extraordinarily valuable for the relational disconnections and alienation.

ADDRESSING DISORDERED SELF-CARE

Our patients evoke in us what they want us to feel or that they cannot feel. In the case of self-care deficits our alarm over so many aspects of addictive involvements alert us to the affective and cognitive deficiencies in our patients that cause them to be unaware of or oblivious to danger, especially those involved with addictions. I have discovered over and over that it is crucial to clarify with my patients that something causes them to react differently to potential and real danger. They do not feel and think clearly around potential or real danger, if they think or feel at all. Long-term psychotherapy may help to get at what that something is—namely, to understand how over/underprotective and traumatizing environments leave them prone to self-care deficits. An interactive and instructive approach is essential to stimulate a growing awareness and vigilance about harm and danger, particularly those associated with relapse to addictive behavior. The feeling of alarm that patients evoke in the therapist should be tactfully shared, and their self-esteem deficits should be examined, as these cause our patients to treat themselves so shabbily and unworthy of self-protection. The range of individual and group treatments we employ should incorporate more sensitivity about self-care deficits. We need to help patients use self-respect, feelings of apprehension/worry, relationships with others, and thoughtfulness as a guide for safe behavior and self-preservation.

Conclusion

I remain convinced that a psychodynamic perspective remains one of the most powerful paradigms to guide clinicians in addressing and modifying the vulnerabilities that precipitate and maintain addictive behavior. The treatments that work do so because they address and relieve the pain and distress associated with addictions. Attitudes of kindness, empathy, support, and instruction are necessary and consistent with a psychodynamic approach for treating patients who suffer with addictive disorders. Individual and group treatments, guided by such a humanistic understanding, provide powerful antidotes to the alienation, dysphoria, and anguish that are so intimately a part of substance use disorders. And finally it bears repeating that to understand and be understood is a powerful correction for the confusion, chaos, and suffering associated with addictions.

References

Allen, J. G., Fonagy, P., and Bateman, A. W. (2008). *Mentalizing in Clinical Practice*. Washington, DC: American Psychiatric Publishing.

Carroll, K. M., Rounsaville, B. J., Nich, C., et al. (1994). One year follow-up of psychotherapy and pharmacotherapy for cocaine dependence: Delayed emergence of psychotherapy effects. *Archives of General Psychiatry* 51:989–97.

Flores, P. J. (2004). *Addiction as an Attachment Disorder*. New York: Jason Aronson.

Khantzian, E. J. (1999). *Treating Addiction as a Human Process*. New York: Jason Aronson.

Khantzian, E. J., and Albanese, M. (2008). *Understanding Addiction as Self-Medication: Finding Hope behind the Pain*. Lanham, MD: Rowman & Littlefield.

Krystal, H. (1988). *Integration and Self-Healing: Affect, Trauma, Alexithymia*. Hillsdale, NJ: Analytic Press.

Miller, W. R., and Rollnick, S. (1991). *Motivational Interviewing: Preparing People to Change Addictive Behavior*. New York: Guilford Press.

O'Malley, S. S., Jaffe, A. J., Chang, G., et al. (1996). Six-month follow-up of naltrexone and psychotherapy for alcohol dependence. *Archives of General Psychiatry* 53:217–24.

Shedler, J. (2010). The efficacy of psychodynamic psychotherapy. *American Psychologist* 65:98–109.

Walant, K. B. (2002). *Creating the Capacity for Attachment: Treating Addictions and the Alienated Self.* New York: Jason Aronson.

Woody, G. E., McLellan, A. T., Luborsky, L., et al. (1986). Psychotherapy for substance abuse. *Psychiatric Clinics of North America* 9:547–62.

CHAPTER 15

A Psychodynamic Perspective on the Efficacy of 12-Step Programs

The author reviews recent developments in psychoanalytic and psychodynamic theory and practice and their applications for understanding and treating addicted individuals. Emphasis is placed on experience near, more interactive, and empathic approaches stressing structural, self-psychology, object relations, and attachment theory in contrast to early classical psychoanalytic models that were impassive, detached, and more strictly interpretive in their methods. The contemporary models are adopted to explain and provide a basis for explaining how and why Alcoholics Anonymous works. From this perspective, addiction is understood as a self-regulation disorder involving difficulties in regulating emotions, self-esteem, relationships, and behavior and how the working of AA address and correct these vulnerabilities.

> After a successful psychoanalytic treatment, a patient is definitely less neurotic (or psychotic) but perhaps not necessarily more mature. On the other hand, after a successful treatment by group methods, the patient is not necessarily less neurotic but inevitably more mature. (Balint 1972, 61)

One view of alcohol dependency and recovery is that Alcoholics Anonymous (AA) removes the "sufficient and necessary cause"—the alcohol—from a person's life and replaces it with the support and comfort of AA (Vaillant 1983). The quote from Enid Balint suggests that AA does far more. Balint was not necessarily referring to AA but she could have been. The group dynamics of AA operate in such a way that it addresses and modifies core problems in regulating emotions, self-esteem, relationships, and self-care-factors that predispose to and result from dependency on alcohol and other addictive drugs (Khantzian and Mack 1994). Beyond that, in our experience, AA works because the group dynamics of the program foster change and growth by serving as a corrective for aspects of personality organization and character flaws of addictively prone individuals involving self-deceit, self-absorption, invincibility, and denial (Khantzian 1995a).

In this chapter, I would like to consider contemporary developments in psychoanalytic and psychodynamic theory and practice and apply them to an understanding and treatment of addicted individuals. These findings derive from structural, self-psychology, object relations, and attachment theory, as well as recently emerging perspectives from relational, intersubjective, and mentalizing paradigms. These approaches are less speculative, more interactive, experience near, and empathically grounded than early classical psychoanalytic models. They converge in a way that helps us understand the vulnerabilities of substance dependent individuals and, applied to 12-step programs, aid in explaining and providing a rationale for how and why AA works. These contemporary perspectives are important because they go beyond and to a considerable extent replace early psychoanalytic theory and practice involving drive theory, a topographic model, and modes of detachment, impassivity, and more strictly interpretive approaches for understanding and therapeutic interaction with patients, approaches that are antithetical to the needs of individuals suffering with addictive disorders. From the perspective of this author, though AA is atheoretical and not considered therapy, the program is truly therapeutic for the problems with which addicted individuals suffer, and these modern models of understanding help to better explain why this is so.

Although I will not be specifically commenting on the dynamics of the spirituality dimension of the program, it will hopefully become evident in what follows how important 12-step programs are in stimulating the transition from the self-absorbing nature of addictive illness to meaningful connections to other in the recovery process. For some it is the connection to the fellowship; for others it is the importance of connecting to a Higher Power, in whatever form that takes; and yet for many it involves a spiritual awakening and search for sources of comfort and meaning in places other than the ones that were found in drug and alcohol solutions. These are potent corrective for the vulnerabilities and deficits associated with addictive disorders.

Addiction as a Self-Regulation Disorder[1]

Understanding addiction as a self-regulation disorder for this author has evolved out of the development of the self-medication hypothesis (SMH) of substance use disorders. The SMH emphasizes that individuals use and become dependent on

---

1. This section is based in part on a recent presentation as the 20th John Bowlby Memorial Lecture titled "The Self-Medication Hypothesis and Attachment Theory: Pathways for Understanding and Ameliorating Addictive Suffering."

addictive drugs because they discover that the drugs change, remove, or ameliorate states of emotional pain and suffering, and, that there is a considerable degree of preference in an individual's drug of choice (Khantzian 1985, 1997). Although the SMH originally placed primary emphasis on painful affect states that were relieved by addictive drugs, as the hypothesis was further developed it focused on a range of painful emotional states that were associated with troubled self-states/self-esteem issues, problematic relationships, and poor self-care capacities that predisposes to dangerous and risky behaviors. Notwithstanding how there has been an evolution in this author's understanding of what addicted individuals self-medicate, I recently summarized the primacy and importance of affect life in the development of addictions as follows:

> Affects are the organizing basis for self-experience (Stolorow et al. 1995), the foundation for a sense of well-being and self-esteem (Kohut 1970, 1977), the currency for human connection and attachment (Bowlby 1973), and a primary ingredient for guiding behavior, especially self-care (Khantzian and Mack 1983). Major trauma and neglect greatly heighten and worsen the self-regulation deficits that are so commonly and persistently associated with addictive disorder. (Khantzian 2014, 227)

A detailed review of addiction as a self-regulation disorder goes beyond the scope of this chapter, but the interested reader can find further elaborations elsewhere of how deficits in self-regulation contribute to addiction (Khantzian 1985, 1995b, 1997, 2003, 2012). I summarize briefly here on these deficits in self-regulation and how they predispose individuals to resort to and discover how addictive drugs relieve the suffering associated with their self-regulation difficulties.

For addictively prone individuals there is much suffering associated with the challenges in regulating emotions, self-esteem, relationships and self-care. Deficits, distortions, and extreme fluctuations in feeling life remain critical factors in the suffering and distress that lead certain individuals to use and become dependent on addictive drugs. For some, affects are absent, elusive, and confusing. For others they are intense and overwhelming. In the former instance, stimulants can be a basis to feel more alive and to counter states of feeling devoid of emotions. In the latter case opiates or obliterating dose of alcohol can help to contain or bear feelings that seem overwhelming and threatening to self or others. When individuals feel defensively cut off from others and feel alone, low to moderate doses of alcohol or the stimulating properties of cocaine can release them from states of isolation and temporarily allow feeling of closeness and warmth that are not ordinarily allowable.

Given how shaky and uncomfortable addictively prone individuals are in the absence of a sense of well-being and poor self-esteem, and thus troubled and unconfident in their interpersonal relationships, it should not be surprising that such individuals would discover the ameliorating effects of addictive drugs on the suffering associated with such dysfunction. Stimulants can help such individuals to break out of their isolation and counter-dependency, and low to moderate doses of alcohol can release individuals from defensive denial of need for others. Opiates and high closes of alcohol can counter narcissistic rage and agitation associated with individuals who suffer with posttraumatic stress disorder (PTSD) and associated borderline personality organizations—conditions that too often cause addictively prone people to recoil from or overreact to needed relationships.

As previously indicated, insufficient reactions of worry, anxiety, and fear in persons with addictive disorders are intimately involved with deficits in a capacity for self-care associated with addictive disorders, capacities that, when present, assure safety and survival (Khantzian and Mack 1983). Such individuals fail to anticipate a range of dangers, especially those involved with addictive disorders. For example, instead of anticipatory responses of shame and guilt guiding individuals to avoid self-harm and danger, such reactions too often follow the unfeeling and unthinking behaviors that otherwise present would avoid the too-often embarrassment, regret, and tragic consequences that result from addictive behavior. In the section that follows, I review how 12-step programs provide correctives for the suffering and difficulties in self-regulation with which addicted individuals struggle.

How 12-Step Programs Correct the Self-Regulation Problems of Addictively Vulnerable Individuals[2]

Bill W., the principal founder of AA, as much as anyone appreciated the psychological suffering that is and was involved in the captivating and pain relieving effects of alcohol in the following quote:

> *Perhaps it took a little time, but it seemed to happen instantly. He could feel his body relaxing, a stiffness going out of his shoulders as he sensed the warm glow seeping through him in all the distant forgotten corner of his being. . . . It was a miracle. There was no other word. A miracle that was affecting him mentally, physically, and, as he would soon learn,*

---

2. This section in part is based on two previous publications: Khantzian and Mack (1994) and Khantzian (1995b).

spiritually. (Bill W.'s first experience with alcohol as reported to his biographer, Robert Thomsen)

As is evident from what has preceded here, it is the experience and conviction of this author that addictive behavior, more than any other consideration, is driven not by pleasure as is so often invoked, but by human psychological suffering. Drawing on the paradigms of self-psychology, and relational and attachment theorists, this conviction is based on the premise that we are more comfort and contact seekers than we are pleasure seekers. That is not to say pleasure is unimportant, but it is temporary and not lasting whereas comfort and contact are more permanent and sustaining. Flores (2004), an attachment theorist, persuasively presents the evidence and forcefully proposes that this is not just a good argument, it is the law. Treatments of addictions that work do so because they address, modify, and resolve the suffering associated with the disordered emotions, self-esteem, relationships, self-care, and troubled attachments. In what follows, I present a case example and review how the 12-step programs operate in such a way as to make this so.

Before proceeding, however, I should distinguish here an "outside perspective" from an "inside perspective." There are many published inspiring and compelling inside views of the extraordinary benefits of AA that I will not recount here. The view I present is an outside one that derives from my exposure to 12-step programs directly and indirectly—mostly the latter—where I have had the chance to witness clinically the corrective value and transformations in my patients who have benefitted from the AA experience. In a recent article I suggested the following:

> To understand and to be understood is a powerful antidote to the confusion, chaos, and suffering associated with addictions. The treatment relationship offers a humane, comforting, and containing remedy to the dehumanizing, discomforting and disorganizing causes and consequences of addictive disorders. (Khantzian 2012, 274)

Although I was commenting on the benefits of individual psychotherapy, I could have just as equally been referring to the benefits of 12-step programs for those individuals who participate and profit from AA. The following vignette robustly demonstrates this.

THE CASE OF DON AND HOW AA TRANSFORMS

Don has been heroic, if not an outright hero, most of his adult life. He exercises his heroism as a gifted, dedicated orthopedic trauma surgeon. As it has now commonly come to be known these days, he is a first responder. For him, it applies whether it is in his well-run community hospital responding to a survivor of a horrendous car wreck, or in some ill-begotten part of the world suffering unimaginable upheaval, where he dispassionately and with exquisite skill exercises his gifts as a remark able fixer and healer.

Well, maybe not so dispassionately. Over the years, his commitment to being the way he was, always ready to respond and what he did, was taking its toll. Subsequent to major catastrophes that he attended, he was beginning to suffer sleepless nights, too often as a consequence of sleep being interrupted by reenactments and visualizations of the situations to which he attended, often the unimaginable nightmarish images being more horrific than the ones he took care of. Yet his family and colleagues were not seeing or aware of the levy his work was placing on him. Later he told me he never talked to his wife, or anyone else for that matter, about any of what he experienced as a trauma responder. In part this was a function of his entrenched penchant to draw his own counsel and to function as if he were a solitary soldier confronting each encounter as if it was his challenge alone. Doing business as usual was also beginning to be complicated by his using increasing amounts of alcohol to quell the breakthrough daytime anxiety and dysphoria that was associated with his care for the injured and maimed that he treated.

His treatment and care of the wounded and the self-medicating of his own emotional distress were brought to an abrupt halt when a family intervention resulted in an admission to a rehabilitation center, where he reluctantly agreed to stay for 30 days. I was a part of that intervention and was worried that his bitter anger and resentment coming out of the intervention would damage his trust of his brother and wife, and subsequently his relationship with me and any opportunity we might have to work on his wounds, stoicism, and dependency on alcohol.

Within two weeks of his discharge from rehab, I was surprised when he called to make an appointment. When we met, though he was far from exuberant about his lot in life and what prospects might be in store with his standing at his hospital, I was impressed that he had decided to attend daily AA meetings and was expressing some satisfaction about its benefits, albeit with some characteristic reserve. Although he conceded the time-line exercises and the psychotherapy provided in rehab were helpful, he said the listening to the stories and the interactions in the AA meetings were what he felt most comfortable with and from which he most benefited. As the end of our first post rehab session was approaching, he expressed the wish that we not necessarily resume weekly or biweekly visits. Instead, he said he preferred to continue the daily AA meetings and to perhaps limit our visits to every other week or monthly. Notwithstanding that I suspected there were elements of resistance to regular visits with me, and that his inbred reluctance to share his fee lings and experiences were mainly operative in his preference to not pursue individual psychotherapy, I was inclined to go along with his preference. Because I was now reasonably convinced that he was accepting that abstinence was the only alternative and that he seemed reasonably stable, though still shaken by the imposition of rehab, I thought I might do better with him for the while to witness and monitor his progress with AA given that he was taking so well to the recovery culture.

That his preference, and my hunch to concede to it, was correct and the right way to go was progressively confirmed over the next two years. Even though there were periods where he expressed deep resentments in his monthly meetings about complication around credentialing and board of registration inquiries (but no sanctioning), for the most part he was increasingly more affable with me, spoke of the friendships he was establishing and valuing through the AA meetings, and openly shared with me how life was getting better.

And then there was one more catastrophic disaster. Predictably, he was there almost immediately. We met subsequently shortly after the disaster, and he seemed upbeat, friendly, and surprisingly open and ready to talk about his experience. He said he was the only surgeon for the first few days in the area where he was working, at first talking about the people with whom he found himself. Although there was a pediatrician, an internist, and a psychiatrist at his site, he described how he depended upon a young technician with a second-grade education as his assistant in surgery. He spoke affectionately of his assistant, as he did of the native nursing personnel who were there to provide, in his estimation, extraordinarily compassionate care and comfort. In several asides it was clear that he had connected with them not only as the doctor in charge but as a respected and respectful friend. I expressed the thought that these connections had offered him a kind of a protection from the impact upon him of the brutal injuries and trauma he had dealt with. He replied emphatically, "Yes, it made a huge difference," yet reminding me that it still was not easy to behold. He gave the example of all the amputations that were being necessitated and the stigma this entailed in that part of the world—mainly because of the complexities and near impossibilities of stump care and working out proper prostheses. And then there were the many inevitable deaths.

And then, spontaneously, he added how embarrassed he was that he had never talked about the nightmares he was experiencing when he first came to see me two years before. In these gruesome nightmares, for example, he said, "Patients would be chasing me and rubbing their wounds in my face." I encouraged him to tell me how it was different now. He reminded me that the fellowship of AA had made a "huge" difference, adding how he now tells his wife "all about that stuff," again saying that was enormous. He reflected that he does it with himself as well as those he trusts, especially friends in AA, and that as painful as it is to do, he now knows he has to. Going out the door, he added, "Now I can lay down and just sleep."

Don's case is a remarkable example of how AA can help a person not only to accept the necessity of abstaining from alcohol to solve life problems, but it can go far beyond that in transforming aspect of a personality organization that can predispose to addictive disorders. It helped Don, who was interpersonally isolated and out of touch with and unable to express his feelings, to become more flexible, progress, and grow in these respects. In doing so, AA enabled him to change and mature in ways that made dependency on addictive solutions less likely.

AA and Problems with Feelings

AA offers human contact, understanding, and self-expression for individuals who are or have become avoidant or unaccustomed to availing themselves of these basic human experiences and needs. Storytelling is the main vehicle. Some benefit more from listening and others benefit from speaking about and expressing feelings they have been unable to express, or are untried in doing so. It helps people who have been out of touch with or unaware of feelings to attend to and take charge of them. Telling and listening to stories helps lonely and despairing people to learn and appreciate they are not alone in their suffering and that there is hope.

Mentalizing theorists emphasize how some of the most central and beneficial aspects of effective psychotherapies involve helping patients to identify, clarify, and put into words their feelings, thoughts, and behaviors (Allen, Fonagy, and Bateman 2008). Twelve-step programs operate in such ways to do exactly that. The support and acceptance that the stories evoke act as powerful corrections for the problems and deficits in being aware of, accepting, and expressing their feelings. The AA approach works in subtle and remedial ways to help alcoholic individuals begin to deal with their emotions in more mature and flexible ways. Participants speak of "learning what life is about." The program helps some to express their feelings and for others it helps to better bear painful emotions.

AA and the Problems with Self-Esteem and Relationships

AA as a group experience counters the predisposing and resulting self-absorption and interpersonal isolation associated with alcoholism. Among the many unflattering characteristics of active alcohol-dependent individuals is their self-centered ways of being and behaving, which is their narcissism. Legitimate debates occur regarding how much the elements of narcissism contribute to or are the consequence of the alcoholism. As so often is the case, the exaggerated sense of omnipotence and inflation of self in narcissistic individuals masks feelings of unimportance and low self-esteem. Harry Tiebout in the mid-20th century was one of the first psychiatrists to promote the effectiveness of AA, emphasizing how it effectively targeted the "egoism" of alcoholics. He proposed that the effectiveness of AA hinged on eliminating the narcissistic element, and trading in the "big ego" of infantile narcissism for a more humble self (Khantzian and Mack 1989). In the program it is referred to as "getting right sized." Whether cause or effect, 12-step programs are ingenious in getting alcoholic persons to reflect on this aspect of their personality, to acknowledge it, and begin to grow and change in modifying this aspect of them that contributes so powerfully to their sense of indestructability and denial of vulnerability to the devastating consequences of unbridled drinking.

The group dynamics of AA forces the appreciation that one is not alone with their problems. Contrary to an active alcoholic's best thinking that they can solve their problems their way, AA helps individuals to appreciate that the problems of human psychological suffering are not best faced or solved alone. Twelve-step programs provide a natural vehicle to address the shattered self-esteem and relational issues that predispose to and result from the ravages of a life immersed in alcohol. Newcomers are met with a simple greeting of "hello" and welcome, a modest but powerful first step to counter and ameliorate the shame and guilt the newcomer struggles with.

Exploration of ambivalence about relationships that AA stimulates creates possibilities of beneficial connections to others. It is in this respect that the connections stimulated by the group experience of 12-step programs are extraordinarily helpful in addressing and ameliorating the attachment difficulties and sense of alienation with which substance dependent individuals struggle (Khantzian 2013).

The storytelling traditions and the sharing of experiences stimulates self-reflection, especially forcing the realization that one must live life on life's term rather than one's own terms. Group psychologies, including the group dynamics of AA, counter feelings of shame and guilt and thus foster meaningful and comforting connection to others. In doing so, the defenses of counter-dependency and self-sufficiency are gently challenged and gradually replaced with genuine care for and about others. The founders and members of AA refer to the importance of the "fellowship" of the program, no mean accomplishment for individuals who, more often, by their own admission, have been "loners."

AA and the Problems of Self-Care

The storytelling traditions in AA directly and indirectly address the problems of behavioral dysregulation, especially deficits in self-care. They do so in that the stories constantly focus on the unthinking and unfeeling behavior involved in persistent drinking and relapse. Participants sharing their stories of the impulsive and self-damaging behaviors involved in their drinking and drug activities cause those telling the stories and those hearing the stories to reflect and to begin to have reactions, thoughts, and feeling of shock and concern that were absent when their alcoholism was active and out of control. Although not labeled as such, the stories cause recovering alcoholic individuals to think and talk about their mindless and thoughtless behavior. A prominent feature of the recovery culture is that participants learn to take matters of self-respect and concerns for each other seriously, but they do it in such a manner that captivates and engages and is not offputting or judgmental. A feature of the program not sufficiently appreciated or understood, but materially important, is that expressions of mutual care and concern are exercised with healthy doses of passion and humor that are attention getting. These responses promote awareness of the errors of one's ways that support and foster addictive thinking and behaviors. Some examples follow:

- "Your best thinking got you here."
- "We're here because we are not all there."
- "I don't get into trouble every time I've been drinking, but every time I've been in trouble I've been drinking."
- "I didn't get here because I drank too many milkshakes."
- My friend who shares that he has a smiley Post-it on his bathroom mirror to face every morning with the caption, "Have a good day, unless you have other plans."

The so-often-referred-to "loss of control" and "powerlessness" of addictive disorders, by many inside and outside the program, is misleadingly linked to the drug and alcohol use alone. What is as least as important and germane is the sense of an inability or powerlessness to control or regulate emotions, self-esteem, relationships, and self-care, problems for which the program acts as a corrective. Even as the program corrects for these issues of self-regulations, what it accomplishes more importantly is personality transformation and maturation that assures more genuine connection to and concern for others. It is in this sense that the veterans of the program make the distinction between abstinence and sobriety.

Comments and Conclusions

AA works because it not only addresses uncontrolled drinking, but more significantly it transforms the life of alcoholic individuals emotionally and spiritually. The attachments that had been made to substances in place of attachment to people are reversed. With abstinence and recovery, self-absorption and preoccupation with alcohol and drugs are replaced by genuine concern for others. AA provides a forum to address the human tendency for self-centeredness and psychological denial. Members are reminded that they suffer with a disease, are powerless to control it, and can get better by going to meetings, ask for help, and not using *today* (my italics for emphasis). These seemingly simple suggestions and aphorisms act as needed important guides and correctives to counter disavowal of vulnerability, feelings of powerlessness, loss of control, and the counter-dependency that so often accompanies addictive behavior. When slips occur and members are riddled with shame and guilt, they are not scolded or banished but are encouraged to remember that they are vulnerable and to learn from their mistakes. AA is a forgiving program for individuals who can be so unforgiving of themselves.

And finally, as with any beneficial therapeutic program, there is the essential ingredient of hope that 12-step programs provide. It is imbedded in the "promise" of the program, which more often occurs: "If you don't drink, things will get better."

References

Allen, J. G., Fonagy, P., and Bateman, A. W. (2008). *Mentalizing in Clinical Practice.* Washington, DC: American Psychiatric Publishing.

Balint, E. (1972). Fair shares and mutual concerns. *International Journal of Psychoanalysis* 53:61–65.

Flores, P. J. (2004). *Addiction as an Attachment Disorder.* New York: Jason Aronson.

Khantzian, E. J. (1985). The self-medication hypothesis of addictive disorders. *American Journal of Psychiatry* 142:1259–64.

———. (1995a). Alcoholics Anonymous—cult or corrective: A case study. *Journal of Substance Abuse Treatment* 12:157–65.

———. (1995b). Self-regulation vulnerabilities in substance abusers: Treatment implications. In *The Psychology and Treatment of Addictive Behavior*, edited by S. Dowling, 17–41. New York: International Universities Press.

———. (1997). The self-medication hypothesis of substance use disorders: A reconsideration and recent applications. *Harvard Review of Psychiatry* 4:231–44.

———. (2003). Understanding addictive vulnerability: An evolving psychodynamic perspective. *Neuro-Psychoanalysts* 5:5–21.

———. (2012). Reflections on treating addictive disorders: A psychodynamic perspective. *American Journal on Addictions* 21:274–79.

———. (2014). A psychodynamic perspective on the efficacy of 12-step programs. *Alcoholism Treatment Quarterly* 32:225–36.

Khantzian, E. J., and Mack, J. E. (1983). Self-preservation and the care of the self: Ego instincts reconsidered. *Psychoanalytic Study of the Child* 38:209–32.

———. (1989). Alcoholics Anonymous and contemporary psychodynamic theory. In *Recent developments in alcoholism*, edited by M. Galanter, 67–89. New York: Plenum.

———. (1994). How AA works and why it is important for clinicians to understand. *Journal of Substance Treatment* 11:77–92.

Vaillant, G. E. (1983). *The Natural History of Alcoholism*. Cambridge, MA: Harvard University Press.

Part IV

REFLECTIONS AND LESSONS LEARNED

In this last section, I have included a number of essays, published in nonacademic forums, articles that have grown out of some of my frustrations over issues mostly, but not exclusively, related to troubling polarizations and unnecessary controversies involving our understanding and treatment of addictive problems. Although chapter 16 was more generally having to do with some day-to-day dissatisfactions at the time I wrote it, I nevertheless link some of the themes I raise in the chapter back to lessons learned from treating the addictions. In chapters 16 through 21, I turn to all the cruel and tragic trends, individual and collective, that are rampant in the ways we view, react to, and fail to appreciate what addictive disorders involve and what to do about them.

I decided that the most fitting way to conclude this volume would be to include one of my most recent publications (2017), titled "Self-Medication Theory and Addiction." I have only referred to the self-medication process as a hypothesis in all my writings, including for the 2017 paper when I submitted it for publication. Not insignificantly, the editor changed it to "theory." Coincidentally, it is consistent with the themes I struck in this final chapter, specifically how widely the concept of self-medication is cited, endorsed, and adopted, thus justifying the designation "theory." So indeed, perhaps, as the editors concluded, the time has come to speak and write of "self-medication theory."

As I indicated at the outset of this book, and in this most recent publication, the self-medication hypothesis provides a humanistic and empathic basis to understand and treat addictive disorders. So I have decided to include this last chapter as my final thoughts for this book. It sums up and appropriately expresses for me what "self-medication theory" provides—namely, what clinicians, scholars, and investigators need to get at to remediate the pain and suffering that drives addictive behavior.

CHAPTER 16

We Are All at Least a Little Lost and Off-Putting

ON TRANSFORMATION

As I approach my 80th year in life, I have come to the conclusion that we avoid a basic aspect of human existence—namely, we are all a little lost and not knowing, and we had better accept this. This is so whether it is the brash young man this morning who challengingly cuts in front of me to turn left when I thought I had the right of way at a four-way intersection; an academic pundit who presumptuously affirms what addictive illness is or is not about (a matter that I have studied and pondered about for over five decades); the interminable standoffs of entrenched politicians unable to come to terms to make our society work better; or the chilling remoteness of the privileged, famous, and wealthy.

Instead of facing this fundamental reality, we posture in ways that counter the feelings of loneliness, uncertainty, and powerlessness that are so basic to our nature. Some strut with attitudes of invincibility which, for example, can be the lot of high-performing athletes. The intellectually gifted speak with unfettered certainty about whatever is on their minds. Those unfortunate among us who have endured childhood trauma, deprivation, and neglect in adolescence and adulthood, may adopt uncaring and troubling solutions of violence, the gang, or addiction to express or hide their vulnerability and the inescapable distresses and pain that are so much a part of life.

Maybe it is because I was a first-generation American, born shortly after my parents came to America. Perhaps it was because of and despite the trauma my parents had experienced in the first genocide of the 20th century in Turkey and, later, great financial hardship when they came to America. They nevertheless remained unassuming, loving, and optimistic. I appreciated the pain and suffering they endured, but I also drew comfort and hope from them for a brighter future and a better world. But there always remained a part of me that was a little unsure and uncertain.

For all I know, the young man who cut me off was simply oblivious to me and in a hurry, but I suspect not. The academic who rigidly sticks to his ideas about the nature of addiction is simply blinded by adhering to a certain perspective. The politicians who squabble are simply motivated by ideological convictions. And who knows what the rich, wealthy, and privileged really consider and experience about their "special" lot in life? In all of this there seems to be so much mean-spiritedness. Whatever attitudes, beliefs, or postures such individuals assume, they likely are so inclined because they draw some comfort or satisfaction from what they do or how they think and behave. But they also pay a price. Feeling secure and so empowered has its advantages but it comes at the cost of setting oneself apart and being less apt to find commonalities and connections with others, a fundamental and necessary aspect of mature human adaption.

Dr. Ernest Kurtz, a student and scholar on the wisdom and benefit of 12-step programs, draws on the lessons of existential philosophers to instruct that acceptance of human limitations is the beginning of sanity for us as humans and the beginning of sobriety for alcoholics. A main lesson I have learned studying addiction is that we are less pleasure seekers (a myth commonly linked to addictive behavior) and more comfort and contact seekers. In the short term addictive drugs and behaviors create the illusion of well-being and relatedness. This goes back to the beginning of life. Scholars of infant development have amassed a large body of evidence indicating the infant is governed not so much by pursuit of pleasure or "oral gratification," but more to seek comfort and contact with his or her primary caretaker.

The human tendency to posture insensitively, arrogantly, imperially, and all-knowingly precludes us from facing and dealing with the lonely, confusing, and inescapably painful realities of human existence. I commonly remind my patients, especially in group therapy, that the worst fate in life is not to suffer; the worst fate is to suffer alone. It boils down to the challenges of creating in our own lives, and in society in general, multiple contexts, groups, and arrangements—therapeutic and otherwise—which foster meaningful and comforting connections and contacts with each other.

Individuals in recovery have learned this lesson well. Their AA meetings succeed in not only removing the offending agent (the alcohol) but most likely, and more importantly, the fellowship has fostered connections and personality growth that transforms them into more mature, caring, and altruistic people. Wouldn't this suit us all better as individuals and as a society?

CHAPTER 17

Tragic Trends in the Treatment of Addictive Illness

Why do so many die as a consequence of addiction? Is it in the inexorable, "progressive" nature of the disease? Or might it be the result of entrenched treatment approaches that repeatedly and increasingly become misaligned with the needs of individuals suffering from addictive disorders? For example, some need, and don't get:

- safety, structure, and support;
- medications for symptom reduction and control;
- nurturance and comfort;
- the company and "fellowship" of others; or
- storytelling and group sharing to understand their "errant" ways.

The list goes on, and every clinician could add what else might be needed or beneficial to address and provide for those suffering from addictive disorders. There continues to be a need for professionals who treat addiction, as well as all health care providers, to continue to fine tune approaches that work best and to avoid approaches that are exclusive or doctrinaire. I write this piece to reach an audience of those who suffer with addictive illness, those who witness it as caring friends and family, and to all clinicians who treat it. I do so to counter attitudes of stigma that diminish empathic concerns for the fate of addicted individuals, and attitudes of therapeutic despair that addictive disorders can engender. And finally, I write it to foster awareness of a problem in the addiction field, where parochial attitudes and practice can be harmful for individuals in need of treatment.

At any given time, we learn of the death of one more celebrity as the media blazons us with such tragic and unwelcome news, a most recent example being the death of Philip Seymour Hoffman. Their achievements and promise, and for some celebrities their notoriety, and the magnitude of such loss, bring us up short. We wonder what addiction is and why it is that it so often results in such deadly consequences. We are left to worry whether it could have been prevented. Celebrity status succeeds in drawing media attention to the scourge of addiction, but we must not forget the countless incidents throughout society, among the rich or poor, gifted or ordinary, and promising or stuck individuals who unheralded and ignominiously suffer the same fate.

Clearly effective models and approaches for understanding and treating addictive illness exist. These include 12-step programs, relapse prevention, cognitive behavioral approaches, harm reduction therapy, motivational interviewing, medication-assisted treatments (MATs), and dialectical behavioral therapy. In my clinical experience, modified psychodynamic individual and group treatments are extremely effective in addressing and resolving the emotional and behavioral problems that drive addictive disorders. Shedler (2010) has documented robust evidence that supports the efficacy of psychodynamic psychotherapy. Few empirical studies show such approaches work for addicted populations, but Shedler's findings apply to treatment of addictive disorders, in my experience. Such application needs further empirical study.

One of the problems in treating addictive disorders is polemics. The debates and controversies go on and date back a half century: Is addiction a disease or a symptom? Do psychiatric disorders cause addiction or is it the other way around? Is it environment or heredity? That debates are rancorous and often bitter is bad enough, but worse, they play out tragically in treatment when adherents of one approach or another rigidly apply a particular model alone to the exclusion of others.

Sadly—and in some cases disastrously—affected individuals are never offered alternative approaches after one option fails. Too often in my own practice, a patient is referred for consultation by a psychotherapist who has adopted a symptom approach alone, trying to get to root causes of drug and alcohol abuse without considering first the need to get the addictive behavior under control; or on the other hand, the patient who has tried and failed 12-step work for decades is told that he or she hasn't bottomed out or "doesn't want" sobriety.

Having authored ideas and perspectives of my own that have received fairly wide recognition (positive and negative)—such as the self-medication hypothesis of addiction (SMH), addiction as a self-regulation disorder, and the psychodynamics of addiction—I have experienced the attack and sting of polemic criticism and outright dismissal of my work and ideas. One example I came upon dismissed the SMH as "dangerously false and misleading" (DuPont 2007). In another case, a doctoral candidate informed me that her Institutional Review Board (IRB) warned her that she should not refer to self-medication in studying a population of chronically relapsing heroin addicts because the IRB felt it was risky and could precipitate relapse.

Of course, I am not alone in feeling the bite of criticism from colleagues. It comes with the territory. However, when it comes to addiction, the issues involved too often hinge on life and death. Rigid adherence by practitioners can jeopardize the course of one's addictive illness, including fatal consequences.

Recommendations

To treat effectively is to avoid the pitfall of approaches that derive from polemic and exclusive adherence to a particular treatment model. Instead, there is a need to combine and flexibly integrate elements of what we know works, whether it be 12-step treatment, individual or group psychotherapy, SMART recovery, medication-assisted treatments, and so on, in permutations and combinations acceptable to and compatible with our patients' needs. And finally, in response to the five bullets about shortcomings in treatment I outlined at the beginning, I would offer some final reflections:

- The structure, connections, and support provided by 12-step programs are natural correctives for the risk and shambles entailed with addictions, and despite its unacceptability to some, clinicians should encourage patients to expose themselves to the Alcoholics Anonymous (AA) traditions to discover whether the advantages and benefits the program provides will suit them. When individuals reject AA, it should not necessarily be considered denial or resistance, and alternative approaches should be considered.
- Many patients need medication management for addiction and co-occurring psychiatric disorders, which fuels the need to self-medicate symptoms associated with these conditions. (It is worth remembering that some of the highest co-occurrences with addiction are PTSD and bipolar disorder, conditions in which despair, rage, and agitation beg for amelioration and relief.) Medication-assisted therapies, such as methadone and buprenorphine, should clearly be considered, especially when a range of psychosocial treatments are not working.
- Kindness, empathy, understanding, and patience—these are powerful elements that should be basic to whatever psychotherapeutic approach is adopted, including facilitated 12-step programs; they are powerful antidotes to the discomfort, shame, and guilt heavily woven into the fabric of addictive problems. Confrontation should be avoided, but in extreme cases when necessary, when self-harm and danger are imminent, it must be done in a way that preserves self-esteem.

- Although AA is not considered psychotherapy, it truly is therapeutic in the sense that the fellowship and connections it provides work powerfully to reverse loneliness and isolation, factors that so commonly predispose to and result from addiction.
- Group therapies, including 12-step groups, provide interactive and validating experiences. Storytelling and sharing help members to reflect on their unmindful and risky behaviors and to pursue more thoughtful and measured ways to correct attitudes and actions associated with addictive behaviors.

Having focused in this piece on some dangerous attitudes and practices that threaten treatment outcomes and can actually endanger patients, it is worth mentioning that addictive disorders are far from a hopeless condition. Many patients get better. Addictions so often represent misguided attempts to deal with life challenges that involve troubled feeling, self-esteem, relationships, and self-care. They have opted for chemical solutions in place of human relational ones when they have felt unable to deal with these challenges. Effective treatments create pathways to help find such solutions. In my experience, patients who have found these solutions are some of the most admirable and mature individuals with whom I have worked.

References

DuPont, R. L., and Gold, M. S. (2007). Comorbidity and "self-medication." *Journal of Addictive Diseases* 26 (Supplement 1):13–23.

Shedler, J. (2010). The efficacy of psychodynamic psychotherapy. *American Psychologist* 65:98–109. http://www.apa.org/pubs/journals/releases/amp-65-2-98.pdf.

CHAPTER 18

Insights on the Insanity of Addiction

So much has been said and written about addiction, much of it so wisely put by individuals in and out of recovery. One popular adage is "the definition of insanity is doing the same thing over and over again and expecting a different outcome." In clinical terms, one of the most distinguishing diagnostic features of addictive disorders is that those affected continually and repeatedly revert to their addictive behaviors, despite the devastating negative and adverse consequences.

In my own career and investigative studies as an addiction specialist spanning many decades, I have emphasized that a primary factor that contributes to repeated abuse is that addictive substances temporarily relieve emotional pain and suffering that otherwise feel unmanageable or intolerable. That is, those who endure such distress self-medicate, and they wittingly or unwittingly provide support for the self-medication hypothesis (SMH) of addictive disorders, a theory that has received much endorsement and at least an equal amount of criticism and rejection (Khantzian 1985, 1997).

On occasion, I somewhat satirically comment that I believe in the SMH more on some days than others. Although I continue to believe that it is a powerful paradigm to explain addictive disorders, today was one of those times when I found myself thinking it does not satisfy the complexities (or perhaps the subtleties) involved in the bedeviling, repetitious, self-harming behaviors associated with addictions. An email from a former patient with whom I had parted ways because I relocated my office to another community stimulated my thoughts about the irrationality of addiction and doubt and curiosity about the SMH aspect of addiction.

Case Vignette

Matthew is a 55-year-old gifted author and college professor of English studies. After struggling for many years as a heavy drinker, he sought out professional help with only modest progress in obtaining control over his drinking. He finally established abstinence and a protracted period of sobriety (five years) before he started treatment with me. He then immersed himself in AA meetings, where he felt supported and found a caring sponsor to work with him.

For reasons not entirely clear but at least to some extent related to recent stressors (some related to chronic musculoskeletal pain), he resorted to periodically drinking large amounts of alcohol. The following e-mail typified that pattern, in this case indicating that his current drinking was in part celebratory:

> *Dear Dr K,*
> *I finally felt okay physically last week, when my class began. I had a great week, so much so that I wanted to celebrate/prolong and drank a bottle and a half of wine Friday night. Saturday was a total loss, but I managed to get out and buy one bottle of wine, which I consumed. Feel okay now and am ready for 4 straight days of classes.*
>
> *Not worried about drinking during the class, but certainly when it ends. The whole thing is very strange. I guess my life was turned upside down by the pain in recent months, not able to go to early morning meeting, etc. But something has to give . . . haven't quite figured it out. Don't feel committed to sobriety.*
>
> *Thanks so much for your text. Would love to come see you, but obviously I need to find someone in the area, sooner than later.*
> *Best, Matt*

I responded to his e-mail as follows:

> *Dear Matt,*
> *Get back to basics. That should include someone to work with you on the insanity of addiction. You know what to do as well as anyone else, and that is to get a safety net of others who care about and love you. YOU CAN'T DO THIS ALONE.*
>
> *I would also add that I am not entirely surprised about your notion that when you complete your course, you will be more apt to drink. Perhaps success creates the illusion that you can control the uncontrollable and be immune to the consequences of drinking.*
>
> *And should you continue to delay in finding someone, come see me in the interval for a sanity check.*
> *EJK*

I was reminded that persons addicted to substances find countless reasons to drink and drug—to grieve, to celebrate, to heighten feelings, to reduce or drown feelings, to get a job done, to drink when a job is done, and so on. Obviously, the reasons to self-medicate are myriad and the motives, seemingly contradictory.

My response to Matt was guided in part by my unyielding, evolving curiosity and interest in what it is that governs and drives the needs and issues that perpetuate addictions. So notwithstanding the criticisms of self-medication motives, the repetitive nature of the "insanity of addiction" does not necessarily contradict. Rather, it begs the question whether addictive behaviors accomplish or fix anything for those who repeatedly resort to it.

To Matt's credit, he followed up with several e-mails and a phone call to indicate that he was more aggressively seeking out an addiction counselor locally to obtain support and to regain control of the drinking.

When addicted persons in recovery speak of the puzzling sense of powerlessness and inability to control their drinking, as Matthew suggests in his e-mail, they also often indicate how the irrationality of it is so painful and bedeviling. As I indicated, the irrational component challenges me as well, on some days more than others, including whether the ideas and theories of addiction psychiatry are sufficient to address and explain what seems so unexplainable and confusing.

I offer a few thoughts here, drawing on my clinical experiences and ideas about addiction, which might shed light on what often can seem irrational and incomprehensible. Although modern neuroscience research has yielded important findings on how substances alter the brain and contribute to addictive patterns of use and misuse, such brain changes and mechanisms alone are insufficient to explain the complexities of dependence on alcohol and addictive drugs. I do not suggest that I have all the answers, but I believe that clinical study and treatment of addiction offer valuable insights into repetitious, self-harm behaviors, as unreasonable as they may seem.

In treatment, my patients consistently reveal their life-long difficulties in dealing with their feelings. They have been plagued by issues of poor sense of self and low self-esteem. Their relationships with others suffer, and they find it difficult to practice self-care. Often they fail to appreciate very real danger—in their surroundings and especially those associated with addiction. I refer to these issues as the human challenge of self-regulation. Persons at risk for addiction are underdeveloped or deficient in some or all of these areas.

In my experience, in the context of experimenting with addictive substances, some people *discover* (italics for emphasis) that addictive substances provide short-term relief from the pain, suffering, and dysfunction associated with their problems in regulating their emotions, low self-esteem, and difficulties with interpersonal relationships. These factors then malignantly interact with deficits in self-care to make addictive attachments more likely.

Thinking about addiction as a self-regulation disorder "helps" in part to explain how addictive substances assist in regulating a wide range of challenges. Considering addiction from such a perspective provides some measure of understanding for what seems so unreasonable, irrational, and incomprehensible.

Returning to Matthew and his dilemma: he knows that resorting to alcohol will be devastating, but he nevertheless feels powerless to avoid that prospect. As we so often say in our work as psychiatrists and mental health professionals, people have their reasons for what they believe, say, and do, as unreasonable and irrational as it may seem. Addicted individuals, including my patient Matthew, do not have exclusive claim to this aspect of human existence.

References

Khantzian, E. J. (1985). The self-medication hypothesis of addictive disorders: Focus on heroin and cocaine dependence. *American Journal of Psychiatry* 142:1259–64.

———. (1997). The self-medication hypothesis of substance use disorders: A reconsideration and recent applications. *Harvard Review of Psychiatry* 4:231–44.

CHAPTER 19

The Cruel Scourge of Addiction

AN ADDICTION PSYCHIATRIST'S CLINICAL VIEW

The cruel scourge of addiction keeps hitting home and the headlines keep blazing that it is of epidemic proportions. At least two to three times a week media accounts—in our local newspaper as well as the *Boston Globe*—herald people succumbing to and dying of addiction, most of them young.

Last week the dose of cruelty got heavier for me. A father and mother were found dead by their ten- and eight-year-old old children from presumed heroin overdoses. This was in my hometown, no less. Additionally, this morning another account revealed the pathetic theft of a donation box intended for Christmas gifts for underprivileged children, stolen from a nearby store. The perpetrator was a young man addicted to heroin. An unrelated story in the same edition recounted the plea bargaining of an addicted, intoxicated, 21-year-old, unlicensed woman who struck and killed two cyclists, injuring two others. And again, I recently noticed in an obituary for a man, an only child in his 20s, whose parents were either bereft or courageous enough to disclose in the obituary that he had died of a drug overdose. Although I am a psychiatrist who is trained and disciplined to understand and treat these disorders, these ongoing stories and accounts leave me feeling helpless and despairing, I expect much like the family and friends who endured all these tragic losses.

Addictive disorders are the consequence of complex factors involving biological, psychological, and social influences that weave their way into the fabric and evolution of the illness. Over the past 15 years the problem has been compounded by the increasing availability of prescription opiates, in particular oxycodone. When individuals become addicted to medically prescribed opiates, and they become more difficult and expensive to obtain, they switch to the more readily available and less expensive heroin. Over time or immediately, they individuals resort to intravenous injection. However, availability alone is not a sufficient factor to account for all the tragic consequences of deadly heroin overdoses.

What I offer here is a psychological, psychodynamic perspective, one in which there has been far too little attention. A major focus of my five-decade career has involved treating people in recovery while studying, lecturing, and writing about addictive disorders. It is written from a perspective that draws on my in-depth exploration of the emotional and behavioral vulnerabilities that predispose to and result in addictive disorders. Such an approach, often combined and integrated with other approaches, has had important beneficial effects on recovery and outcomes for my patients in treatment. Colleagues and students adopting such a perspective report similar findings and results.

Unfortunately, in an era where studies of addiction treatment rely so heavily on empirical evidence, the findings from a psychodynamic approach and the case study method (i.e., practice-based evidence) have fallen out of favor, thus making it more likely the findings from such an approach do not pass muster for acceptance and publication in peer reviewed publications. Because of this, such valuable findings go unnoticed or are underappreciated. So this piece is offered for peers, scholars, and students of addiction to consider clinical and psychological dimensions of addictive vulnerability that warrant further exploration, study, and application for treating addictive disorders.

Before proceeding, a disclaimer is in order. Critics of explorative and/or psychodynamic treatments all too often assume practitioners adopting such methods wait on getting to the root causes of addiction to produce abstinence and sobriety. Of course, anyone doing so (whatever their orientation) are remiss, if not grossly mistaken. Modern day methods that effectively address the need for abstinence and control at the outset—12-step programs, extended rehabilitation confinement, medication-assisted treatment (MAT)—should and need to be adopted to ensure stability and safety first. It is then that investigative study of and correction for root addictive vulnerabilities are in order to address the most bedeviling and pernicious aspects of addiction—namely, relapse.

I am admittedly not dispassionate about the lot of my patients whom I have treated and studied. Besides the complexities that need unravelling when considering causes and consequences of addiction, the issues are further complicated by competing concepts and approaches that too often are pitted against one another, rather that integrating and considering what models for understanding and treatment or combination of treatments will best serve the need of any particular person in need of help.

Too often our reactions and attitudes about addiction are misguided by stereotypes and misinterpretations. A couple of the more notorious ones, that have roots in recent and past clinical and scientific models, are that addictive behavior is driven by pleasure seeking and/or suicidal motives. This is a terrible misunderstanding about addiction that stands in the way of our collective and individual need to feel more empathy for those who succumb. Based on my experience and that of other clinicians who work with addictive disorders, it becomes inescapably apparent that addiction is rooted in human suffering and unhappiness, not pleasure seeking or self-destructive motives. It's the bad news and the good news about our lot as humans. It is what I refer to as "the challenge of self-regulation." We are not hard-wired to face the human challenges of regulating our emotions, self-esteem, relationships, and behaviors, especially our self-care. Some get disordered in some or all of these areas and great pain and distress results, causing such individuals to resort to addictive solutions to cope with these challenges. Otherwise when we more successfully meet, overcome, and master these challenges, we come out more flexible and adaptable as human beings. As I put it in a recent publication, the alternatives proffer for dissatisfaction and misery, or for satisfaction and joy (Khantzian 2012).

The distress and dysfunctions involved with the challenges in self-regulation for addictively prone individuals have varied origins. As indicated, I will focus here primarily on the pain and suffering at the core of addictive illness. As alluring and seductive as addictive substances seem, they are not universally appealing or captivating for those who experiment with or try them. Many try them, but only a minority becomes dependent upon them. However, susceptible individuals experimenting with these drugs discover that something is set right for them. It is not by chance that people with mood disorders, posttraumatic stress disorders (PTSD), pre-psychotic conditions, and schizophrenia are especially vulnerable. There is an inordinately high co-occurrence of these disorders with addiction. They are very painful conditions that share in common intense threatening feelings to self and others involving agitation, rage, and aggression. At the other extreme, feelings are elusive, cut off, or confusing, and individuals may self-medicate the dysphoric feelings associated with such threatening, vague, and persistent emotional states.

One need not suffer with a psychiatric condition to discover that addictive drugs can ameliorate distress. For a variety of reasons having to do with growing up or disturbing environmental influences, certain individuals suffer because they are discomforted or threatened by painful emotions that cause persistent distress not readily identifiable or associated with a psychiatric disorder. For others, addictive drugs provide short-term relief from feelings of low self-esteem and may lessen associated difficulties in getting along with other people. You have to love yourself to get along with others. Little wonder that clinicians and patients alike speak of the "fix" that individuals derive from their drug of choice. And yes, although individuals experiment with many drugs, they do navigate or prefer particular ones.

For example, opiates are powerful agents to dampen intense violent and angry feelings. Furthermore, in low to moderate doses alcohol softens individuals' defenses to have feelings about self and others that they ordinarily cannot experience or allow, and in obliterating doses alcohol can knock out a whole range of unwelcome feelings. Stimulants cast a wider net and have their appeal because they can counter low self-esteem for those suffering with depression, can boost energy levels for people who need to maintain expansive mood or activities, and can act paradoxically to calm and focus those who suffer attention and hyperactivity problems (Khantzian 1997).

So what about treatment? As a colleague of mine said a long time ago, "One of the best kept secrets in medicine is how treatable these conditions are." In my estimation this still holds true, and furthermore, we have many more tools now than we had then. Individuals get better.

However, there remain complications and hurdles. Needless to say some addictive disorders are more challenging and problematic than others. Often, especially in the case of opiate dependency, the problem of chronicity is a major one. We do not have the resources and programs to diagnose early and often enough to counter the powerful physical and psychological dependency these drugs produce, especially when duration has been protracted. Additionally, if dysregulated emotions are predisposed to opiate dependency, the course of addiction heightens the problems of intense and dysregulated emotions.

For the opiate and other drug dependency disorders, we indeed have effective treatments. These include a number of medication-assisted treatments (MATs) such as buprenorphine, methadone, naltrexone, and others; a range of new and old psychotherapies such as CBT, MET, DBT, and psychodynamic therapy; 12-step treatments; and extended rehabilitation programs. In addition, when carefully evaluated, diagnosed, and treated, individuals with co-occurring psychiatric disorders can benefit on both fronts when a skilled clinician combines different psychosocial interventions in a flexible and individualized fashion.

The problem, however, of mixing and matching treatment options to meet patients' needs remains a big one, as is the related issue of what patients will and will not accept. It is not a well-kept secret, and an unfortunate one, that various approaches get pitted against each other and often there is a failure to consider alternative or combination of approaches when a particular one is not working. I have had the unfortunate experience of witnessing extreme cases when intensive psychotherapy was used to get at root causes of the addiction, but there was a failure to consider treatments that would have addressed unbridled drug and alcohol use. At the other extreme, an individual had attended 12-step meetings for decades at the insistence of a counselor despite repeated relapses, and alternative treatments had never been considered. In such cases, entrenched, doctrinaire approaches can have tragic consequences.

Addiction is not a hopelessly chronic and unremitting problem dooming those affected to all the cruel and tragic consequences that we witness on a daily basis. It should not necessarily be so. Rather it is incumbent on us as citizens, clinicians, and affected "consumers" to insist and expect of ourselves, each other, and our political and professional leaders to afford, cultivate, and establish the wide range of resources and treatments, flexibly applied, that can assure comprehensive, effective, and alternative programs and treatments that will improve chances of getting better and recovery. Otherwise, the unrelenting heartbreaking accounts of addiction will persist at epidemic proportions.

References

Khantzian, E. J. (1997). The self-medication hypothesis of substance use disorders: A reconsideration and recent applications. *Harvard Review of Psychiatry* 4 (5): 231–44.
———. (2012). Reflections on treating addictive disorders: A psychodynamic perspective. *American Journal on Addictions* 21 (3): 274–79.

CHAPTER 20

Life Lessons Learned from Addictions

I have been working with individuals who have succumbed to and recovered from addictive disorders for the better part of five decades. It has been an adventure taking me into the realms of human vulnerability, suffering, and resiliency. The journey has also shown me that addicted individuals have many of the same life experiences we all encounter. In the realm of human psychology, we all face issues of survival and getting along with each other. Our common challenges include regulation of our emotions, self-esteem, relationships, and self-care. Put more simply, to study addiction is to study the psychological challenges we all face. In what follows, I offer some vignettes drawn from clinical experience and daily life that allow us to consider some of the lessons learned from addiction.

The Two-Part Secret to Life

My patients who have experienced the benefits of recovery have taught me the two most important ingredients for their success: show up and hang in there.

To run the risk of sounding corny or simplistic, the two-part secret is an effective guide to dealing with many of life's problems, and recovering addicted individuals learn this well. There has been ongoing controversy over the past several decades whether 12-step programs are the preferable approach for addictive disorders. Some of this debate is legitimate and some of it polarized and unfortunate. As with most effective therapeutic regimens, when adhered to the results are beneficial. In Alcoholics Anonymous (AA) and related programs, there is a saying: "More meetings more sobriety; less meetings less sobriety; no meetings no sobriety." I offer a recent clinical example.

CASE VIGNETTE

> Nancy, a 57-year-old patient whom I hadn't seen for several years, suddenly called me late one night. It was evident that besides being intoxicated, Nancy was frantic about her condition and its effect on her work and career. She asked for help "getting some rest" and getting detoxified from her heavy reliance on alcohol. I gave her an appointment for the next morning for an evaluation and referral to an appropriate program for detoxification and rehabilitation.
>
> When I first saw her the following morning, I was struck by her haggard appearance and rambling manner—a far cry from the poised, attractive, and well-spoken person I remembered. Although she had abstained from alcohol for nine years and had participated in regular AA meetings, after a divorce from an abusive husband she had stopped going to meetings and resumed periodic drinking. Over the past couple of years, her alcohol consumption increased and she was now drinking heavily. Initially she was resistant to my suggestion that she be hospitalized but finally agreed to self-commit for detoxification. She called me that evening, more lucid and articulate, and expressed relief to be there and mentioned that she had attended a good AA meeting.

At our family Thanksgiving dinner six months earlier, I had shared the two-part secret to life with 10 of our grandchildren. I told them that I had learned the secret from my patients and that I was thankful that their parents adhered to this idea and always showed up for their children, hanging in, for example, by driving them to athletic and social events. I said how thankful we were for our grandchildren successfully sticking with their academic and athletic activities. I reminded them that all of this was not without disappointments and setbacks, but that they were succeeding by persistence, again emphasizing our gratitude for that. I was pleased several days later when two of my children mentioned how impressed the grandchildren were with my Thanksgiving thoughts.

I believed that Nancy's comment about "a good AA meeting" in the detox program might be a hopeful sign that she would get back to the basics of showing up and hanging in there. She needed the connection with others to correct her tendency to isolate, which was greatly amplified by her drinking. She needed to share her shame and guilt for her relapse, to benefit from a caring and forgiving environment, and to be supported by people who could help her work through her feelings about losing control and loss of self-esteem.

I may seem preachy but, more hopefully, instructive in reminding my patients (and my grandchildren) that success in life requires paying attention to the basics, starting with showing up and hanging in there.

Look Both Ways before Crossing the Street

Self-care, which some individuals who are prone to addiction lack, involves basic habits of health and safety. More specifically, it affects how individuals think, feel, and behave around dangerous and risky situations. The rule of crossing the street is a basic one—but it likely goes back further than that. Think of the toddler in the family room who bumps into a coffee table. Most parents know enough to comfort and soothe the child and caution him or her to be careful. However, some parents hit the table and say, "Bad table!" That's the wrong message. The toddler needs comfort and guidance, not a message that attributes the mishap to external environmental hazards.

Too often careless and dangerous behavior of addicted individuals is simply attributed to impulsivity, stimulus seeking, and risk taking, when in fact we fail to consider how such an individual's guidance systems (technically I refer to it as an ego function/capacity) for self-care and safety are underdeveloped or absent. Patients with addiction disorders think and feel differently in the face of danger, especially those involved with addiction and related behaviors. But these kinds of behavioral lapses and shortcomings are on a continuum for all of us. You need not have an addiction to suffer this kind of lapse. In what follows, I share maddening instances that involved operating an automobile, some of which test the limits of my self-care and safety.

There's an alley for cars off the parking lot of my office building that leads in and out of the lot. The way out of the alley is a blind corner with no indication of traffic on the exit out of the lot. When I leave, I proceed with extreme caution because anyone driving out of the exit can't see me. I continue to be dumbfounded by how little attention is exhibited by drivers zipping out of the lot with no thought of caution. It seems to be a clear setup for an accident. I suppose this seems like a minor hazard compared with the wide range of dangers we all encounter on our highways, but it still unnerves me that leaving my office feels like a daily opportunity for a major mishap. Perhaps I fuss too much, but maybe if we all fussed a little more, the world would be a safer place.

Tailgating also puts me and others in jeopardy. I sometimes glibly share my reactions about this with my patients to make a point about safe behaviors. Namely, I say there are two types of tailgaters—the mean ones and the oblivious ones. I emphasize the latter, but both greatly aggravate me (usually expressed not so delicately). I lament that there seems to be so little margin for safety with such driving.

But I leave out my own contribution to lapses in judgment when I angrily make some gesture (non-obscene of course) to tailgaters who place me and my passengers in danger. My wife has to remind me, and I have to remind myself, that it is at least as dangerous to react to tailgaters as it is to tailgate.

Working with patients in recovery, I learned to pay close attention to my feelings and thoughts as a reaction to my patients' stories of the dangers and risks associated with their addictions. I echoed those reactions to my patients so that they could appreciate and understand their lack of alarm that so often left them at risk. But, lapses in worry and thought fall on a continuum. The lessons learned by addicted patients in recovery about safe living should instruct us all about the value of caution and worry. When feelings of anxiety and fear are absent, we are often put in harm's way; when they are extreme, we are paralyzed. The right dose of worry will guide us more than imperil us.

Disputes and Debates about Heredity

There are far too many disputes and polarizing arguments about the nature and treatment of addictive disorders. The influence of heredity is among the most notable. Scholars, clinicians, and the public debate its influence. Alcoholism is a prime example. Concordance rates for alcoholism among identical twins are 50/50: if one twin suffers from alcoholism, there is a 50 percent chance that the other twin will have the same disorder. Beyond twin studies, it is less clear how influential heredity is in the development of alcohol dependence.

A grandmother who had consulted me about her daughter's alcohol misuse and, later, her granddaughter's addiction wrote to me recently raising the question about heredity in a poignant e-mail:

> Dr. Khantzian,
> Not knowing how family mental issues can affect other generations I am sending you a summary of what I know of the families on both sides.
>
> My mother suffered from depression and anxiety the last 35 years of her life. My brother Ted struggled with depression from his early 20s and used anxiety meds as drugs until he was 55, when he committed suicide. I have been treated for depression since 1976. Stewart [my daughter's son] has been treated for depression but is not in treatment now. And as you know Sharon [my daughter] has dealt with drugs and depression. Thank God it seems that now it is under control. She still sees Dr. F. My other daughter is also being treated for depression.
>
> My husband was treated for depression over the last 12 years of his life. His sister's son who had been on drugs committed suicide when he was 18. His sister's daughter who is in her 60s was diagnosed as bipolar many years ago. Meredith's [my granddaughter] uncle committed suicide

several years ago. I do not know if drugs were involved or if he had depression. It is so frightening to see Meredith's drug use and depression. Thank you for your help.

It is interesting how a narrative often makes a more compelling case than an empirical study. In the case of the grandmother, heredity jumps out as a possible cause of much suffering, disability, and tragic consequences. But if it is hereditary, it is not clear what is inherited. Is it a specific gene or is it temperament? Or is it a more complex interaction, with one's childhood environment and aberrant DNA molecules, that renders so many to the fate that the grandmother and her family succumbed to? I learned from Meredith's father, with whom I also consulted, that Meredith's mother was abusive and neglectful. In addition, I had a chance to meet with Meredith about decisions for a rehab confinement to overcome a dependency on heroin. She revealed to me a pattern of emotional instability and major difficulties in controlling her behaviors. Her father's accounts of her erratic behavior, and Meredith's own description of her behavioral and emotional difficulties, appeared to be more consistent with a borderline personality organization, a condition that more often originates and is rooted in environmental influences and less so in genetics.

The lesson here is that once again, reductive conclusions about human development, whether they are about environmental or biologic factors, often obscure more than they clarify. The grandmother's tale, most recently focusing on her granddaughter's behavioral and addiction problems, begs the issue of complexity. The grandmother's account of the apparent family biological loading, as compelling as it seems, leads to more questions than conclusions about our nature and susceptibility to the range of human troubles that befall us.

Some Final Musings

Beyond the lessons about persistence, self-care, and the complexities involved in causation offered here by those who suffer and recover from addictive disorders, there is more that can be learned from individuals who endure and mend. But a final message here is to gather in a few of them at a time to assure acceptance and empathy in tolerable and learnable doses. For those who endure these conditions, as well as for ourselves, who to varying degrees are challenged with these vulnerabilities, there is an opportunity to cultivate a kinder understanding of addicted individuals—and to see that we, too, can err or falter from similar human shortcomings.

CHAPTER 21

"Psychophobia" and Getting It Right

It remains a major peeve of mine that we still keep missing some of the most fundamentally important reasons why addictive substances and behaviors are so absorbing and compelling. The following is based on a condensed version of an article I recently wrote for the website FIX. Dating back four decades, the distinguished scholar and psychoanalyst Leon Wurmser wrote of "psychophobia" in relation to our disinclination to get at the psychological roots of addiction. From my own work and perspective, working with my patients spanning five decades, it is my belief that the phobia has at least a twofold reason—reasons that originate in our patients, and ones that originate in us as clinicians and investigators—namely, confusing and unbearable emotional pain and suffering causes susceptible individuals to avoid their distress and opt for addictive solutions. The experience is contagious. If we are not careful, we too succumb to the avoidance because the depth and intensity of the suffering is commensurably unendurable for those of us who witness and treat it, thus the "psychophobia" and the tendency to not get at the roots of addiction.

We still don't get it right when it comes to understanding addiction. The most recent example of our failure to appreciate what makes addictive behavior so compelling is the burgeoning widespread addiction to the synthetic opiate oxycodone—with all of its tragic consequences. We keep reacting as if the problem is the potency of the drug itself that leads to the escalation and progression to the more deadly intravenous use of heroin. The example that is most frequently encountered is the instances where oxycodone was initially prescribed for some medical or surgical problem, but then the person becomes "hooked." And of course there is the example of adolescents experimenting with addictive agents as a presumed and invariable stepping stone to become addicted. As the psychoanalyst Sandor Rado instructed at the turn of the 20th century, it is not the drug

253

but the urge to use it that causes addiction. Most of us by now appreciate that addictive substances are not universally appealing.

I offer another example that has recently caught my attention as yet another mischaracterization and misunderstanding of what addiction is about. This one has to do with recent clinician warnings that addicted individuals on the street and in correctional settings are seeking out Seroquel®, the powerful antipsychotic drug, to "get high." The phenomenon is referred to as a "Q Ball," drawing parallel to street use of "speedball" injections (a combination of a stimulant and heroin). It is one more pejorative and stigmatizing characterization of addictive behavior when individuals use the drug. Some characterize the drug as a sedative. The term "sedative" does not do justice to the effects of medications like Seroquel. Medications in this category are powerful agents to quell states of agitation, intense fear and uncontrollable rage and violent feelings. Recent reports, for example, indicate that quetiapine is effective in treating patients who suffer from borderline personality, a condition in which the aforementioned intense painful emotions predominate. Opiate pain medications have similar actions. As a returning combat veteran suffering from all the violent feelings of rage and anger associated with his PTSD put it, "I don't use the heroin to get high; I use it to feel normal." Pharmaceuticals such as Seroquel are powerful calming agents, which in good part explain their appeal. Yet, unlike addictive drugs, Seroquel does not cause tolerance or physical dependence.

Opiates may similarly be used by persons who have difficulty managing their rage and aggression, which I posit are more often linked back to earlier traumatic exposure to violence and aggression. In this manner, opiate abuse functions as a temporary adaptive response that mutes and attenuates disorganizing and threatening rage and aggression.

So I argue that simplified explanations for the seductiveness of drugs are insufficient explanations for the development of addiction, whether it is alcohol, cocaine, marijuana, oxycodone or Seroquel. The use, misuse and sometimes dependence on these substances are driven by a meaningful and purposeful connection between the inner state of the individual and the effects of the person's drug of choice. As psychoanalyst Debra Rothschild has pointed out, in addiction theory and practice "the object of study should be the individual rather than the substance."

The fact is that individuals who experience extreme physical trauma (e.g., painful burn conditions), and are treated with opiate pain killers, in the largest majority of instances do not become addicted. What more likely happens is a vulnerable person discovers that such drugs counter more than the feelings of physical pain. Rather, the drugs grab hold of susceptible individuals because knowingly or unknowingly they suffer with coexisting psychiatric conditions and painful psychological feelings and states. A recovering alcoholic physician, a reserved and reticent man, described himself as a "born-again isolationist" and, in exquisite and colorful language, described in group therapy how the preparation and consumption of a gin martini "fixed" him—the scent of the bitters, the crackling of the ice, and so on. Then he exuberantly exclaimed, "I could feel free, be one of the guys, I could join the human race!"

Addictive drugs, as powerfully compelling as they can be, are not universally appealing. Whether in non-medical experimentation or legitimate medical use, most individuals exposed to these drugs do not become addicted. We still tend to explain the appeal of addictive drugs on the basis of reward and pleasure ("the high). Then, if it is not pleasure or physical pain that causes addiction, why are some of us more vulnerable than others to addiction? Beyond biological addictive mechanisms of tolerance and withdrawal, and genetic predispositions, we have had enough extensive clinical evidence backed by empirical studies to conclude that addictive disorders are related to the powerful effects addictive drugs have on a range of co-occurring painful feeling states and psychiatric conditions, thus giving them their appeal. For those so predisposed, the action of addictive drugs, short term, are experienced as a magical elixir and corrective. And one need not suffer from a painful psychiatric condition, however, to find addictive drugs appealing. Those who endure excessive painful or intolerable emotions are also more likely to find inordinate relief and comfort in addictive drugs. If there is "reward" associated with addictions, it is less the reward of pleasure, but more the reward of relief from intense psychological suffering.

CHAPTER 22

The Theory of Self-Medication and Addiction

The Self-Medication Hypothesis

Throughout the span of my career, I have adhered to the maxim that to understand and to feel understood is a powerful antidote to relieve human psychological suffering. Treating individuals with substance use disorders is no exception. Too frequently, people who have succumbed to drug addiction have heard dire predictions from family, friends, and clinicians of what the drugs do *to* them—a reaction that more often than not is unhelpful. Such reactions heighten the shame and guilt that persons with substance addiction heap upon themselves (as does society at large) and contribute to the already considerable burden of stigma.

In contrast, it is more empathic and fruitful to ask, "What did the drug do *for* you?" The self-medication hypothesis (SMH) of addiction is embedded in this inquiry—an inquiry that I pursue with all my patients. It is a powerful and relationship-building way to start treatment with patients. It invites exploration and understanding of the critical feelings and related issues that predispose one to use addictive drugs.

SELF-MEDICATION

The self-medication hypothesis, a theory about addiction, was first published in 1985 as a cover article in the *American Journal of Psychiatry* (Khantzian 1985). It focused on how and why individuals are drawn to and become dependent on heroin and cocaine. An updated version was published in the *Harvard Review of Psychiatry* in 1997 with application to conditions that had not been previously considered (Khantzian 1997). The hypothesis of self-medication derives from clinical evaluation and treatment of thousands of patients (practice-based evidence) spanning five decades. It is a theory that has been and continues to be endorsed. It is widely and regularly cited and endorsed by clinicians and investigative scholars, as evidenced in research websites such as Research Gate, Academia.edu, and Google Scholar. In an article in the *American Journal of Psychiatry*, Mark S. Gold (2000) concluded that it was one of the most "intuitively appealing theories" about addiction.

Yet the theory has also been trivialized and dismissed. The expression "self-medication" has become a household expression that detracts from the emotional suffering and complexities of feelings that are at the root of a person's need to self-medicate. And, it has been dismissed outright in some quarters. But, alternative theories that get at the root of understanding addiction have been few and far between. Theories are important because they help to identify the facts.

Despite the extraordinarily wide inroad of addictive drugs in our society, especially the scourge of opiate dependency and all its tragic and deadly consequences, it is bewildering and disconcerting that we have so little understanding of the reasons for drug addiction. Perhaps part of this is that the recovery culture has designated and popularized alcoholism and addictions as a "disease," emphasizing the lasting consequences of drug effects on the brain. Neuroscientists have similarly concluded addiction is a "primary disease," which underscores brain pathways that explain the physiological bases for addiction and relapse. As one neuroscientist said, "Addictive drugs hijack the brain."

This perspective has stimulated breakthrough findings on underlying brain mechanisms and pathways that provide a biological explanation for addiction, but there have been few or minimal corresponding explorations of why addictive drugs have such a powerful psychological appeal or hold on individuals who succumb to addiction. The SMH provides a valuable investigative and clinical paradigm to address this challenging issue.

Table 22.1. The Self-Medication Hypothesis

The self-medication hypothesis maintains that suffering (not pleasure seeking) is at the heart of addictive disorders such that:

1. During the short term they relieve painful feelings and psychological distress.

2. There is a considerable degree of preference in a person's drug of choice, but it isn't as though a person "chooses" a drug; rather, while experimenting with various drugs he or she discovers that the effect of a particular drug is experienced as welcome because it changes or relieves feeling states that are painful or unwanted for reasons special to that person.

Whether it is in the offices of prescribing physicians or in the environs of young people exposed to or experimenting with addictive drugs, only 10–20 percent of users become addicted. It begs the question, "Why is this so?" In the pursuit of answers to this question, the SMH has provided a generation of clinicians with an effective path to help them and their patients understand why this is so and to work out alternative solutions (see table 22.1).

EMOTIONAL STATES

Feelings (e.g., sadness, fear, anxiety, anger) are powerful governing emotions in many aspects of our lives. They determine how we regulate ourselves; they are the basis by which we develop a sense of self-esteem and who we are; they are the foundation for a sense of well-being; they are the currency for human connection and attachment; and they are a primary ingredient for guiding our behavior, especially our capacity for self-care, which guides us in the contexts of risk and danger but is often underdeveloped in persons prone to addiction.

Feelings can be a source of comfort and well-being, or more ominously they can be powerfully unsettling and threatening. It is in this latter instance that drugs can become captivating and addictive. Troubling or disturbing feelings persist for a range of reasons. Some originate in early childhood development as a consequence of trauma or neglect. In adults, emotional states become evident as symptoms or are expressed in temperament or aspects of their personality. For some, distressful feelings are intense, volatile, and threatening. In others, feelings

Table 22.2.   Emotion-Altering Actions of Addict Drugs

Drug class	Action
Opiates (e.g., oxycodone, heroin, morphine)	Reduce intense feelings of anger, rage, agitation
Depressants (e.g., alcohol, benzodiazepines, barbiturates	
Low to moderate doses	Relax restricted, tense, anxious feelings
High doses	Obliterate distressing emotions
Stimulants (e.g., cocaine, amphetamines, methylphenidate)	Activate and energize depressed individuals; augment hypomanic individuals; calm and improve focus for persons with ADHD
Cannabis	Both stimulating and sedating, depending on the symptoms

remain inaccessible and confusing, rendering the sufferer vulnerable to a nameless interminable dysphoria. For yet others, the painful emotions are rooted in more readily identifiable co-occurring psychiatric conditions.

It is not so much that these individuals seek euphoria, but rather the aim is relief of dysphoria. It is not surprising that individuals with any of these conditions could become attached to the powerful change in emotional state that drugs can provide, especially persons who are prone to addiction. Table 22.2 briefly summarizes the effects of some emotion-altering drugs.

As suggested, dependency on addictive drugs may or may not be associated with co-occurring psychiatric disorders. Conversely, in conditions such as PTSD, borderline personality, and bipolar disorders—conditions in which anger and rage can predominate—the disproportionately high co-occurrence with opiate addiction is too great to be by chance (Darke 2013).

Conclusion

SMH is a theory that gets at the human psychological underpinnings of addictive disorders. It does not compete with approaches that emphasize biological or social factors. More likely, the perspectives complement each other. If judiciously integrated, they can enrich our approach to unravelling and solving the elusive equation of addiction. Such an understanding and perspective is in the best humanistic traditions of science, medicine, and psychiatry.

References

Darke, S. (2013). Pathways to heroin dependence: Time to reappraise self-education. *Addiction* 108:659–67.

Gold, M. S. (2000). Treating addiction as a human process. *American Journal of Psychiatry* 157 (11): 1892–94.

Khantzian, E. J. 1985. The self-medication hypothesis of addictive disorders. *American Journal of Psychiatry* 142:1259–64.

———. (1997). The self-medication hypothesis of substance use disorders: A reconsideration and recent applications. *Harvard Review of Psychiatry* 4:231–44.

Credits

The author gratefully acknowledges permission to reprint the following:

CHAPTER 1

Khantzian, E. J. Understanding addictive vulnerability: An evolving psychodynamic perspective. (Target article with commentaries.) *Neuropsychoanalysis* 5 (2003): 5–21. Reprinted by permission of the publisher (Taylor & Francis Ltd., http://www.tandf online.com).

CHAPTER 2

Khantzian, E. J., and Weegmann, M. Questions of substance: Psychodynamic reflections on addictive vulnerability and treatment. *Psychodynamic Practice* 15 (2009): 365–80. Reprinted by permission of the publisher (Taylor & Francis Ltd., http://www.tandf online.com).

CHAPTER 3

Khantzian, E. J. Addiction: Why are some of us more vulnerable than others? *Counselor: The Magazine for Addiction Professionals* 9 (2008): 10–16. Copyright © 2008 by Health Communications Inc. on behalf of the publishers. www.counselormagazine.com.

CHAPTER 4

Khantzian, E. J. The capacity for self-care and addiction. *Counselor: The Magazine for Addiction Professionals* 12 (2011): 36–40. Copyright © 2011 by Health Communications Inc. on behalf of the publishers. www.counselormagazine.com.

CHAPTER 5

Khantzian, E. J. The self-medication hypothesis and attachment theory: Pathways for understanding and ameliorating addictive suffering. In *Addictions from an Attachment Perspective: Do Broken Bonds and Early Trauma Lead to Addictive Behaviours?*, edited by Richard Gill. London: Karnac Books, 2014. Reprinted with kind permission of Karnac Books.

CHAPTER 6

Khantzian, E. J. The self-medication hypothesis as a problem in self-regulation. In *Understanding Addiction as Self Medication: Finding Hope behind the Pain*, 13–20. Lanham, MD: Rowman & Littlefield, 2008. Reprinted with the kind permission of Rowman & Littlefield.

CHAPTER 7

Khantzian, E. J. The self-medication hypothesis revisited: The dually diagnosed patient. *Primary Psychiatry* 10 (2003): 47–54. Reprinted with the kind permission of *Primary Psychiatry*.

CHAPTER 8

Suh, J. J., Ruffins, S., Robins, C. E., Albanese, M. J., and Khantzian, E. J. Self-medication hypothesis: Connecting affective experience and drug choice. *Psychoanalytic Psychology* 25 (2008): 518–32. Copyright © 2008 by American Psychological Association. Reproduced with permission.

CHAPTER 9

Mariani, J. J., Khantzian, E. J., and Levin FR. (Cover Article). The self-medication hypothesis and psychostimulant treatment of cocaine dependence: An update. *American Journal on Addiction* 23 (2014): 189–93. Reprinted with the kind permission of John Wiley and Sons.

CHAPTER 10

Khantzian, E. J. The psychodynamics of addiction and its treatment—an interview. *New Therapist* (September/October 2013): 5–9. http://www.newtherapist.com.

CHAPTER 11

Khantzian, E. J. Reflections on group treatments as corrective experiences for addictive vulnerability. *International Journal of Group Psychotherapy* 51 (2001): 11–20.

CHAPTER 12

Weegmann, M., and Khantzian, E. J. Interview by Martin Weegmann (Reflection on group therapy). *Journal of Groups in Addiction & Recovery* 1, no. 2 (2006): 15–32. Reprinted by permission of the publisher (Taylor & Francis Ltd., http://www.tandfonline.com).

CHAPTER 13

Weegmann, M., and Khantzian E. J. Dangerous desires and inanimate attachments: Modern psychodynamic approaches to substance misuse. In *Addictions: Psychology and Treatment*, edited by Robert Patton, Paul Davis, and John Witton. New York: John Wiley and Sons, 2017. Reprinted with the kind permission of John Wiley and Sons.

CHAPTER 14

Khantzian, E. J. Reflections on treating addictive disorders: A psychodynamic perspective. *American Journal on Addictions* 21 (2012): 274–79. Reprinted with the kind permission of John Wiley and Sons.

CHAPTER 15

Khantzian, E. J. A psychodynamic perspective on the efficacy of 12-step programs. *Alcoholism Treatment Quarterly*. 32 (2014): 225–36. Reprinted by permission of the publisher (Taylor & Francis Ltd., http://www.tandfonline.com).

CHAPTER 16

Khantzian, E. J. We are all at least a little lost and off-putting: On transformation. *Psychiatric Times*, September 25, 2013. http://www.psychiatrictimes.com/blogs/couch-crisis/we-are-all-lost-and-off-putt. Reprinted with the kind permission of UBM.

CHAPTER 17

Khantzian, E. J. Tragic trends in the treatment of addictive illness. *Psychiatric Times*, March 18, 2014. Reissued in *Psychiatric Times* (Lead/Cover Article) 31, no. 5 (May 2014):1–2. http://www.psychiatrictimes.com/addiction/tragic-trends-treatment-addictive-illness. Reprinted with the kind permission of UBM.

CHAPTER 18

Khantzian, E. J. Insights on the insanity of addiction. Commentary, *Psychiatric Times* 33, no. 3 (November 2015): 41–42. http://www.psychiatrictimes.com/addiction/insights -insanity-addiction. Reprinted with the kind permission of UBM.

CHAPTER 19

Khantzian, E. J. The cruel scourge of addiction: An addiction psychiatrist's clinical view. Counselor Connection, 2015. http://us5.campaignrchive1.com/?u=0a96915d1b284a d7deb377594&id=29fe70a83a&e=5cde87df96.

CHAPTER 20

Khantzian, E. J. Life lessons learned from addictions. Commentary, *Psychiatric Times* 32, no. 10 (October 2015): 28–29. Reprinted with the kind permission of UBM.

CHAPTER 21

Khantzian, E. J. "Psychophobia" and getting it right. *American Academy of Addiction Psychiatry* 33, no. 1 (Spring 2017): 8. Reprinted from the spring 2017 newsletter of the American Academy of Addiction Psychiatry (AAAP).

CHAPTER 22

Khantzian, E. J. The theory of self-medication and addiction. *Psychiatric Times*, February 21, 2017. Reissued in Commentary, *Psychiatric Times* 30, no. 11 (November 2013): 37. http://www.psychiatrictimes.com/blogs/couch-crisis/we-are-all-lost-and-off-putting -transformation. Reprinted with the kind permission of UBM.

Index

12-step programs, 146, 217, 235; classical models and, 218; group therapy compared to, 167. *See also* Alcoholics Anonymous

AA. *See* Alcoholics Anonymous
abandonment, 80, 82, 88
abstinence, 242; from CD, 141–43. *See also specific topics*
abuse, 185; normative, 80; sexual, 80–82, 184; traumatic, 80–82, 111–12, 183–84
abused businessman, 80–82
adaptation: developmental deficits and, 13–14; in psychodynamics, 3–4; psychopathology as, 12–13, 12n2; special, 13–14; treatment alliance and, 14–15
"addictive drives," 66
"addictive personality," 104
addictive vulnerability. *See* vulnerability
ADHD. *See* attention deficit hyperactivity disorder
adolescence, 9–10, 132; nicotine dependence and, 62
affect, 113. *See also* disordered affects; drug choice and affect research
affect regulation, 132–33, 152, 201, 219; attunement and, 86–87. *See also* feelings

African Americans, 173. *See also* drug choice and affect research
aggression, 10; opiates and, 120, 254
Aharonovich, E., 121
Albanese, Mark, vii, 115
alcohol, 24, 57–58, 70, 220; depression and, 152–53; "disease" of, 258; as drug of choice, 128, *129*, 130–31, 243–44; dysphoria and, 194–95; energy and, 200; individual therapy about, 84–86; isolation and, 238–39, 254–55; methadone and, 175–76; NIAAA, 3–4; PTSD and, 116; recovery and, 7, 45, 47–51, 199–201; schizophrenia and, 59; sedation from, 120; self-regulation and SMH, and, 99–100; self-soothing from, 192; SMH and, 77; spark from, 85–86; superego and, 164; traumatic abuse and, 111–12; in vignettes, 84–86, 163–64, 221–24, 248
alcoholic husband, 84–86
Alcoholics Anonymous (AA), 7, 45, 47–51; control and, 162; feelings and, 224; fellowship of, 218, 223, 225, 232, 236; group dynamics of, 217–18, 225; humor and, 226; on life lessons, 247–48; narcissism and, 224–25; powerlessness and, 226–27;

About the Author

Edward J. Khantzian, MD, is professor of psychiatry at Harvard Medical School and past president of the American Academy of Addiction Psychiatry. Dr. Khantzian is a distinguished scholar, psychiatrist, and analyst, specializing in addictions for more than fifty years. His other work includes *Treating Addiction as a Human Process*, *Addiction as a Human Process*, and (with Mark J. Albanese) *Understanding Addiction as Self Medication: Finding Hope behind the Pain.*

About the Contributors

Mark J. Albanese is director of Adult Outpatient Psychiatry and Addiction Service, Cambridge Health Alliance, and assistant professor of psychiatry, Harvard Medical School.

Frances R. Levin is Kennedy Leavy Professor of Clinical Psychiatry at the College of Physicians and Surgeons of Columbia.

John J. Mariani is associate professor of clinical psychiatry at the College of Physicians and Surgeons of Columbia University and research psychiatrist at the New York State Psychiatric Institute.

Jesse J. Suh, PsyD, is a clinical psychologist and clinical assistant professor of psychology in psychiatry at the University of Pennsylvania Perlman School of Medicine, Center for Studies of Addiction, and maintains a private practice in Philadelphia, Pennsylvania.

Martin Weegmann is a clinical psychologist and group analyst working in private practice and for the National Health Service in London. He is a trainer and teacher. His latest book is *Permission to Narrate: Explorations in Group Analysis, Psychoanalysis, Culture* (2016).

Made in the USA
Las Vegas, NV
28 October 2024